Praise for Don R. Campbell and the REIN System

[I am] extremely impressed with the quality of information and integrity that is stressed by the entire team. *Real Estate Investing in Canada* really opened my mind and completely changed my vision. The Real Estate Investment Network [REIN] has given me the ability to meet like-minded people and access to an enormous wealth of information. Best decision of my life.

— *Jeff Worth*

Over the past two years, I have been using these strategies, which have led me to a hundred times better lifestyle and a portfolio worth over $8 million. Thank you, Don and REIN!

— *Dan Barton*

This program and Don's book have completely changed the focus in my life. The program is fantastic. Getting the information, and then some, right from the "horse's mouth," is worth the thirty hours of attendance. Thank you to REIN for helping reshape and redirect my focus and energy!

— *Kelley Star*

Fantastic array of tools to help me succeed in real estate. One word: confidence. I now feel that I have the tools and the system to move my real estate investments into the stratosphere. Thank you. I look forward to seeing the results of my actions over the next months and years.

— *Brian Creed*

This program helped reaffirm that positive outlook and confidence are the cornerstones of success. The information provides the peace of mind to invest in real estate and be profitable. The level of integrity while handling business certainly matched my personal outlook. I look forward to interacting with REIN in the future.

— *Brian Code*

Wonderful—exceeded my expectations. The bonus was having Don Campbell turned out to be sort of like a humorous life coach! I was considering acquiring an additional property or two, but my horizon has just been expanded. (I'm thinking 10 or 15 now!) I liked the continual reference to goal setting and believing that I can, and should, realize those goals/dreams.

— *Laura Duggan*

What an excellent program! This information makes it so simple to become a successful professional real estate investor. I particularly love the fact that there is no grey area. Honesty and integrity are paramount to being a member of REIN.

— Christine Nelson

[An] amazing, eye-opening experience. Being a Realtor, it's helped me stream-line my business approach with investors. Helped me filter out the things that take too much of my time in searching for quality investment properties. Finally, a proven system. Thank you, REIN!

— Chris Belanger

Extremely comprehensive, current, well-researched, and tested information. I appreciate the ultra ethical approach that is both taught and modeled. Thanks for all you do to invest in us.

— Karen Marshall

Full of great tools and knowledge to help me reach my goals. Definitely the best use of any money I've ever spent on a course. I have come out of the Quickstart with a firm goal, the motivation to attain my goal, and the knowl-edge and tools to start attaining these goals. It will change my life.

— Will Noble

This is a meat-and-potatoes organization that avoids the fluff. REIN sets the standard for all other investment networks out there.

— Shane Brewer

The Quickstart program truly gave me insights on what and how to look at investment properties. I never would have learned all I needed to know except through mistakes. Undoubtedly it has saved me thousands of dollars already. I feel empowered and knowledgeable to go out and start looking for my next property and realize my dream.

— Carol Coote

Excellent, practical, and removes all the guesswork, fear, and emotions from the transaction. A fool-proof system.

— Maureen DeFreitas

Terrific systematic process flow of analyzing investments. There are no longer any subjective opinions regarding properties. This system has minimized all the fears I had in terms of real estate.

— Carmen Luk

JoAnne! Live Your Dreams! Don

51 SUCCESS STORIES FROM CANADIAN REAL ESTATE INVESTORS

DON R. CAMPBELL
with Joy Gregory

WILEY

John Wiley & Sons Canada, Ltd.

National Library of Canada Cataloguing in Publication Data

Campbell, Don R.
    51 success stories from Canadian real estate investors / by Don R.
Campbell ; with Joy Gregory.

ISBN 978-0-470-83916-4

    1. Real estate investment—Canada. 2. Residential real estate—Canada.
I. Title. II. Title: Fifty-one success stories from Canadian real estate
investors.
HD316.C317 2007   332.63'240971   C2007-907018-3

Production Credits
Interior design and typesetting: Natalia Burobina
Cover design: Jason Vandenberg
Printer: Printcrafters Inc.

John Wiley & Sons Canada, Ltd.
6045 Freemont Blvd.
Mississauga, Ontario
L5R 4J3

Printed in the United States of America

2 3 4 5 6 7 8 9 10 PC 18 17 16

This book is printed with biodegradable vegetable-based inks. Text pages are printed on 60 lb. Rolland Enviro 100. 100% post-consumer waste.

Table of Contents

PREFACE
"So What's in It for Me?"

This is unlike any "success story" book you have ever read. Sure, there are stories of people who have done well in their life—some of whom started with nothing and now are living the "freedom lifestyle"; however, let's be realistic. Those types of stories are enjoyable to read as you live success vicariously. But they prompt the inevitable question you, the reader, are asking yourself: "So what's in it for me?"

That's right; when it comes right down to it, we are all tuned into the same radio station in our head: WIFM, and I applaud you for that outlook. In today's fast-paced society, if you're not looking after yourself, no one else will.

On the flipside, once you get clear on your direction and start looking after yourself and your finances, others will jump at the chance to help you out. In other words, once you become committed to your future and lead your life according to plan, others will do whatever it takes to help your vision turn into reality. Other committed people truly enjoy helping others with like minds.

How do I know? Quite simply, it happened to me and I've seen it happen to thousands of your fellow Canadians. It all begins with you and your commitment to what you truly want to create in your life.

My personal success story is filled with people showing up in my life at exactly the right time when I needed their guidance, knowledge, experience or assistance. These coincidences only started to occur after I became extremely clear on what my wife, Connie, and I wanted to create in our lives. Once we defined our "Personal Belize" (as described in Chapter 3 of *Real Estate Investing in Canada*) and started to tell people about it, positive occurrences and coincidences just started to happen. That's not to say that everything has been easy. Believe me, there have been times of mental, physical and financial struggle along the way, but the focus on our long-term vision helped us over these road bumps and helped us to enjoy the smooth parts of the journey. There were many excuses we could have used to stop us travelling on our dream path. Friends who said we were crazy, family members who said we worked "too hard," so-called professionals saying that our dreams were too lofty—those dream-stealers are out there. The key is to not get into a discussion justifying why you are on your life path. The best solution is to ignore them (even when that is very difficult to do) and stay focused on what you want to create for you and your family. It's your life, not theirs.

A great way in which to do this on a consistent basis is to surround yourself with like-minded people who are already well down the pathway you have chosen to take. The more of these positive and supportive people you have in your life, the faster you'll be able to proceed towards your dreams. I call these people dream-supporters.

Dream-stealers do their best to steal your energy and your confidence by distracting you with reasons why *not* to do something, while dream-supporters conspire to help you make it happen. The choice, to me, quickly became obvious as I started on my path to success, and I hope you, too, will come to see the same wisdom.

If you want to play bass in a blues band, or want to travel around the world, or write the next great Canadian novel, or work with charities to help those less fortunate, or learn to paint, all I can say is, no matter what your age or your financial position, do it! Find a way to arrange your life and your finances to make it happen sooner rather than later. Stop dreaming and, like those in these stories, start doing.

John Lennon said it best: "Life is what happens while you are busy making other plans." Make your plan, execute it to the best of your ability and then deal with the road bumps along the way. Life throws us all curve balls whether we are moving forward or we're stuck in neutral, so you might as well be moving forward towards your life goal.

That all being said, let's get back to your favourite radio station, WIFM. So what's so different about this success story book versus others? There are four key differences:

1. The book is completely focused on stories about everyday Canadians creating above-average success in Canadian real estate. They come from investors I've met and worked with across the country over the last 15 years. Every single one of them has used the strategies described in my first book, *Real Estate Investing in Canada*.

2. Each of the stories reveals mistakes or something personal about the storyteller so that you can see that the reality of life as an investor is not all sweetness and light, and so you can learn by avoiding the mistakes they made.

3. Importantly, the book you have in your hands directly addresses and answers the question "WIFM?" With each of the success stories, I will show you landmines you need to avoid. I'll highlight lessons you can learn from the investor's mistakes and I will provide you (and the storyteller) with action steps that you can adopt in your life.

4. You will develop your own game plan for the future, as you'll find pieces in each story that you can model in the future so that you are propelled forward on your chosen path.

By the end of this book, you'll know the key action steps and turning points that these successful investors used to start living their dream. This book may well be the start of surrounding yourself with like-minded successful people who will work with you to help you achieve what you want to achieve. To facilitate this, as you read the book, make notes in the margins, bend pages that you find especially helpful to you and feel free to highlight mistakes you truly want to avoid as an investor.

The stories are divided into four categories titled: Overcoming Personal Adversity; Family and Friends; Jumping Off the Cliff; and Following Proven Systems. Having them grouped like this allows you to easily refer back to a particular section if you ever need to reference certain action-steps or lessons.

You are about to discover that real estate investing is not a get-rich-quick scheme; true success comes to those with a long-term view and a focus on the three keys: systems, relationships and follow-through. With these in alignment, life works together with you and positive coincidences begin to happen. If you allow them to get out of alignment, life will feel like a long, hard struggle.

After reading and enjoying these success stories, I trust that you will begin, or continue, to allow others to assist you along life's path and you'll start watching for positive coincidences as they occur in all aspects of your life. Once you get clear in your mind where you want to go, the pathway becomes very clear.

ACKNOWLEDGEMENTS

Success in any aspect of life is all about taking charge of the future, not just waiting for it to happen. Success is not measured by the number of dollars in your bank account or the number of toys in your driveway; you've truly achieved success when you get to the point of not knowing whether what you're doing is work or play. Success is not a destination; it is a way of thinking and a way of living life, regardless of your income or net worth. There are many unhappy multimillionaires and many very happy people living on minimal income, so obviously, mindset is the key.

This book is dedicated to everyone who has, or wants to, take charge of their own success and start living their life today as a happy and successful person.

This book is also dedicated to the 75 people who contributed to the 51 success stories in this book. Their willingness to tell their stories while being fully open, honest and vulnerable is a sign of their character. Only by sharing the good and the bad of their journeys are we able to learn the many lessons they've learned along the way. They've now marked the path for others to follow. Every reader of this book owes them their thanks.

A very special thank you must go to Calgary writer Joy Gregory, whose dedication and insights made this book possible. Through her, the stories came alive and set the stage for an entertaining and informative read that can change lives.

Share your stories, good or bad, long or short, on Canada's Real Estate Discussion Forums at www.myreinspace.com.

INTRODUCTION

"A success story book—how is that going to help me?" asked Richard, the rookie investor you met in the first book in this series, *Real Estate Investing in Canada*. He and I were sitting in our usual Starbucks for our monthly get-together.

Since Richard began his journey as an investor just a few short years ago, Richard and his wife Emma's lives have changed significantly. As a quick recap: He had been working at a job he didn't enjoy; he had been forced to fly back early from his holidays while his family stayed at a beautiful resort, and he had been frustrated. I met him on that flight and decided that this was a person who needed a hand up.

In *Real Estate Investing in Canada* he learned the complete process of finding financial freedom through investing in real estate. He discovered the 12 keys to analyzing a city, town or neighbourhood in order to determine whether it is poised for growth or poised to decline. He also discovered checklists on how to analyze a property (right down to the last dollar) to determine if it would be a good investment. And, in that short time, he even discovered how to negotiate the deal and build his team so that he and Emma can focus on the priorities in their life—their family.

Now, a few short years later, Richard and I still meet on a monthly basis as he continues to add to his portfolio, deals with property management issues and discovers how to attract joint venture capital for his next purchases. It is at this regular get-together that he heard about the "success story" book you now have in your hand.

"How is it going to help me?" Richard had asked. "I don't want to read about other people's success—I want my own."

"Richard," I responded, "you've heard me speak about the importance of surrounding yourself with like-minded people who are doing better than yourself so you can learn the lessons they've learned, avoid the mistakes they've made and follow in their footsteps along your success journey. Well, this book will help do that for you."

51 Success Stories from Canadian Real Estate Investors is designed with one very clear goal in mind, and that is to provide Canadian real estate investors with an instant team of "like-minded people" who are already on the path to real estate success and who have seen the landmines, and the goldmines, and want to point them all out to us. These are just a few of the hundreds of success stories we have captured over the 15 years of working with investors across the country and around the world, and when you **register this book online at www.realestateinvestingincanada.com** you will be given access to many more, including audio recordings from these and many other investors.

In this book and through the online stories, you will discover the key breakthroughs that became the catalysts of success—how average Canadians created above-average results. For instance, you'll hear from and learn the lessons of:

- A single mother of three who had to start her financial life over with limited employment skills.

- A young couple, just starting out, who live in Japan and invest successfully in Canadian real estate.

- A man who has overcome severe dyslexia to become a leader, a trainer and a very successful real estate investor.

- A couple who have been married for over 35 years whose relationship was renewed and revitalized because they began investing together.

- A young bachelor-waiter who, within two short years, has created a growing real estate investment company from scratch.

- A mother and daughter who work closely together to create a wealth foundation for their family.

- A number of sister-and-brother and other family-member teams who pooled their resources and their knowledge to make a better life for all families involved.

- Many investors who, in mid-life, decided that the job path they were on was not going to help them create long-term wealth, so they completely changed directions (despite years of university training and expertise for their current jobs) and found happiness and financial freedom where they never expected it.

- A pastor and his wife who are using the income from their real estate to help them live their passion of making a difference in their community.

- A man forced into bankruptcy who, instead of hiding behind this excuse, turned his life around and now owns properties across the country that fuel his fun and exciting lifestyle.

- Many average Canadians who started with nothing and have created above-average results in their life.

- And many more stories from people, aged in their 20s to their 70s, who have overcome adversity, made mistakes and changed their life paths to create lifestyles they previously only dreamed about and thought they would never have.

You may currently be investing in real estate or just considering it. You may be sick and tired of your job and want to know what others in your position have done to "jump off the treadmill" and land on their feet. You may be looking to learn some of the lessons that others have learned along the way so you can shortcut around the mistakes. Whatever it is you are looking for, you will find it in these stories.

You will see that many of the people featured in the stories had issues they could have easily used as excuses to not take action. Let's be honest, we all have these potential excuses in our life that we can use. What you'll discover is how, in order to break from the average masses, you have to take actions that others aren't willing to—just like many of these investors have.

As I told Richard on the warm summer morning in Starbucks, "We all need to be surrounded by and mentored by those who have already taken the path we're on." And this book will give you 51 potential mentors and over 100 lessons that were learned along the way. Learn from others already on the path, start from wherever you are and take forward steps, no matter how big or small, towards your ultimate goal.

Enjoy this book. I look forward to seeing your success story, big or small, in the next edition! Please feel free to send it directly to success@ reincanada.com.

Sincerely,

Don R. Campbell

HABITAT FOR HUMANITY UPDATE

As you may already be aware, the authors donate 100% of the royalties from all three of our books (*51 Success Stories of Canadian Real Estate Investors*, *Real Estate Investing in Canada* and *97 Tips for Canadian Real Estate Investors*) directly to Habitat for Humanity. To date, the amount of money we have been able to raise, with the generous assistance of the members of the Real Estate Investment Network™, now exceeds $250,000, every single penny of which goes directly to helping build homes for those in need.

I would like to thank the many retailers who have also helped support these books and this worthy cause. I urge everyone to *find a cause you believe in and do what you can* to support it with your time, your money or your expertise. Every little bit helps, and every little bit makes our society better. Thank you for buying this book and helping to support Habitat for Humanity.

SECTION 1

OVERCOMING PERSONAL ADVERSITY

SUCCESS STORY #1
REAL ESTATE BRINGS THE FAMILY TOGETHER

Donna Hamilton

At first, I minimized what I did as the deal-maker and manager in a joint venture partnership. We may not be putting up the money, but we are doing the work. I get that now.

It wasn't the wear and tear of a nine-to-five job that kept Donna Hamilton up at night. A waitress married to a refractory bricklayer whose high-demand job kept him on the road and away from his young family, Donna saw a future that looked lonely and financially insecure.

Money was an issue, but time was even more scarce. It was nearly impossible to work any of her shifts around Luke's schedule, especially since he was exhausted on rare days off. "We never even had so much as one weekend off," Donna recalls. "It was just work, work, work."

In 2000, just days before their second daughter was born, Donna bought her and Luke's first investment property, a condo. "We inherited good tenants," she says. "We put up $10,000 [the property cost $65,000] and in September of 2006, it sold for $165,000. It would have gone for about $250,000 if we'd held onto it for a few months longer." She utters the last sentence without a hint of regret. Frightened people may try to move forward while looking back. But Donna Hamilton is no longer frightened.

Soon after buying that first property, Donna followed a suggestion made by two trusted friends and enrolled in a Quickstart program. The program's message was powerful, but the Real Estate Investment Network's (REIN) $200 monthly fees sounded astronomical. Instead, she set out on her own, buying two more properties before realizing that $2,400 a year was a cheap way to strengthen her business with some of the real estate investment community's best economic data and support.

Six years later, the 41-year-old mother of six- and nine-year-old daughters is glad she made the investment. "I would not have 15 properties if it wasn't for REIN," she says. "REIN has helped with everything. That's where I learned to screen tenants, it's where I learned to set up joint venture partnerships, it's where I learned how to find quality tenants."

Quality tenants turn the wheels of Donna and Luke's investment business. Most of their tenants are families, young couples or young executives who want to live in the settled communities of West Edmonton. That clientele tends to stay put, meaning fewer turnovers and more opportunities to develop positive relationships.

In the early days of their investing, Luke kept his day job. When his job slowed over the winter months, he renovated houses. That boosted cash flow, but had a negative impact on their family life. "Luke was never really home," says Donna "If he wasn't away working, he was home—but logging long hours on renovations."

This year, her husband of 17 years took a giant step back from his job, freeing more time for renovation deals and more of the hands-on details of property management. Best of all, he's now able to drop what he's working on and go get the girls from school if Donna needs more time with a deal, or to look at property. "Honestly, I'm good at finding good deals. But I figure I've looked at 300 to 400 houses. It definitely takes a lot of my time."

Looking ahead, Donna estimates they have more than $100,000 in equity in every property they own. It's money they'll use to finance more purchases. They'll also bring in more joint venture partners, a business decision that brings its own set of due diligence.

Early experience with JVs showed the value of clarity. When one partner saw the money that could be made flipping a particular property before others thought it was time to put it on the market, they bought him out. Their planned renovation of that property took more than six months. "But we were focused on the bigger deal. By the time it goes on the market, we figure our profit will be a couple hundred thousand."

One of her first JV deals taught a bigger lesson. Here, eyes wide open, Donna used her partner's money to finance the deal. In return, Donna and Luke handled the renovation—and took a cut of the profit. Before that, she wondered why investors who put up the JV money often took only 50 percent of the profit. Once she'd worked through the process, she realized her time was worth a 50-percent share!

As time goes by, she's learning new ways to value her own time. Luke now shares more of her parenting responsibilities and property management. She's also hired cleaners to get property ready to rent. "What took me two full days, they do in a few hours," she says. "With the girls at school, that's time I now spend visiting property or talking to lenders."

What she won't change is her commitment to making sure her offers include a cover letter specific to the deal on the table. The letters, which introduce her and Luke, as well as their business plan, lay the groundwork for what she hopes will be a working relationship with a vendor. "I know it's got me deals. One time, I didn't get a for-sale-by-owner property. But the guy phoned me to tell me why. I think he read my cover letter and felt like he owed me a personal explanation. That's pretty incredible."

With plans to buy more single-family homes in the Edmonton area, Donna is honing her knowledge of investment and refinancing options. She's also kicked up her "get it in writing" approach to due diligence. That happened after a recent deal was complicated by a lender's reluctance to meet terms she thought had been firmly negotiated. The big lesson there: Lenders can and do change their minds. And it can cost you, so make sure everything is in writing

Another time, she was shocked when a lawyer asked her to sign papers saying she was not refinancing her principal residence to buy investment property. Determined to stay out of the grey area, she marched back to her mortgage broker to make sure everyone understood that was exactly what she was trying to do (and she wasn't going to lie about it!).

Donna's the first to acknowledge she's got a lot to learn about real estate investing. But she's equally quick to say that what she does know about the business she genuinely enjoys. She likes the mental challenge of the purchase. She likes the creative side of renovations and the relationship side of landlording. She likes knowing it's the reason she, Luke and their girls have taken wonderful family vacations to Hawaii, Phoenix and British Columbia. She likes knowing real estate is the reason her husband is at home nights (and volunteers at the kids' school during the day).

Describing herself as someone who's "gone through life always chasing a dream," Donna admits it's tough to talk about what this business means to her family. "It makes me feel like crying," she confesses, her voice cracking with emotion. "Truly, I never thought life could be this good."

———— ❈❈❈ ————

Don Campbell's Observations

Donna's family story is a heartwarming look at what real estate can do for you over and above any financial rewards. Money was obviously not the main result of Donna's focus; it was the lifestyle that the money would help to provide.

Donna had to overcome quite a number of roadblocks, many of them based in old beliefs. Once she broke through these old patterns, through sheer determination, her positive results began to appear. Donna, like many of those in this book, could have easily hidden behind her adversities, but her family was too important. Nothing was going to deter her.

Another insight that is unique to Donna's story is the admission that she has looked at up to 400 potential properties to find the few that fit her portfolio. Many beginning investors stop in frustration after looking at as few as 10 properties and not finding any that work. They hide behind the easy and completely inaccurate excuse of "All the Good Properties Are Taken." These investors are usually those who have a money focus. Finding gems takes some effort, and having a long-term focus not on money, but lifestyle, will help keep you focused.

The third lesson Donna provides us is a system lesson. She has adopted the "Cover Page" strategy full on. For every offer she submits, she attaches a cover letter addressed directly to the vendor. In it she explains her deal in simple, easy-to-understand language and gives them reasons to choose her offer over someone else's. This direct line of communication to the vendor makes it easier not only for the realtors in the deal, but also easier for the vendor to say yes, even if there are competitive bids for the property.

ACTION STEPS

1. Who in your life can you positively influence by becoming successful in real estate investing?

   _____

   _____

   _____

   _____

2. Do you currently use the Cover Letter Offer Strategy? If not, what is holding you back from using this proven deal maker?[1]

_____

_____

_____

_____

3. If you ever find yourself frustrated by not being able to find properties that fit your investment system, it is important to change your perspective. Finding real estate is like finding the perfect flat skipping rock on a beach that has been visited by thousands of people before you. The rock is there, but on a busy beach it just takes more time to find it. You would find it more quickly if you had a few people working with you on the hunt. The same is true for a busy real estate market; there are deals to be found in every market condition. However, in an active real estate market it takes more time (and more relationships) to find the gems. Who do you have helping you? Realtors? Relatives? Current tenants?

_____

_____

_____

_____

4. Re-read Chapter 7 titled "Skipping Stones to Success" in _Real Estate Investing in Canada_.

---

1 For more details, see Chapter 12 titled "Placing Your Offer and Getting It Accepted" from _Real Estate Investing in Canada_.

SUCCESS STORY #2
VETERAN PASTOR USES REAL ESTATE TO MAKE A DIFFERENCE IN THE COMMUNITY

Scott Lewis and Laurie Lewis

Ours is not a rag-to-riches story. It's about a slow and steady journey towards increased resources for our family and for those whose needs we can meet through our abundance.

When young couples show up at the door of his church for premarital counselling, pastor Scott Lewis likes to talk to them about money. He knows financial issues are behind a lot of failed marriages, precisely because few people really know how to talk about money. From where he sits, that's a mistake. "If you think about it, money really is more important than a lot of the other stuff," he suggests. "Not only because you need it to secure food, shelter and clothing, but also because of what it lets you do in the world."

A pastor and teacher in church settings for almost 17 years, Scott currently leads a fledgling non-denominational Christian congregation in Sarnia, Ontario, a city of about 72,000 people nestled on the banks of Lake Huron. He and his wife, Laurie, bought their townhouse-style condo in 2000. A year later, calculating that their church work would not necessarily be the only source of income they would need, they launched into real estate investment and bought a duplex with two semi-detached units.

The thrill of that purchase was soon masked by the raw angst associated with their new role as landlords. The first tenants came with the property—and gave notice a month after the deal went through. Given that one never cleaned and the other had a large family that left considerable wear-and-tear in its wake, Scott and Laurie made the best of things and used the break to spruce up the units.

The litany of tenant issues continued to grow. One tenant had a pit bull and never cleaned up after the dog. Another had caused a kitchen fire that left smoke damage. One used such foul language that her phone calls left Laurie exhausted, and sick with stress. Add to that late-night calls over maintenance issues and tenants who moved without notice and it's little wonder Scott and Laurie questioned the wisdom of their investment decision. "This was all in the first few months of owning the property," recalls Scott, now able to roll his eyes and laugh about the experience. At the time however, "it was awful."

When a man from their church talked to them about his new work managing properties, the Lewises listened with open ears. They were so strongly moved by their recent experiences as landlords, they told him they felt ready to sell their investment property. "He sat at our kitchen table," says Scott, "and recommended we try property management first."

The transition took a while, but the experience was wonderful. Nearly six years later, that property continues to net $250-$350 a month. They've also refinanced the property twice, enabling them to purchase two more properties.

Because traditional lenders turned him down, the duplexes were bought with the help of a mortgage broker Scott found via the Internet. He was grateful for her help, but soon discovered they'd hit another investment wall. With four properties, including their own home, they just didn't have anything to offer as a down payment on another property.

Those who seek, find: Scott found what he was looking for by reading *Real Estate Investing in Canada*. That book inspired his search for more information about ways to invest in Canadian real estate. Days after he finished the book, he put down an offer on a fourplex under repossession. They bought that complex in June 2006 and added another duplex just three months later. "We went from 6 individual rental units to 12 in a single year and leveraged the new purchases with refinanced money from other properties and a personal line of credit," notes Scott. "All of a sudden we were able to buy property without needing to put very much of our own money into the deals."

Scott, who became a father to baby Ronan, a son, in 2003, credits Don Campbell with teaching him the value of building a "team" he can now count on for advice and support with various deals and issues. That helped him and Laurie grow their investment portfolio. Knowledge gleaned from reading real estate books and attending seminars also helps them find creative solutions to pressing problems. When their new church needed to reduce some of its own costs, Scott took a cut in salary, using his and Laurie's investment portfolio to take pressure off their church community. He also used his growing knowledge of investment to negotiate lower payments on their own home.

While he still believes debt can be dangerous unless managed with care, he and Laurie envision a time when their real estate investments will help them support others doing charitable work. "I no longer think in terms of having 'just enough to survive until we die,'" says Scott, who plans to add more properties in 2007.

Instead, he dreams about using his own family's cash flow to help others, and maybe even help other investors make money so they also have more to give away.

Scott's dual roles as pastor and real estate investor may take some by surprise, but he has thought a lot about money's place in the world. He takes inspiration from the great evangelist, Paul, a tent-maker who sold his products (the first mobile homes, no less!) to finance his international ministry.

"As I see it, there are two reasons why money is entrusted to us," says Scott. "First, to provide for those under our care, and, second, to give away to those who have need. This makes abundance a good thing, since it can be used to generate—and improve—a multitude of resources that enrich the lives of people in many ways."

─────

Don Campbell's Observations

I can't speak for Scott and Laurie, but from what I know of them they were already living their passion when they discovered real estate investing. Scott, as the pastor of his congregation, had committed his life to making a difference in and being a leader of his community. He was living his calling, despite it not being the highest paid profession in the world. And that is the number one lesson we can take from Scott and Laurie's story.

The financial rewards that can accrue to you through properly investing in real estate can help support the kind of life you want to live. You may want to be a spiritual leader such as Scott; you may wish to pursue the arts as a career choice; or you may have the talent and desire to coach non-professional athletes full-time. There are many careers with rewards that are not counted on a profit and loss sheet, or in a paycheque. For those who choose these career paths and don't do it for monetary reward, they do it to follow their passion or dream. But what many don't understand is that there is no need to live an impoverished life just because you choose a calling that doesn't pay well.

When you speak with some in these professions they are almost repelled by the thought of wealth, believing it to be a bad pursuit. Well, that is an amazingly selfish attitude. Abundance and wealth is a blessing that we must not shy away from. Through abundance we can live our passion and at the same time have a major impact on our community through charity work.

A very wise man, Patrick Francey, once told me that, if you have the ability to create a lot of wealth, and you have a noble cause to support with it, you are being incredibly selfish if you choose not to create this abundance. He went on to say that by not using your talents and your knowledge to maximize the wealth you create, you are forcing extra hardship on those you would have been able to help with these funds and the extra time it will help create in your life.

As with Scott's story, real estate is not about personal wealth, it is about supporting the career he chooses and making his community better at the same time. He understands that he couldn't have done it on his own and has built a strong team around him to support his business venture, which in turn provides him with more time to follow his true calling as a community leader.

Don't hide behind financial struggle as a noble cause. Find a way to use abundance so you can follow your passion, no matter how much it pays you as a career. Please, make a difference.

ACTION STEPS

1. If you had zero money worries, what would you pursue with your life?

    _____

    _____

    _____

    _____

    Don't wait to go after this passion. Find a way in which you could start slowly today; then as your real estate portfolio begins to provide you with financial backing, begin to pursue your passion with increasing fervour.

2. What is the number-one charity or cause that you would support fully if you had the choice?

_____

_____

_____

_____

Don't wait to start supporting your favourite cause. Find a way—and it does not have to be financial in nature—to begin. Contact them and explain your situation; you may be very surprised at how a small effort from you can make a huge difference.

I will start supporting (or increasing my support) for the above cause by (date):

_____

SUCCESS STORY #3
PERSEVERANCE OVER LIFE'S MAJOR HURDLES, NO MATTER HOW HIGH THEY ARE

Irene Gluckie

It's okay to ask for a better deal. And never take "no" for an answer.

"Are you going to fix that?" asks the young man sitting at the kitchen table as his landlady, Irene Gluckie walks by. Her tiny tool box (measuring a scant 12 x 3 x 4 inches) in hand, she smiles at what she's come to see as a question born more of ignorance than sexism. The 59-year-old former schoolteacher turned real estate investor owns 21 properties and is what others call "handy." She's also smart. "Well, I am going to try," is her quick reply to the unbelieving, "and if I can't fix it, I know someone who can."

The daughter of Polish immigrants who came to rural Saskatchewan carrying more than their weight in painful memories of the Second World War, Irene has learned to focus on the job at hand. She's all about getting the job done and getting it done right.

Irene, a mother of four, bought her first investment property when still married in the early 1990s. The deal went sour and the Gluckies lost $40,000, a crippling amount for a couple with young children. Shaken, but wiser, her second attempt involved a $10,000 investment in a Fort McMurray townhouse. She figures that property is now worth $300,000. "I say that with a big grin," she says, "because I still own it." Better still, a strong economy and good relationships with her tenants means it's remarkably little work. "When my tenants are going to leave, they set me up with friends of theirs. I still carry out my tenant check, but this system has really worked for that property."

Closer to home, she also self-manages the 21 other homes in her portfolio. Success on the investment front has come through experience, including some with tenants-gone-bad, but the real story behind Irene Gluckie goes well beyond what she does for a living. It speaks of a willingness to help other people—and it cries out from a resilience born of the life lessons no one seeks.

Her third child, a baby daughter, died in 1979. Born with a congenital heart defect, the baby only lived for a few months. The child's death left a gaping hole in Irene's heart. In 1994, still coping with the end of her marriage and supporting three teenagers, she entered what she calls the "buying phase of my investment business," eventually buying about a dozen of the properties she still owns today.

She was also working full-time as a teacher focused on adolescent students with special needs. Her board moved her to a school that required a special-needs teacher known to be strong in math and English. Irene smiles at the irony behind the move. "I didn't know English when I came to Canada with my parents. My mother used to tell me, 'We came here with two hands each, and you.'"

Irene felt fulfilled by teaching and pleased with how her real estate portfolio augmented her family's future. The pain of her daughter's death dulled with time.

And then the phone rang.

In August 2002, her second-born and only son, Lindsey, died in a plane crash near Maple Ridge, B.C. He had been only a few days shy of his 25th birthday. The tragedy forced Irene to leave a job she loved. She remembers a young counsellor telling her that she was depressed and needed to be honest about that before she could get better. "I refuse to be depressed," was Irene's response. "I am grieving. And what's more, I have lost two children—and I have the right to grieve."

In the end, it was her real estate that kept her going. "Without that," she says, "I might have been one of those people who stayed in bed all day and never answered the phone."

Once a teacher, always a teacher, and Irene credits her classroom experience with helping her teach people to be responsible tenants. Over the years, she's helped several joint venture partners buy their own properties. More recently, she set up a rent-to-own deal for one of Lindsey's friends.

"Some of my tenants seek my opinion on different things happening in their lives and that's okay," she says with a laugh. "But I take my business very seriously. When I counsel new tenants about my rental policy, I am very honest. I tell them, 'Paying your rent on time is very important. In the hierarchy of things, it's next in line to breathing.'"

Her reputation for wise negotiation makes Irene a go-to person for fellow investors in her life. Ten of the 14 properties she tried to buy from June 2006 to June 2007 are in her portfolio, at least in part because she finds ways to make deals work.

And the time she spends counselling other investors is well spent. "The more you give, the more you get back," insists Irene. "I don't expect the people I help to come back and help me. I expect them to help others."

That vision of what it takes to make the world a better place is the reason Irene spearheaded an effort to get REIN's female members involved with Habitat for Humanity's Women Build projects in Edmonton.[1] The need to give back is also why she chooses to spend more time assisting her mother. The need to pay-it-forward is why she chooses to spend time with her family and plans to pass on a legacy, as well as part of their inheritance, long before she leaves this world.

Interestingly enough, her advice to would-be investors who don't know if they "can" do it is similarly all about taking action in the world. "All of us have a little voice that natters at us about what we should or should not do. If it keeps you from being the person you want to be, ignore it. If you want to do something, learn how to do it. And then do it. Plain and simple."

Don Campbell's Observations

Irene has been handed more hurdles in her life than many, and still she has come out the other side an amazing woman. Strong in her convictions and focused on making a difference to the many people she touches in her life, she has a no-nonsense approach to her future.

Irene has become what I like to call a quiet leader and motivator. She is out there making a difference for her tenants, her business partners, her fellow investors and her community, all while not seeking the spotlight or praise. She just has a clear focus and a clear vision.

Once again, as we have heard in others' stories, it was the real estate that kept her going, both financially and emotionally, as the major hurdles were put up in front of her. Having heard Irene's story, I now often speak

---

1   Her drive for this worthy cause was the catalyst for 100% of all of Don R. Campbell's author royalties going directly to Habitat for Humanity. By introducing this cause to Don, Irene has helped raise over $250,000 so far. She is to be congratulated for making such a huge difference.

to those who are just starting out in real estate investment and I tell them, very clearly, that you never know what life will throw at you, so why not get going today so that your financial foundation is already being built. Don't wait for a traumatic event to make a major change.

There are many lessons we learn from Irene's story. Persistance, focus, focus on the family, and on on. However, the most important subtext to her story comes out in the last paragraph. Shakespeare said it well: "To thine own self be true." Irene says it even better: "If it keeps you from being the person you want to be, ignore it." A lesson we can use in all areas of our lives.

SUCCESS STORY #4
Don't Wait until a Near Death Experience to Get Started

Greg Bueckert

I like knowing my business provides an important service.

In 2001, an ailing Greg Bueckert was told he had less than six months to live. Just home from a pleasure trip to Mexico, he'd picked up an opportunistic infection while scuba diving in ocean waters teeming with invisible bacteria. Invisible but nasty, those bacteria were bringing him down fast, compromising vital organs and leaving their host in physical ruin.

A pharmacist with a better-than-average understanding of where medicine comes up short, he agreed with the prognosis. Greg had one teenage daughter and two teenage stepchildren, so he turned his practical attention to getting his estate in order. "My father owned a lumberyard in the Medicine Hat area," Greg recounts. "But he also owned about 20 revenue properties and when he died, they kept my mom going for more than 30 years. I'd dabbled in real estate investment for years, and now I wanted that kind of legacy."

A member of REIN since the late 1990s, Bueckert says he was already comfortable with investing: "I sold about 20 houses and 2 hotels in 1999, mostly in what I now understand was a fit of frustration over other business issues. Looking back, I realize I probably saved the wrong business when I kept the pharmacy and let the properties go. It was definitely a decision that was impacted by emotion instead of real estate fundamentals, which I really do try to follow most of the time," he says with a quick laugh.

Six years later, Greg is alive and well, thanks to medicines that performed well above expectations. Better yet, a real estate portfolio born in crisis is thriving. Centred on a long-term buy-and-hold model, he owns 22 properties, most of them in Medicine Hat. A few others are in Calgary and Edmonton.

"I took what could be called a very linear path to investing," says Greg. "By the time I sold the pharmacy to focus on investing, I already had some experience and some money. For the most part, I invest alone, although that's changing thanks to a couple of big projects in the works."

One of those projects involves a $10-million-plus retrofit of a former school in Crowsnest Pass, west of Medicine Hat. Whereas others may look at the site and see a green-roofed cube of a building, Greg sees 18 condominiums, likely owned by weekend and summer tourists from Calgary, Medicine Hat and Lethbridge. With some of the region's best hiking and ATV trails nearby, as well as an extensive cave system reputed to offer North America's finest spelunking, Greg says that recreation-minded buyers are just waiting for a development like his Cameron School project.

While the details of that development haven't fallen in place as quickly as he'd like, Greg is shopping the deal to European investors and figures construction will be well under way by the fall of 2007. He's also dreaming about the penthouse suite, which he'll keep for himself.

The rest of his portfolio includes condos, an apartment block and duplexes. He also employs four full-time tradespeople, up from one just four years ago, and depends on them to deal with property maintenance issues and to renovate homes he's purchased to upgrade and sell in Medicine Hat's lucrative re-sale market.

While he loves the demolition side of a reno project, Greg has learned to hire out basic property management. He doesn't want to collect rent cheques. He doesn't want to hear about every tenant and maintenance issues. But he does like to be around people who understand what his business is about, which is why he routinely makes the three-hour road trip to attend REIN meetings, where he can share news of high-intensity investment business, without people thinking he's either crazy or greedy.

When people say he's lucky, Greg rolls his eyes. Having come back from the brink of his own serious illness, and having weathered the pain of a recent divorce, he knows his success isn't about luck. It's about his knowledge of the local market, where he's lived all of his life. The people who only see the success don't see him scouting poster boards in local shopping centres or driving around to follow up on referrals. They don't see the relationship he's built with his tradespeople, men whose work, and lives, he respects. They don't see his willingness to take action in relation to their own willingness to talk about investment as if it's something they can't do, or wouldn't stoop to do.

"The word 'landlord' is like a bad word to some people. I know I provide an important service. And I like knowing that my business provides an important service."

That sense of service helped him make a dream come true for his own mother. When she was 85, he took her out to the tiny hamlet of Schuler, not far from Medicine Hat, where she hoped to see her parents' home. "I drove out there only to find a big hole where the house once stood. She was disappointed, but we toured the town and returned home. Subsequent to this, my sister traced our family history and discovered that the house had been moved into Medicine Hat sometime during the 1940s."

Greg tracked down the owner, and brought it back into the family. "It is now completely renovated and safely returned to family ownership."

Novelist Thomas Wolfe may well have been right when he wrote, "you can never go home again." But thanks to real estate investing, Greg Bueckert proved you can bring the homestead home again (and please your mother in the process!).

⎯⎯ ❦ ⎯⎯

Don Campbell's Observations

Luck is all about positioning yourself in the right place at the right time, and Greg has done just that. When an investor studies the economic fundamentals of a market, and cuts through the hype and fear that surrounds the real estate market, they can become very "lucky."

I'm sure some considered Greg's father lucky to have accumulated 20 revenue properties before he passed away. His mother was probably considered lucky because the income from those properties kept her well for over 30 years, and now people consider Greg lucky because the 22 properties he has purchased have performed so well in a strong market. When in reality, luck had nothing to do with it. Careful planning and execution created the results, not luck.

Greg probably didn't feel so lucky when he returned home to a diagnosis of six months to live. But, from past experience he knew his family would be taken care of through the proceeds of his property portfolio, just as his mother was.

"Lucky" is something others call you to justify their inaction. They won't call you smart as it may infer that they are not. Lucky is a safe word for others to use when you're doing well, but it is a word that discounts the hard work that the other person has put in to create their results.

The secondary lesson we learn from Greg's story is that if you allow emotions to enter into the investment equations, poor decisions are often made. For Greg it was making the decision to sell 20 houses in 1999 because other frustrations in his life boiled over and he thought that liquidating a strong real estate portfolio to save a weak business was the right decision. He had fallen in love with saving the business, rather than allowing himself time to analyze all of his options and remembering how important a real estate portfolio was to his family after his father died.

What's ironic with this situation is that you can be sure that when people listen to him talk about liquidating his portfolio right before the big boom hit, they don't call him unlucky, but rather refer to the decision as a mistake. And that's the second lesson. When you win in life, others will call you lucky; when you make a mistake, these same people will not call you unlucky but will say "you made a mistake." You never win in their eyes; those who think that way are often those who are fearful of making a mistake. But if we were to live our lives in fear of what others think of our decisions, we would deliver mediocre results.

Greg is anything but mediocre. He is creating a financial legacy, he is making a difference in other people's lives. Let them call him lucky. I'm sure he's okay with that!

ACTION STEPS

1. Take the word "lucky" out of your vocabulary. Replace it with a statement like "congratulations, well done!" Here's an example:
   Old way: "Wow, you sure are lucky to have invested in those properties that have gone up $100,000."
   New way: "Congratulations on investing in those properties that have gone up $100,000. Would you mind showing me how I can do the same?"

2. What three people do you know who have created results you would like to duplicate?

- _____
  _____
- _____
  _____
- _____
  _____

3. Contact these three people and congratulate them on their accomplishments, acknowledging that it must have taken some courage and hard work to create that result. Then ask if they would mind sharing their experiences so that you could follow their path. You will be very pleasantly surprised at the results. You are only looking for one out of the three to say yes to sharing their experience; if you get responses from all three, that would be very "lucky" for you!

SUCCESS STORY #5
FROM THE BRINK OF DISASTER TO THE BRINK OF SUCCESS

Jules McKenzie

Our fundamental error was buying older properties, particularly in our little town, where some of those houses are over 100 years old. We didn't have a specific plan, or the funds to complete these major renovations.

The plan was simple. Living in Orillia, Ontario, Jules and Ange McKenzie would buy undervalued old houses in need of repair, fix them up and hold them as revenue properties to supplement monthly cash flow. Using a U.S.-based investment strategy that taught them how to boost their credit card limits and access highly leveraged lines of credit, they would secure their family's financial future with properties that increased in long-term wealth. It was a strategy that cost them $35,000 in up-front fees and it was brilliantly designed to keep them laughing all the way to the bank.

Two years later, there was no time for laughter. "We tried to model the successful results of the U.S. students," says Jules, a police officer with the Mnjikang Police Service. (He's been with that service for six years and was an Ontario Provincial Police officer for 11 years before that.) Instead of success, however, he and Ange accumulated $140,000 in high-interest debt, cost their family of five several stressful moves and pushed them to the brink of bankruptcy all because they followed an American-based investment system that didn't take into account that Canada's market is very different.

A couple of years after launching their revenue property business with that first strategy, they could track most of their properties in lost savings and mounting debt. By the time they tallied repairs and electrical upgrades, commission and the need to cover part of the purchaser's down payment, one of their first properties cost them about $20,000. Another deal on an eightplex cost them $27,000 when a dispute with a contractor led them to walk away from the deal. Yet another fixer-upper robbed them of $30,000.

The turning point came in August 2003 when Jules joined the Real Estate Investment Network.

A year later, armed with a few better investments and a whole lot more Canadian-specific knowledge, a professional credit counsellor helped the family get into a legal process by which they could avoid bankruptcy. Under terms negotiated with their creditors, the McKenzies kept their existing properties, which, by then, were generating enough revenue to cover all expenses.

Jules recalls that the move to a Canadian system signalled a massive "shift in what we were trying to do." From near bankruptcy, their portfolio has since grown to include 43 properties held with joint venture partners, as well as two single-family homes, including one with a suited basement.

"Our fundamental error was buying older properties," Jules reflects, "particularly in our little town, where some of those houses are over 100 years old. We didn't have a specific plan, or the funds to complete these major renovations."

Now firmly focused on buying town houses and condominiums, they find their condo fees cover most exterior maintenance costs. Following our new-found systems to analyze and buy real estate has taken the guess work out of cash flow projections. "We're able to set up what I call generational wealth," says Jules. "We're investing on the basis of economic fundamentals and we're confident our properties will continue to appreciate. So far, we have nine joint venture partners and they trust their money with us because we have adopted an informed approach to investing."

Ange laughs when asked how they put some of the tougher lessons to work in their investment business. It turns out one tenant, provided with "free" water, provided a laundry service for an extended family. With that experience under their belts, their next rental unit included a coin-operated washer and dryer that paid for itself in about 18 months. "Our gains haven't come without costs, because it's been a struggle for us," she admits. "But I feel like we can at least see the light now—and we're almost at the end of the tunnel."

Her optimism is fuelled by a May 2005 deal to buy 38 town homes with joint venture partners.

Jules found the deal, then brought in six JV partners and dropped his personal share to 25% to make it work. "Why 25%? Well, I figure that 25% of something is better than 100% of nothing," says Jules. "Besides, this property is managed by a great property manager and I just have to manage the manager."

That long-term approach to their investment business feels darn good compared to the stress of earlier get-rich-quick strategies, he adds.

If he has any regrets about where he's at right now, Jules, now 39 years old, concedes it's that his father is not alive to see him taking care of his family. A 17-year police veteran, Jules McKenzie grew up on a First Nations reservation in Quebec, where the cycle of poverty ran deep and basic amenities, like clean running water, ran scarce. A dedicated advocate for First Nations people, Jules' father taught his children to seek a legacy of financial independence. "I remember watching my dad fighting for native rights and native self-determination when I was a child," says Jules, who figures a fair portion of his personal stick-to-it-iveness is the inheritance of both genetics and example.

Jules likes moving through the world secure in the knowledge his father would approve of what his son has done to put his family on the path of financial independence.

Jules and Ange are grateful the REIN Group became part of their lives when it did. The systems helped them tremendously, and they're helping others by sharing what they've learned about investing. To that end, their new investing philosophy and style begs the question, *How can I help you?* Guided by that philosophy, they're helping a couple of Ange's siblings invest in real estate and they mentor other novice investors, too. "I am proud that I can take this experience and help others to not make the same mistakes that I made, either by assisting them or having them invest with us," says Jules.

— ∞ —

Don Campbell's Observations

Jules and Ange have returned from a devastating start. We can all learn about fortitude from this wonderful couple. If anyone had an excuse to give up on their vision of financial security, they sure did. Yet, they chose to ignore that excuse and instead find a way around it.

The easy option would have been to declare bankruptcy and hide behind it. Of course, the easy course is not the best course in most cases, and that has been proven in their story. Jules and Ange stepped up to the plate and took full responsibility for their situation and faced the consequences.

The strength and confidence this has provided them will last for the rest of their lives. There will never be a problem too large for them to solve, as they just cleared a huge hurdle with confidence.

Taking responsibility for the situations in our lives, although not easy, provides strength. When we pretend to ignore tough situations in our life, they don't go away. They just sit in the back of our minds constantly chattering and sapping our energy. I'm sure you've heard the 3:00 a.m. voice of worry, when you wake up and immediately you start thinking of the key situation that hasn't been dealt with. The more of these unresolved situations we carry along with us the less happy, healthy and wealthy we can become. The basis of this unbalance comes from focusing on the past and the regrets this rearward focus can bring. Only by taking responsibility for their cleanup, no matter how uncomfortable that may be, can you start creating the life you truly want.

It is very simple to test this out yourself. Identify a situation that you have chosen to ignore, take responsibility, whether you believe it is your "fault" or not. Then go and deal with it directly. After the uncomfortable cleanup is done, you will feel physically lighter and you will have freed up space in your brain for more creative thoughts. You'll come to enjoy this new feeling and start looking for other situations that need your attention.

Throughout this very stressful time, their family stuck together, kept their long-term focus and have come out the other side stronger, more confident and substantially better off financially, all for taking responsibility and not being afraid of saying "no more!"

ACTION STEPS

1. Is there a problem or situation in your life that you've decided to ignore rather than confront? If so, what is it specifically?

   _____

   _____

   _____

   _____

2. What are the three action steps you will take to start the process of dealing with this situation?

----

3. By what date do you wish to have this situation cleared up so you can start focusing on the future?

Celebrate the cleanup of this uncomfortable situation, then repeat the above three steps on the next situation. As an added hint, don't create any more of these emotional anchors. When a situation like this shows up in your life in the future, rather than ignore it, deal with it directly

SUCCESS STORY #6
IF AT FIRST YOU DON'T SUCCEED . . .
FIND A BETTER MENTOR!

Domenic Mandato

That property was a heartache, but I learned a lot about managing prop-
erty and I learned a lot about finding solutions instead of being dragged
down by problems. More than anything, I learned I could do this.

Domenic Mandato remembers the property that nearly broke his spirit.
With a basement suite plus two suites upstairs (one two bedroom and one
bachelor), it had all the markings of a cash cow. He owned a handful of
investment properties scattered across the country, but this one in Maple
Ridge was close to his Vancouver-area home. It looked like the ideal property on which to cut his property management teeth. Unfortunately for
Domenic, very little went according to his plan. The two suites upstairs
were sporadically rented, and tenant issues slashed into the time he had to
renovate the basement suite before tenants could move in. "I remember
feeling physically sick when I turned onto that street," he recalls, "because
nine times out of ten, something was going wrong."

When Domenic decided to sell the house, one of his contacts offered
$200,000, a nice increase from the $155,000 he'd paid, even after $15,000
in upgrades were included. When Domenic wavered, the buyer cut his
offer. Before long, only $150,000 was left on the table. "I was devastated,"
he says. "But my biggest fear was that maybe I wasn't cut out for real estate
investment. I believed this was my future and it wasn't working."

In the end, his wife, Rosa, encouraged Domenic to give the place another go. Following up on a comment made by the same buyer who kept
dropping his price, they converted the upstairs to a single suite. "Lo and
behold," says Domenic, "it ran great for about 18 months." A couple of
years later, in 2003, they sold it for $195,000, using the money to help
their family relocate to his new job in Calgary.

A business development manager for an automation company in
Calgary, Domenic took his first real estate seminar back in 1999. The
deal on their first family home closed that same year and, with Rosa expecting their first baby, they used a line of credit to buy property with an

investment firm that sells property at its seminars. Following similar leads, they also bought into a triplex in Montreal and a couple of properties in Ontario. None of these turned out exactly as the information indicated. Frustrated, but with no way to prove his investments were not delivering what he thought he'd been promised, Domenic clung to the notion he could generate long-term wealth via real estate—if only someone could help him out. In fairness, at least one of the educational programs he paid for included mentorship—sort of. Domenic was darned disappointed to learn their version of mentorship meant he paid good money to be "on the phone with what felt like 100 other investors." To make matters worse, those same mentors told him they couldn't answer his "Canadian" questions.

Chagrined by his first stab at property management and frustrated by the failed mentorship, Domenic broached the subject of real estate investment with the realtor who helped them find a home in Calgary. That guy put him onto REIN, and it changed Domenic's life. "I'd been burned so many times before," he says, "so I asked an awful lot of questions. I was excited to find out Don Campbell himself led the meetings and I joined in June 2003."

A few months later, he attended a Don Campbell presentation on buying multi-family properties. Determined to move his portfolio in that direction, Domenic followed leads—and started buying.

Now parents to three young children, ages seven, four and two, Domenic and Rosa owned 62 units by July 2007 and were negotiating for 42 more. All of the units are in economically strong areas.

The toughest part of his business right now is juggling a day job alongside management of his real estate holdings. He understands the value of that paycheque and appreciates how his job brings him in contact with some of the senior executives pulling the expansion strings on Canada's oil and gas industry.

There is a strategy for coping with that anxiety, confides Domenic. "It's called planning for the future. I've got some good properties in place and with rents increasing over time, cash flow will be good, too. There is no question in my mind I will be a real estate investor for many years to come because it is now so enjoyable."

Domenic bases that forecast on a mid-2007 portfolio that tipped the scales at $10 million—not bad for a guy who bought his first investment property with a line of credit, then came close to walking away from real estate investment when tenants got the best of his unsophisticated land-lording skills.

But let's get one thing straight: Domenic Mandato appreciates a lesson when he sees one. When Domenic thinks about that house back in Maple Ridge, B.C., his memories are tempered by more recent experiences and his later success. "That first property was a heartache, but I learned a lot about managing property and I learned a lot about finding solutions instead of being dragged down by problems." Domenic's voice falls quiet before he adds, "more than anything, I learned I could do this."

It's that knowledge that spurs him forward—and has his eyes looking up—w-a-a-a-y up. "I can see myself moving into commercial property." Translation: He'd like to be the bucks behind some high-rise commercial space.

In the meantime, Domenic surrounds himself with successful people and people who support him. That wisdom nurtured his real estate port-folio's success during the transition from single to multi-family housing, and it helped him raise $2.5 million in investment dollars from family and friends. When opportunity knocks, Domenic also opens the door, even when it means he's really helping someone else out. His advice to an im-migrant friend, for example, prompted the friend to take an occupational leap of faith and concentrate on his photography skills. His business took off, and he thanks Domenic for the inspiration.

For his part, Domenic is just happy to help others recognize oppor-tunities in their lives: "If I examine my life, if I look at my success, then I have to be honest and say it owes a great deal to the people I've met and the people I've surrounded myself with, like Don [Campbell] and the REIN group. They've catapulted me to the next level of investing. By the same token, if I have one thing to warn others about, it's to stay away from people who are negative. You want people who will help you move forward, not people who want to hold you back."

Don Campbell's Observations

A great lesson from Domenic's experiences is the one he learned regarding mentorship. It is tremendously important to ensure that the mentor you have is currently helping you to achieve results. It is easy to coach theory, but a good friend of mine gave me these rules for choosing a mentor:

- They must not be theorist; they must have real-life experience.

- They must have a higher net worth than you. If they are going to teach you how to be financially successful, they better already have more wealth than you as proof that their system will work for you.

- If they are providing you with investment research, they should not also be selling you the investment (stocks or investment property) as this is biased influence and a conflict of interest. A mentor is a mentor; a salesperson is a salesperson; both are important to have in your life. They just shouldn't be the same person.

Now, these three points sound very black and white, maybe even a little harsh, yet it does give us something to ponder. To whom are we listening in our lives? Are they looking after our best interests, or their own? Where do we get unbiased research before we make decisions?

An underlying message from Domenic is that the mentor should have expertise in your geographic area so that he or she understands the subtleties of your market. For instance, if you are investing in Canada, find a Canadian support team; if you want to invest in the United States, look for an American team as a mentor and make sure they have real-life experience and lived through both up and down markets, so they can advise you in all market conditions.[1]

The second lesson we learn from Domenic is that it is still very possible to keep a full-time management job of more than 40 hours per week while building a large portfolio of real estate. In fact, he's already built his property total up to $10 million and he really only started to build it in late 2003. It is often preferable that you do keep your job, as it will be easier to arrange mortgage financing on your investments.

1   For more details on how to choose an unbiased mentor, see tip #10 in *97 Tips for Canadian Real Estate Investors* by Don Campbell (Toronto: Wiley 2006).

Due to their focus on properties in economically strong areas, if Domenic and Rosa sat back and let the market take care of their current portfolio, they would be extremely happy with the returns in the coming years. However, their systems are now in place so it would be a pity to stop now with the potential they have as a family. They're focusing on the positives, working through the roadblocks and setting themselves up to create a wonderful legacy. All it took was a slight change of direction; small changes can lead to large gains.

ACTION STEPS

1. Who are the three people who have the most influence over your financial decisions? (It's okay if you put yourself on the list):

    * _____

    * _____

    * _____

2. Do you feel that they are unbiased in their recommendations? Rate each one:

    * _____

    * _____

    * _____

3. Are there any changes you feel you need to make?

    _____

    _____

    _____

    _____

SUCCESS STORY #7
SINGLE MOM OF THREE FINDS A WAY TO MAKE IT HAPPEN

Tana Wheatcroft

I'm learning to be smarter. And it's working.

Tana Wheatcroft was living someone else's nightmare. Thirty-three years old, newly separated and the mother of three elementary-school-aged kids, she was intimidated by what she knew to be true. She knew, for example, that she needed an independent income, no small feat after being a stay-at-home mom for 13 years. She also knew that her kids needed her, perhaps more than ever, and that few jobs (and quite possibly none she was qualified to do) could keep her at home before 9 a.m. and after 3 p.m.

More than anything, she knew she and her kids had to find a way to be okay—and that she was responsible for making that happen.

"So, while some investors go looking for what they want to do, I focused on real estate investment very early," recalls Tana. "It was something that had interested me for a long time. Now I just wanted to do it."

At the time they separated, Tana and her husband were renting out the other half of the duplex in which the family lived. That experience, and a chance introduction to REIN via a magazine article, took her to her first meeting. "It was obvious to me, right from the beginning, that this group was going to help me get started and I soaked up the information they were giving."

But it wasn't easy. Still reeling from the emotional turmoil in her life, and completely intimidated by the knowledge and raw enthusiasm that swirled around her at REIN meetings, Tana went to the meetings, but avoided contact. "I swear I didn't talk to anyone in that room for six months."

After six months of regular attendance, she drove three hours to a city she'd only visited once before for a workshop. "I left that meeting absolutely empowered," says Tana, her dark eyes sparkling at the memory. "Empowered—and determined to buy—I literally drove around the streets looking for a house for sale."

The one she found had all the markings of a winner. "I saw two others on the same street that could eventually be bought and torn down for a multi-family building. I got that house—and I was bursting with enthusiasm."

What she didn't see were the problems a more experienced investor might have clued into, or at least recognized as issues to be dealt with. First, the home was old, a fact that complicated her quest for insurance, with seven companies turning her down. The home was also located in a neighbourhood that teetered on the cusp of gentrification. That's the process that transforms run-down but affordable neighbourhoods, typically in the inner city, into communities with rapidly escalating prices. Savvy investors know there is a significant difference in tenant profiles pre- and post-gentrification. Tana wasn't that savvy yet. Her first tenant experiences were horrid.

She had to evict one set of tenants. Their successors used the property for a marijuana grow-op. Tana shakes her head. In spite of all that, the deal made money—and it convinced her she was in the right business.

Her mistakes weren't all behind her, though. "At one point," she says, "I had to sell a lot of properties, including the duplex we were living in. I was holding 40 properties and trying to manage them all myself. Looking back, I was cocky. I was listening to other people and not doing my own due diligence. That's not what I had learned over the last six months."

What she did learn is to find solutions, not wallow in the mess. To get her business back on track, Tana took a deep breath, sold some properties and redoubled her due diligence.

Today, with her oldest child having graduated high school in June 2007, the single mom's portfolio includes 21 properties. Held with 12 joint venture partners, they include single-family homes in Calgary, Edmonton, Sherwood Park, Sylvan Lake, High River and Okotoks.

She's done some renovate-and-sell, but right now she prefers to find properties that have potential, negotiate a solid deal, and then sell these contracts to investors who have the time and talents for completing the hassles of the renovation-upgrade.

Back on the home front, her kids form another part of her investment team. Now 18, 16 and 13, they help with the yard work and cleaning of her rental houses. Her 16-year-old daughter also helps her organize and send out letters to people who might be thinking of selling their homes.

"What I'm very good at is finding properties," says Tana, who values the input of a particular real estate agent. He frequently calls her with potential deals and in return for helping her source competitive prices in different markets, she always pays full commission if he's part of a successful deal. "I'm not interested in negotiating lower rates. He's good at what he does and I appreciate that."

He also understands that her market is focused on properties located in neighbourhoods in ethnically diverse communities. "It's a demographic that works for me," says Tana. She can provide quality housing for quality people. Whereas tenants in other parts of the city shy away from paying top dollar for great quality homes, this demographic is characterized by multi-generational families who pool their incomes to pay for good-looking, well maintained homes.

Over time, Tana has added mortgage brokers to her team, so they are chasing the banks for her; a move she calls "one of the smartest things I've ever done." She's also learned to hire bailiffs if eviction is an issue. "This isn't about me; it's about people not meeting their obligations. I had to learn that, too."

Experience may be a tough teacher, but it's a good teacher, too.

"I find it kind of ironic that other investors now phone me to ask about problems they're having," observes Tana, "but I guess I do have something to say. I've made some mistakes, but I've paid attention to those mistakes, too—and I'm not going to make them again!"

Don Campbell's Observations

A single mom of three children would have her hands full at the best of times, but Tana didn't let that stop her from taking control of her future. She had very limited income, she was a stay-at-home mom, her kids were her number-one priority and there weren't many jobs she was qualified to get. If she had an excuse to become a victim of circumstances, she had all of the pieces.

Lesson one from Tana, no matter where you are currently, financially, emotionally or geographically, today is the perfect time to start on your future and not hide behind your past.

Sure, you'll make mistakes but at least you're moving forward. She found a group of people who were willing to teach her the mistakes they've made and the strategies they've used to win in the game of real estate. She sat back, listened for half a year building her knowledge base. Then, and only then, did she start to take action. She had the patience it takes to learn a new craft and understood that she wasn't running a race.

Now, just a few short years later she has not only built a strong financial foundation, she has been able to influence her children in more ways than even she knows. The entrepreneurial spirit she has transferred to them will serve them very well in whatever career they choose . . . a much better lesson than playing victim would have given them.

It is important to remember that all of our actions influence others in our lives, even if we don't immediately see it. Whether it is our children, our parents, our siblings or our friends, we influence them as they influence us. Our choice is whether to be a positive influence or a negative influence. Being negative is the easy way out. Tana chose the more difficult road to give her children the opportunity of a lifetime by living in a positive-focused family atmosphere—and look what it has provided her on so many levels. Now Tana is becoming a leader in the investment community, transferring her knowledge and experiences to others. We all need more people like her in our lives.

Sure she's made mistakes and is bound to make others in the future, but that's not going to hold her back from achieving her family's "Personal Belize."

ACTION STEPS

1. What three people do you have the most influence upon in your life?

   _____

   _____

   _____

   _____

2. What type of leadership are you providing these people?

   _____

   _____

   _____

   _____

3. What three people most influence your life?

_____

_____

_____

_____

4. Thank those who are positive influences. They may not even be aware of their influence.

5. If one or more of the people you have identified is a negative influence, find a way to not allow their poor outlook to affect your thoughts. Surround yourself with positive influences and life will become more fun and success will be drawn your way.

SUCCESS STORY #8
FOCUS ON THE POSITIVE—BUT DON'T IGNORE THE RISKS

Diane Duckett

Fear is normal. Every deal I go into I ask myself, "What's the absolute worst thing that could happen to me?" Usually, the very worst thing is not so scary after all.

Teenaged children have a way of making their parents feel like they know absolutely nothing. So imagine single mom Diane Duckett's elation when her 17-year-old daughter won an in-class competition by following in her mom's footsteps. That's right. While her classmates used their fictitious million bucks to buy hot cars, clothes and, in a few cases a principal residence, Diane's daughter bought two residential properties. Both generated rental revenue—and equity.

In fairness, the kid had a good teacher.

Diane's been buying revenue property since the late 1970s. When she and her now ex-husband relocated to Calgary in 1997, after having moved throughout the world with his position in the British government, they bought a principal residence. A year later, they bought a revenue house down the street. Four years later, that second property became Diane's separate residence.

It's also the headquarters of a real estate investment portfolio firmly centred around a niche market for executive suite accommodation available at monthly rates. By the fall of 2002, Diane had bought her first apartment-style condominium in Calgary's Lower Mount Royal. Two years later, she had five condos in two different buildings in the same area and, she says, "I was hooked."

Diane also owns two properties in South Africa, acquired in separate deals that date back several decades. She outsources their management, but self-manages all of her property in Calgary, where she sticks to a business strategy that aims for 100% occupancy. To that end, she outfits each unit with everything from blenders to blow dryers, art work, CDs and dried flower arrangements. Each Home From Home (which is her company's name, too) also includes cable and Internet access and rents for slightly under market rates. Again, that's part of a deliberate strategy to keep each unit occupied.

Diane left full-time employment so she could manage her business and spend more time with her kids, now 15 and 17. In early 2006, she became the money partner in a similar business venture in Edmonton where she's currently the JV in five executive suites located in newer buildings.

That same year, she took $12,700 from her kids' personal savings (birthday, Christmas and grandparent gifts) and invested in another Calgary property. When that partnership ended, she took the $45,000 she'd earned with that partnership investment and pumped it right into another property all with the goal of creating a financial foundation for her children.

And what do the kids think? "You don't think I told them, do you?" asks Diane with an infectious laugh. While she's big on them saving for their future, she's not so big on letting them know how much money they have squirrelled away in investments on top of an education savings plan. She wants the money to be there when they need it, but shivers at the thought they would "expect it."

That said, she does expect her daughter and son to help do things like move furniture and they may even pitch in and help, when they're not working at their own jobs, with some between-tenant cleaning.

Diane admits the lure of the deal remains strong, even though she's not actively looking for new property. That's why she likes meeting a group of fellow investors on a monthly basis. She likes hearing about what other investors are doing, the breakthroughs they've had and the mistakes they've made. It is a continual learning experience.

"The best thing of all this is that I've got freedom," says Diane. "I don't have to push somebody else's papers around any more."

She's also got time to plan her 2008 journey around-the-world with Kirsty and Andrew at her side. Kirsty will have just graduated from high school. Andrew will be going into Grade 12.

"I think I did overcome a fair bit of adversity to get where I'm at," she concludes. "But I'm here now. And I love it!"

Don Campbell's Observations

Adversity is obviously not a stranger to Diane. As a single mom she has been able to not only create a financial foundation for her children but also leave her full-time employment to focus on her real estate and providing leadership to her children. That's great, when you consider that she only started investing on her own five years ago.

That's the biggest lesson that Diane teaches us with her story. If you allow yourself time, and you stick with your system, real estate can change your whole financial picture and get you through any adversity you may have in your life. If you do it right, you'll be having so much fun and be so busy living your life that you won't have any time to think up excuses for not taking action. When you are committed to your pathway, life is incredibly rewarding ... but only if you are truly committed.

The second lesson that comes through clearly is that she found a niche she enjoys and makes good business sense and she works hard to be the best at it. Sophisticated investors like Diane know that the more specialized you become the more long-term success you can create.

ACTION STEPS

It took Diane approximately five years to get to where she is starting to really enjoy the fruits of her real estate investments. With that in mind ask yourself these questions:

1. Where were you financially, emotionally and geographically five years ago?

    _____

    _____

    _____

    _____

2. Where do you truly want to be five years from today?

    _____

    _____

    _____

    _____

3. Will the pathway you took over the last five years get you to where you want to go?

_____

_____

_____

_____

4. If not, what are you going to change to make sure you get there?

_____

_____

_____

_____

SUCCESS STORY #9
LEARNING DISABILITY IS NO EXCUSE FOR NOT BEING SUCCESSFUL

Philip McKernan and Pauline McKernan

I won't pretend to harbour some romantic notion of Canada. This is a country I genuinely like, but I'm setting up a real estate investment business here because it's the right time and place. This country is an economic powerhouse and Europeans don't know that yet.

Philip McKernan is a student of the global village. He has travelled the world in search of the finest wines and best coffee beans, all in the name of good business. By 2005, major business organizations, schools and post-secondary associations in Ireland, the land of his birth, were inviting the 33-year-old to talk about what it means to build a successful business from the ground up. Others were hiring him as a personal coach. What they really wanted to know was how he got so darn smart, so darn fast. And Philip loved it.

But it wasn't what these people thought they knew about him that captured his imagination. He was intrigued by what they didn't know.

Better yet, he realized he no longer had to hide the disability that virtually crippled his own formal education. In fact, he knew the dark side of his success story could probably help some people in the room, since life's demons come in all shapes and sizes.

A native of Dublin and the youngest of three boys, Philip concedes his home was "probably more competitive than others. I think that is a good part of the reason I don't have much trouble taking action when others might take a second look." What he did have trouble with was reading.

While in school, his learning disability went undiagnosed. But it manifested itself in fierce psychological pain. Emotionally speaking, young Philip was devastated by his inability to understand how his friends learned, and why he couldn't seem to decipher the same information from the written page. The pain grew physical and intense: "I spent the last six years of school, the years young people are supposed to be spreading their wings and starting to find things that interest them for the future, with an absolute knot in my stomach. It felt like the way your stomach feels the minutes and seconds leading up to the moment you jump off a bungee platform. I was nearly sick to my stomach. And every day was like that."

Philip was gut-wrenchingly afraid he was going to be asked to read out loud. The fear set in motion a series of coping strategies. Avoidance was paramount. What he didn't know then was that his disorder was not uncommon.

Philip McKernan is dyslexic. A learning disability that manifests itself in problems perceiving the printed word, dyslexics encounter various degrees of difficulty with reading and spelling. When business success proved easy, given his willingness to work hard to excel in competitive markets, Philip mastered coping skills never taught in school. At 35, the vestiges of the disability wreak havoc in only one area: "I cannot spell," says Philip.

Years later, a natural dexterity with the same numbers that once confounded him brought 33-year-old Philip before groups of young students and professionals. The statistical reality of those he looked out on was as clear as the noses on their faces: While no two students experience the same problems with dyslexia, it is the most common learning disability, affecting literacy development skills in up to 4% of the population. Statistically speaking, Philip knew some of the people in his audience would relate to his own disability.

Others, who struggled with issues ranging from bullying to complicated family lives or unfulfilled vocations, would also find strength and wisdom in his experience.

"They could listen to me," he says, "and realize if I could do it, they could do it. It was the first time I'd ever talked about being dyslexic and the story really resonated with my listeners. I started to realize that everyone has a story. People wanted to focus on my success, but what they needed was to learn how hard I worked to get here and how I conquered my fear."

A year later, his entrepreneurial spirit piqued by what he was hearing about an economic boom in Alberta, Canada, Philip found himself in Edmonton at a book signing with Don Campbell, president of REIN Canada. The investment opportunities made almost immediate sense. But there was more. When Don Campbell talked about how real estate investors were using their financial success to meet personal goals, Philip was intrigued. If he could use this vehicle to make enough money to support himself and his wife, Pauline, he could spend more time inspiring young people with his personal story.

By October 2006, Philip and Pauline (they married in 2004) were buying property in Edmonton. They held six single-family homes, then jumped from that market into development and are currently analyzing a $52-million, 160-acre development just outside Alberta's capital city.

They had relocated to Edmonton by May 2007, buying a principal residence and launching McKernan Property, the only European company solely focused on the Alberta market. They represent Europeans with upwards of $250,000 to invest. The Canadian side of the investment search, Maple Leaf Property, will source Canadian investment partners.

Given his rapport with European clients he got to know in the coffee and wine trades, the transatlantic move was not a prerequisite of doing business here. The bigger issue is confidence, and Philip likes knowing he'll talk to Europeans from the very place he thinks they should invest.

He'd been a regular visitor to Alberta ever since his parents participated in a Calgary house exchange in 1998. He liked doing business here and he also liked REIN, attending four workshops and one Quickstart program while he was still living in Ireland.

Philip's first Canadian property was a JV with another REIN member in October 2006. It cost $120,000 and was worth more than $200,000 five months later. "Even in the height of the boom in Ireland," he recounts, "we did not experience that kind of growth. As a result, we have decided to sell every other property we own in South Africa, UK, France, Finland, and all but one in Ireland, to invest in Alberta."

In late 2006, the Bank of Ireland (Ireland's largest bank) approached Philip about producing a DVD where the accomplished speaker talks about how he thinks students are influenced by family, media, friends and the fears that suppress their dreams. That DVD was sent to every secondary-level school in the country. Down the road, Philip dreams of taking time to produce another DVD and (irony aside) write a book about what it's like to have dyslexia. He wants to give others a window on the world he came from, not so they'll feel bad, but so that they'll look around and see themselves and others from a different perspective.

"Hate is a strong word, but I do have two things in life I hate," says Philip. "The first is fear. The second is regret. It's the fear of doing or not doing things that leads to regret and I see this in people every day. Fear has people all over the world in the wrong job, marriage, financial situation, mental state, physical state, etc. They settle for what they don't want because they are too afraid to go after what they do want."

Thinking back to a rambunctious childhood fuelled by testosterone-laced fun with his brothers, Philip knows fear has its place in keeping people alive. But when it keeps you from being the person you were meant to be, it is "the assassin of dreams" because it denies people a chance to live a meaningful life.

That's not going to happen to Philip McKernan. Better yet, real estate investment will give him the tools he needs to inspire others. "Success comes from learning what you can do. I want to challenge people to live the way they want to live!"

<hr>

Don Campbell's Observations

Learning disabilities are being diagnosed at an increasing rate across the country and around the world. Sadly, in our society, this becomes a label that places people into pigeonholes and in some rare cases these labels are used as a crutch for not living life to the fullest.

Any disability should be taken seriously, yet as we learn from Philip's story, it can also be used as a motivator. The "I'm going to prove my label wrong" attitude has helped lift Philip into the stratosphere as a world-class educator and real estate investor, changing lives in Europe and Canada.

Without a formal post-secondary education, Philip readily admits that he is often pre-judged when presenting to a room filled with highly educated professionals. It used to bother him, but now he places a spotlight on it and turns it into an asset. Sure, there will always be people who think that he should have a formal diploma, but as you see in his story he's not too concerned about what others are thinking; he's too busy out there being a leader inspiring others to be the best they can be in anything they choose.

Philip's success truly began to take off when he partnered up, in life and in business, with his wife, Pauline. With her formal accounting training and joie de vivre, she brings a completely different perspective to the business. This business and personal relationship work so well because of their differences, not despite them. They are stronger together than they would be apart.

And now they've committed to building a huge business and the first step was their commitment to spending much more time in Canada so that they are on the ground taking care of their joint venture partner's money more efficiently, while maximizing their returns. Not many would make that type of commitment and their partners must be very thankful.

On the path that these two are on, you are bound to be hearing increasingly more about them as they become leaders, not just in Europe but here in Canada.

ACTION STEPS

1. What excuse are you currently using on a consistent basis for not taking action?

    _____

    _____

    _____

    _____

2. For the next 30 days, be aware of how many times you are tempted to use the excuse. But rather than use it, find an excuse to take action. In the awareness will come opportunity.

3. Whom can you rely on to help you with this exercise?

    _____

    _____

SUCCESS STORY #10
A Four-Year Journey to a Financially Secure Future

Simone Robinson and Ernest Robinson

The early days in the business were tough. Now we're giving more than we have ever done and are enjoying life like never before.

Simone and Ernie Robinson had a lot on their minds as they sat in the hospital emergency room in the spring of 2007. It was the first serious injury Ernie had recorded in more than 30 years on the job and, with the throbbing pain of torn biceps and tendons pulsing through his body, their anxious thoughts jumped ahead to the future. A journeyman carpenter who'd been self-employed since 1979, a couple of years before their now 26-year-old triplets were born, Ernie earned the family's primary income. By the time of his injury, his company was subcontracted to a window and door company and, with Edmonton's economy fuelling a hot renovation business, Ernie and Simone still counted on the job. They also knew he needed two arms to do it.

As bad as the injury seemed at first, skilled medical staff took care of the arm with unexpected speed. The injury happened on a Thursday, he supervised the job site on Friday, had surgery on Saturday, rested on Sunday and was back at work on Monday.

At the height of all the pain and angst, however, Simone was afraid, but she also remembers turning to Ernie and telling him that they were going to be okay. "Even if he hadn't been able to work for a whole year," she says, "we would have managed, no problem."

That conviction rested on four walls and a roof—only it wasn't the roof over their heads at home in Sherwood Park, a prospering municipality on the northeast edge of Edmonton. The Robinsons had been real estate investors since 2003 and were holding eight properties when Ernie was injured.

"If we'd had to, we could have sold one to give us some income. It was good to know we had options," says Simone.

Those options came with a few lessons attached. In the early days, Simone recalls, "we jumped in and bought three properties very quickly.

Before long, we had five vacant houses and we really didn't know what to do. It did get a little overwhelming."

It also got better. "The first houses we bought were not so great as far as revenue property. The first property we bought provided great cash flow, but was at a very bad address. So when the tenant we inherited moved out, we had to renovate to re-rent it. We chose to quickly sell it and replaced it with a property in a much better location."

In the early days, they also tried their hand at the reno-and-flip. "We did it all wrong," says Simone. They had partners, but hadn't agreed on all that needed to be done. Worse, Ernie booked time off to do the work and brought his paid employees with him. "We lost money, but we learned a lot," says Simone.

With all of those bad experiences channelled into positive lessons, the Robinsons focused on building a better team. By the spring of 2005 they'd met what Simone proudly refers to "as the world's best real estate agent." This agent found them four properties and joint-ventured on one deal.

"For us, real estate investment has created a safety net," says Simone. "Before real estate, we had no corporate pension to fall back on and the construction industry has been pretty feast-and-famine over the years. We had a kind of pay-as-you-go lifestyle, and there was no way to put away thousands and thousands of dollars for retirement."

When updating their wills in January 2007, she discovered their portfolio was valued at almost $2 million, with a loan-to-value ratio of 51.6%. "This is a long way from the $85,000 we started with and we haven't done anything that anyone couldn't do."

They have, however, applied the philosophies and strategies that REIN teaches—and Simone is adamant about the group's role in their success. "We are giving more than we have ever done," she says, "and are enjoying life like never before."

Partnerships with a spouse can be complicated, and Simone admits she's seen other investors sell their properties to maintain familial peace. While she's always kept the books for Ernie's construction business, which evolved with market demand, her role in their real estate portfolio has always been more hands on. "In the end, it brought us much closer together," Simone affirms. "But there were days when neither of us knew what to do with a particular investment problem. All we knew was that we wanted the other to take care of it—and that's disastrous. Learning to be 'business partners' was probably the toughest thing we faced."

Four years after buying their first property (one of two "dogs" they've since sold), Simone and Ernie are confident about a future that includes using Ernie's income to maintain their borrowing power so they can build a portfolio of 12 to 15 houses over the next five or so years. After that, Simone says, they'll keep the best and sell a few of the others "so we have a comfortable income, a workload that doesn't tie us down—and we'll even be able to travel a bit."

In the meantime, they've also set a strong example of self-reliance for those triplets, two sons and a daughter. As of mid-2007, all three own their principal residence, one of which doubles as a suited investment property in a neighbourhood of upwardly-mobile equity.

"I think that one of the tricks with investing is learning to see the glass is half full," notes Simone. "There are days when you feel like giving up. But those usually happen just before all your hard work pays off!" It's always darkest right before the dawn.

Don Campbell's Observations

Ernie and Simone have proven that you can become a success no matter at what pace you wish to build your portfolio. They decided, in order to achieve their goals, build their construction business and stay sane all at the same time, they needed to invest at their own pace and not compare their results with what others were achieving.

This journey to building their financial foundation has taken only four years, and so far they have already increased their net worth (retirement fund) by almost $1 million.

Put yourself in Ernie and Simone's position for a moment. Imagine the sense of relief and freedom you would feel when you realized that even if Ernie couldn't work for a long time that finances were not going to be an issue: their real estate portfolio would take care of them. There are many independent contractors across Canada and whether they are blue or white collar many do not have the luxury of a corporate pension fund or disability insurance to cover them if they can't work. That's a situation that even a small real estate portfolio can solve; it provides a financial back-stop supporting your life.

Now they're able to play a financial leadership role in their circle of family and friends, showing them how they can accomplish the same thing in their lives.

Life and investing do not follow a straight and predictable line, as Ernie and Simone readily admit. However, they used their long-term vision, their positive attitude and their passion for building a strong financial foundation to get them through the rough patches. And in four short years, they were able to sit in the hospital emergency room and focus on Ernie's health rather than worry about finances. That alone has made the journey worthwhile.

ACTION STEPS

1. If you have been investing in real estate for more than 12 months, take a few moments to update your net worth statement. Remember to include current property value and outstanding mortgage principal.

2. If you are happy with your progress to date, congratulations. If you are not, what, specifically, are you going to change, starting today so that you are much happier one year from today when you do this exercise again. Be brutally honest with yourself; to change your results, you must change your actions.

_____

_____

_____

_____

SUCCESS STORY #11
ADVERSITY: THE MOTHER OF CREATIVITY

Brian Smeenk

I don't think I handle risk all that well. But my definition of risk is different from a lot of people's. I'd rather take some risks with money than look back on my life after 80 years and say, "I wish I'd done that."

It didn't take long for Brian and Jennifer Smeenk to decide what to do with the $70,000 she received from her mom's estate in the spring of 2005. A mechanical engineer by training and a real estate investor by choice, Brian had been buying investment property with two business partners for a couple of years. He looked at this new money a little differently. "It came from Jennifer's family, so I wanted it to stay in the family. But I told my wife I was worried about just putting it in the bank where it would most likely end up as a giant plasma TV or some new clothes."

With Jennifer's blessing, Brian hit the phones with a simple message: "I am looking to buy a fourplex. Let me know if you find something I should look at." One of his first callbacks got his attention and with a mortgage broker's help he and Jennifer soon bought a cash-flowing fourplex for $328,000. "I knew I could make that building work," he says, "and that equity appreciation was going to be hot. But I was self-employed and my debt-to-service ratio was probably at 125%, so I wasn't a good candidate for a lot of lenders. I think it's fair to say my mortgage broker had to work extra hard for this deal—and that's what got me the mortgage." It was another lesson learned: make sure you are working with a true investment property–focused mortgage broker.

Looking back, Brian knows that's the mortgage that launched his portfolio down the right path. A year later, he refinanced the building and used about $37,000 to buy something special for his family, a brand new Honda Odyssey for Jennifer, who was by then expecting their third baby. It's one of the few non-real estate purchases Brian readily admits to giving him peace of mind!

A few months later, he was reading public CMHC predictions of an Edmonton real estate market that would gain by an unprecedented 9% over the course of 2006. Behind the scenes, sophisticated investors were saying that was way too low. "I came home from a REIN meeting," he says, "and told Jennifer, 'We don't own enough property.'"

It was time to improve their own living situation, so they went looking for a home in the $350,000 range. Disappointed by what they found, but determined to buy real estate in a market where prices were on a steady up tick, Brian floated the idea of buying another fourplex instead. "What a brilliant idea!" was Jennifer's quick reply.

His next two fourplexes attracted multiple offers, but not before Brian locked in his price. He got his second fourplex for $425,000, $25,000 less than other deals on the table. The third one closed at a list price of $440,000, with a competing offer at $460,000. After $160,000 in renovations that finished in early 2007, his third fourplex appraised at $810,000. The second is his favourite deal to date. He put in $25,000 in upgrades after June 2006. A year later, it appraised at $910,000.

Buoyed by their portfolio's strength, the Smeenks took possession of a new home in May 2007. Their knowledge of the economic fundamentals of the residential real estate market helped Brian estimate that the home was undervalued by $100,000. They took a few months to finish the basement, then moved in with their four kids, ages six, five, three and one, in July.

With three fourplexes and a great family home behind them, Brian Smeenk admits there is a flip side to all of the obvious success. And that flip side has some pitfalls.

Back in the spring of 2002, Brian was disenchanted with his mechanical engineering career and his on-the-side experiences with network marketing. He and Jennifer were expecting their second baby when he got a $15,000 line of credit to take a real estate course that claimed 100% of students earned back their tuition fees before the course ended. "I was hugely naïve," he recalls. "I didn't know anything. I trusted them and although these guys didn't take my money and run, they sold me an absolute dog of a property." A few months and a lot of headaches later, Brian and Jennifer sold the building for a small profit. Making matters worse, between the contract and the closing he'd lost his job and their sole source of income. Ergo, he says, the profit "barely covered the living expenses we incurred during the renovation. It was devastating."

By the end of that year, he hooked up with two other investors. "I was too scared to do it on my own," he admits, "so we started into business together." They bought an eight-unit building and soon learned they could check their exhilaration at the door. They bought the $220,000 building with $50,000 down. Less than a year later, they learned it was a local haven for drug dealers and users. It wasn't just the real estate investment partners who had trouble with the tenants; Brian remembers sitting across the street and watching a SWAT team swarm one unit. About 18 months later, they sold the property. They turned a small financial profit and pocketed a massive education in landlording.

By this time, Brian was working his third job in mechanical engineering, the degree he earned in 1999. Hindsight tells him he was never cut out for that profession, but he has no regrets about his five years earning the degree, nor the engineering jobs he took to support his family while getting his feet wet in real estate. He knows he earned that piece of silver on his pinkie finger—and he knows it cuts some serious respect in a province that boasts more engineers per capita than any other.

The determination to stick with his engineering day jobs changed dramatically on Sept. 22, 2003, the day Brian brought home his third pink slip. He decided he was through with engineering. A month later, he signed up for a Quickstart program, a weekend he paid for with his credit card. "I went to that seminar without my partners and was blown away," he relates. "The other course I took encouraged a kind of cloak-and-dagger approach to every deal. At Quickstart, here was a guy telling me I had to be absolutely honest with everyone, including my banker." His message to his partners: "I'm joining REIN. And if you don't, I'm out of the partnership." Integrity and honesty in all his dealings are that important to Brian.

Still burned by his $15,000 lesson in how not to buy real estate if you want to be successful, Brian remembers sitting at the back of his first REIN meetings, pretty much oozing skepticism. "I kept trying to find something that didn't fit. Something that was wrong. Something that was unethical."

By January 2004, the partners felt reassured they were on to something good. They relaxed, started putting their new knowledge to work—and bought their 17 properties in their first year as members.

When the partnership ended after four years, Brian walked away from their portfolio with more than $1 million in cash. He and Jennifer also owned three fourplexes by the time he left and were on the lookout for more. Using equity from previous purchases, he'd like to own 20 to 25 fourplexes and half-duplexes by the time his portfolio peaks. He expects they'll all be in the same area and he'll likely continue to handle his own property management.

He'll also keep getting up when his kids rise at 7:30 a.m., take time to travel with his family of six and enjoy their new home with its beautiful view of the green space it backs onto. "My whole perspective of what I can and can't have has changed," he says. "I used to think about things that I couldn't afford. Now I think about things and ask myself, 'How can I afford that?' It makes a world of difference in how you approach life."

While engineers aren't widely known for their interpersonal communications skills, Brian feels that real estate investment has made him a better communicator and, in the process, a better person. "I've been backed into some corners by doing some things a sophisticated investor would tell you never, ever to do. I've gone into deals, for instance, where I really didn't know what I was getting myself into. I don't do that anymore—but it's because those early experiences really taught me a lot."

Reflecting on his own experiences in real estate, Brian says it's easy for market newcomers to "over-analyze this business and underestimate their abilities. This isn't rocket science and it's not get-rich-quick. It's slow and steady wins the race—as long as you understand the 'race' is about long-term financial security."

―――∞∞∞―――

Don Campbell's Observations

Brian and Jennifer's ride on their way to success has not been a smooth and straight line, and nor will it be for any real estate investor. Successful investors, like Brian and Jennifer, turn the setbacks they experience along the way into opportunities to adjust their investing system to avoid future problems. Unsophisticated investors have a tendency to play a "poor me" victim role when inevitable adversity strikes and then use this as an excuse to not take any further action. They become stuck in the past, rather than focus forward.

Brian and Jennifer had all of the opportunities in the world to stop shooting for their goal:

1. Their first experience with a property was bad.
2. Brian lost his job, their sole source of income.
3. Their first real estate training experience turned bad.
4. He had an unpleasant experience with the property in his first partnership.
5. His first real experience with landlording was a nightmare.

However, even with these setbacks, they persevered and are now beginning to reap the benefits. Sure, there must have been days in which they questioned what they were doing; most active investors have those days. They kept their focus on the horizon rather than the day-to-day bumps along the way. It is always good to remember the old proverb "The faster you row the boat, the less it will rock."

Another lesson we can learn from Brian and Jennifer's journey is that real estate investing is not as complex as some people would have you believe. It's not a race against anyone—it's all about what you want real estate to provide you with and never letting someone steal your family's dream.

ACTION STEPS

1. Brian stepped out of his comfort zone to become a better communicator and therefore a better investor. What do you feel is the biggest personal weakness that may be holding you back?

   _____

   _____

   _____

   _____

2. What steps, comfortable or uncomfortable, can you take to assist you in strengthening this perceived weakness?

   _____

   _____

   _____

   _____

3. By what date will you act on Step #2 above?

    _____

    _____

4. Most importantly, what strength do you have that you can accent and
    use to your advantage?

    _____

    _____

    _____

    _____

SUCCESS STORY #12
DON'T WAITE TO TAKE ACTION, NO MATTER WHAT YOUR AGE

John Waite and Nicky Waite

Hindsight is a cruel teacher. Looking back with the knowledge I have today, the biggest mistake I've made in real estate was selling out in the late 1970s and early 1980s. I should have studied economic fundamentals about where the market was really headed, rather than react to media headlines, and stayed the course.

John Waite bought his principal residence and his first real estate investment properties at the age of 28. Twenty-two years later, he'd sold most of his investments and was financially bankrupt after a successful kitchen cabinet manufacturing company he owned and operated was declared insolvent on his 50th birthday. Fifteen years after that, he's back in the real estate investment business, owns 30 properties and is comfortably well off.

Well, that's not quite true. Some might call him rich, given that his wife, Nicky, is still at his side after 40 years and they divide their time between travelling the world and indulging their two grandchildren. There's also that priceless collection of Rolls-Royce motor cars to consider. His 1929 Phantom I Pall Mall Touring Limousine won the Most Elegant Car award at an All-British Field Meet car show held in Vancouver in May 2007. His 1966 HJ Mulliner Rolls-Royce Silver Wraith Touring Limousine earned the People's Choice award at the same show the previous year. He also owns a 1969 T-Type Bentley. All three cars are a steely testament to how he's used excess revenue from other ventures to fund a real estate portfolio that now lets him and Nicky enjoy the time and financial luxuries associated with true freedom.

John figured he first learned about real estate investing the old-fashioned way, from his father. But he says his dad "never really taught me why he was investing in real estate, and when he died at the age of 58, the opportunity to learn from him was gone."

Still, the spark of real estate ownership was lit. In 1970, John and Nicky bought their first home in North Vancouver, then invested $2,500 each in two undeveloped lots (representing 25% down). They sold those lots a year later for $12,500, providing $2,500 in profit, thus making 100% return on investment (ROI) less interest on the loan.

In fairness, some investors may gloss over the interest payments, preferring to focus on gross as if it represented a pure profit. John Waite couldn't do that. Not after all he'd been through!

Keen to build on their early success, he and Nicky soon bought an investment property in east Vancouver. They paid $18,600, put $1,500 down and included a 10% interest take-back-mortgage from the vendor. They then installed a basement suite, recorded good cash flow and chalked up their first experience with buy-and-hold revenue property.

After taking a weekend investment course, John honed his skills at using low down payments to buy more property. Over the next few years, they ended up with "a total of seven houses, two in partnership with close friends."

An avid reader, John figured he knew what was coming next "and that real estate would not continue to increase." He divested his portfolio, buying silver in its stead, and was out of most of his real estate investments by the time mortgage rates exceeded 20% in 1982.

Through all of this, John worked as a professional engineer. He has degrees in engineering science from Oxford University and in water resource engineering from the University of California and spent 22 years working on the design, planning and licensing of hydroelectric projects, most with BC Hydro.

When he lost his job in 1985, John went into business for himself and bought a kitchen cabinet manufacturing company. The last of his real estate investments was sold in 1986 to buy new machinery for the growing business. "The company prospered for six years and then went bankrupt in the seventh," recalls John.

The experience was devastating—and made more traumatic by the fact it happened on John's 50th birthday. "I lost everything other than the house owned by my wife, Nicky." She'd insisted their assets be split when he went into business, a move that kept a roof over their heads during the darkest times.

There are moments in our lives when we crumble or stand tall. In 1992, John Waite stood tall. He liked the cabinet software his company had been using. So he approached its U.S. owner to ask to represent that product in a sales territory that covered B.C. and Alberta. "They said 'yes,' and my next business was born. Over the next 15 years, I took over the whole Canadian market and built up the business from scratch to more than $2 million a year. After a while, that gave me more income than I needed to live off, and I put the excess into mutual funds."

He also started to think about his dad's real estate investments and those he and Nicky held in previous decades. He bought his first condo properties and soon owned properties in Edmonton, Cranbrook, B.C., and Guelph, Ontario. Before long, he says he was dreaming of a "virtual apartment block made up of units in many different places across Canada." He figured the strategy spread his risk through different markets, leaving his overall portfolio less subject to changes in individual markets.

That approach changed in 2003, when John, living in B.C., attended a seminar and learned more about what was happening in Alberta's real estate market. From there, he took in his first REIN seminar, learned about market focus "and by the end of the weekend I had purchased a 12-unit apartment building." It was one of 15 buildings in a complex with 176 units in total.

That experience, tied to an economy now firing on all cylinders, cemented his and Nicky's conviction to invest in Alberta rather than anywhere else in Canada. "Over the past several years," he says, "we have converted most of our mutual funds, together with ongoing surplus income, into real estate. We now own 30 properties, and our retirement is secure."

Managing that portfolio is a hands-on business for John, but he doesn't do it on his own. "One key to our success has been that all of our properties are professionally managed. Another is that we have built up a team of professionals, including realtors, lawyers and mortgage brokers."

He also likes his information hot—and from the source. Although he lives in British Columbia, he goes to REIN meetings in Edmonton as often as he can, at least six times a year. He counts on the economic research and the association with other successful investors. "That connection to REIN gives me the confidence to continue to expand our investments because REIN teaches me which economic fundamentals to watch."

In 2007, John sold his cabinet software sales business to four of his key employees. He looks forward to the day when he's no longer involved in that business at all. "Our priorities now are enjoying life and enjoying our grandchildren." Sounds easy. But only John and Nicky Waite really know how long the journey's been.

⸲⸲⸲

Don Campbell's Observations

From bankrupt back to success in a few short years, just by changing their focus. What a difference a focus on economic fundamentals has made in John and Nicky's life. With this new focus they can confidently make their investment decisions, no longer having to guess or react to headlines.

They've also discovered that real estate markets, like all financial markets, are living and breathing entities that respond to different stimuli. These markets always have plateaus or cleansing times as they progress upwards. No market can continue in a straight upwards trajectory without taking a break. It is during these breaks that the unsophisticated investors panic and sell, while sophisticated investors, such as John and Nicky, take action and buy.

Like many others in this book, they did not allow their first bad experiences to knock them off their chosen path; in fact, those experiences forced them to adjust their system and made them better investors over the long run. Their new system doesn't allow them to repeat their earlier mistakes.

Just a few short years after bankruptcy, John and Nicky are now living their passions, married for over 40 years, driving classic cars and living their life to the fullest, and they did it having to start all over again at age 50. It has not been an easy journey, but it would have been a lot more difficult if they had allowed their initial financial woes to stop them in their tracks. No "poor me" victim mentality for these amazing people.

ACTION STEPS

1. If you had to start all over again financially today, what would you do differently?

_____

_____

_____

_____

2. What's stopping you from making these changes today and moving forward?

_____

_____

_____

_____

SUCCESS STORY #13
THE GRASS ISN'T ALWAYS GREENER ON THE OTHER SIDE

Trudi Johnston and Val Novak

You can search high and low for the pot of gold. But sometimes what you really need is in your own backyard.

There is a heartbreakingly beautiful scene in one of Robert Munsch's most loved children's books, *Love You Forever*, where a son drives across town to rock his aged mother to sleep, secure in the knowledge of all she did for him when she was strong and healthy. Trudi Johnston lives that story. Her business partner, Val Novak, is a Czechoslovakian immigrant living a hybrid version of the same tale. But make no mistake. These women say they're privileged to have time to spend with their loved ones. They also say real estate investment makes it possible.

Trudi, 51, recently helped her father make a tough decision to find her mother full-time care in a home for people with Alzheimer's. When her dad moved into the family home Trudi shares with her teenaged daughter and second husband (he has three older children and she has one older daughter), Trudi made a commitment to visit her mom daily and to be there when her mom is tucked into her bed at night. It sometimes means supper isn't on the table, she says, "but that's okay. My mom was always there for me and I will be there for her."

Val is 43 and her version of the beloved Munsch story about the cycle of family life begins a few pages earlier. With an eight-year-old and another daughter in high school, Val found full-time employment wreaked havoc with her efforts to be the parent she wanted to be. Having escaped Communist Europe and moved to Canada in 1988 with a husband, no English, $400 in cash and two battered suitcases between them, Val now feels blessed to be able to take every second Thursday and spend it making soup with her daughter's Grade One class. When the older daughter gets a day off school, they plan day trips to the mall or special lunches.

In and around their family responsibilities, Trudi and Val are real estate agents whose realty work supplements their real estate investment. They met while working at what Val describes as a "nine-to-nine" job in sales. Exhausted by the rat race and looking for change, they started investing in real estate together about five years ago. But their early experiences were daunting. "We were really inspired to get into real estate because it offered the potential to generate an income, give us more time with our families and create long-term wealth," says Trudi. "But the first organizations we joined weren't helpful. We managed to get through it, but there was lots of pain. When that all fell apart, we really struggled. We had put a lot of work into making it a success and it cost us time and money we couldn't get back."

By the time they went to their first REIN meeting in 2006, the friends had created and stabilized a $1.1-million portfolio of five properties. They were keen on more investing, but equally wary of action. "It was like we had this wall in front of us," says Val. "We were very frustrated by our other education event experiences, and I know I absolutely did not want to go through that negative experience again."

Enthused by the solid structure and system REIN offered, Trudi and Val flew to Vancouver for their first Quickstart program. It was a long way to go from their homes in Toronto. "It was the right thing to do," Val adds. "No one knew us, people were very friendly and we had a whole weekend to talk about what we really wanted to do, and how we would do it." This weekend away, fully absorbed in planning and designing their business, became their turning point.

By then, both had their real estate licences. It was another way to maintain control of their time and generate some income while building their investment portfolio and their network, explains Trudi. As their portfolio grows, they expect to focus on the Durham region of southern Ontario. That focus makes it easier to find properties and will ease property management, which will likely be handled by Trudi's husband, Dennis. "We're developing our network and things are falling into place," she says.

Looking back, Val admits it was "financial suicide" to give up her full-time job. "But if I hadn't done that, I would not have been able to become a realtor and focused on investing. My husband, Charles, and I joke that he pays the bills now and I am the one taking care of our financial future."

She is also setting an example far different than one she could have set for her daughters in Communist Czechoslovakia, where women were largely excluded from business. "On the last day of my life, I want to be able to look back and see that I was a good role model for my girls. I want them to be two confident women who can stand on their own feet."

Trudi also likes to maintain a balance between personal and professional responsibilities. Her youngest daughter is working on her pilot's licence and is an avid sailor. Her 24-year-old is in the Canadian Armed Forces.

Like Val, Trudi knows it would be good to go beyond their local area and invest in another region where a strong economy, low vacancy rates and consistent property appreciation nurture a lucrative investment market. But they follow the "Get Real" focus they've learned at REIN meetings. For them, says Val, getting real today is all about business decisions that give them more time with their families.

Trudi agrees. Better still, "Real research behind the headlines has also helped us understand why Durham is a great place to invest for us. Truly, everything we need to be successful is in our own backyard."

Don Campbell's Observations

Trudi and Val know what they want and they are not afraid to go and get it. The best thing they've ever done was to take a weekend away from all distractions to design their business, create a vision and make a plan of action. Many beginning investors have a tendency to jump into the investment arena without first setting out a long-term plan or having a proven system to follow. Not having a plan or system is how disasters begin.

Because running a business or an investment portfolio can be overwhelming, all investors and business owners should pre-book time away from the business at least twice per year. This is not holiday time, and nor should it be booked during family holiday time. This is time fully focused on assessing the direction of your business, looking at your plan and accomplishments, and making sure that everything still fits.

Myself, and many other successful business owners, have taken this strategy to a whole new level by taking one full day per week to focus only on items and actions that impact the future of our businesses. I call it my "Forward Focus Friday." Of course, we didn't get there right away: first it was one day per quarter, then once day per month and now it has graduated to one day per week. During this day I only deal with:

1. Building strong relationships that support the business's future goals;

2. Developing systems or strategies for the business or our clients;

3. Writing and creating; and

4. Reviewing, and making corrections to, the direction the company is moving in order to ensure we are operating according to our philosophy.

Anything that has to do with cleanups of past projects, or dealing with current operations is put on hold for a scheduled cleanup day. They are not allowed on "Forward Focus Fridays." Val and Trudi have proven the importance of taking the time to plan as they have quickly become leaders in their investment society.

Trudi and Val also learned a valuable lesson of not allowing past experiences to hold them back. I can still remember when they first attended a REIN event. They had crossed arms and were very hesitant. You could see that they were waiting for the proverbial "other shoe to drop." I don't blame them at all: they had been burned badly before and were wisely very skeptical. However, once they discovered that they had found a safe place in which to live their real estate passion, and that there wasn't anything behind the curtain, their business began to skyrocket.

A healthy level of skepticism is important; just don't let it get in your way of finding what you're looking for. Being a constant skeptic is easy: you don't have to do anything but sit back and watch life pass you by. The key lesson is once you do find the system that fits your philosophy of life, commit to it 100% and go after it. Make it happen!

Just dipping a toe in the water is a habit that many chronic skeptics have. They never fully commit to a plan, even when they see it working for thousands of others. And, because they don't 100% commit, the system invariably lets them down and they can smugly walk away saying "I knew it wouldn't work." What they don't know is that it didn't work because they didn't make it work. So in essence they were doomed from the start.

It would be hard to imagine anyone starting with less than what Val started with, landing in a new country with only $400 in her hand. And now look at what passion, drive and a wonderful partnership has brought these two partners. They are well on the road to achieving all that they wanted in their family, in their finances and in their lives. Their healthy skepticism has served them well.

ACTION STEPS

1. On a scale of 1 to 10 (10 being the highest), rate your level of skepticism.

   _____

   _____

2. Have you tried investment systems or businesses before in which you didn't do very well?
   ❑ YES   ❑ NO

3. Looking back at these experiences, can you honestly say that you 100% committed to the system?
   ❑ YES   ❑ NO

4. If no, why not?
   ❑ The system wasn't proven.
   ❑ I didn't believe it would do as it said.
   ❑ I was sold the system under false pretences.
   ❑ I knew going in that it wouldn't do very well.
   ❑ Other: _____

5. If you checked off any of the excuses above, you may wish to examine what dream you were chasing that made you start the system and why your current filter system didn't weed it out before you started.

   _____

   _____

   _____

   _____

SECTION 2

FOCUS ON FAMILY AND FRIENDS

SUCCESS STORY #14
FREE COLLEGE EDUCATION FOR YOUR KIDS

Donna Sylvestre

You can use real estate to pay for your child's expensive education. How great is that?

Donna Sylvestre was torn. Part of her was sad the eldest of her two daughters wanted to leave home to attend college and her heart ached to think Amanda would be living a couple of hours away from their family home in Edmonton. Another part of her was pleased to see her daughter take deliberate steps towards the future. Further comforted by the fact Amanda planned to make the transition with two girlfriends, Donna found herself doing what Canadian parents across the nation are called to do before the start of every post-secondary academic school year: She tucked in the apron strings, took a deep breath, got her kid into the car and drove to the chosen city, in this case Red Deer, to try to find her daughter a decent place to live. And that's when a different kind of reality hit home.

"When we discovered it would be $900 to rent an apartment, I started to consider other options," recalls Donna. Before long, she was talking to a new home builder and putting together a deal that would see the family build a half-duplex for $129,000. With monthly payments that tallied $700 for the mortgage and another $100 in taxes, "the three gals had a three-bedroom home with much more space and Amanda and I had an investment."

By putting Amanda in charge of everything from interior design details to lining up and working with tenants, both of whom paid $350 a month, her mother gave Amanda the kind of real-world education they don't offer in school. "I put down the down payment and qualified for the mortgage and both of our names went on the title," says Donna. "Since this was Amanda's permanent residence, we qualified for 5% down."

In return for all her work on the property management front, Amanda received a 25% share of the property's equity. To help her really grasp the cost of living and learn the value of what real estate investors call "good debt" (the kind of debt that makes you money!), Amanda also paid $350 a month in rent. The deal has proven especially sweet not just financially but also from a life lesson perspective. Two years later, the property is worth $250,000. "Do the math," says her mom. "It was a win for both of us on so many levels. From the profits, Amanda's full schooling is paid for. She will be one of the few who leave school without any student debts holding her back from getting on with life. I win because I was able to own a hassle-free investment property that gave my child a headstart in her financial life." And it all occurred because Donna looked at the problem from a unique perspective.

Another plus: "Amanda experienced a lot of pride of ownership while living there. It was her place, and because she was responsible for making mortgage, tax and utility payments on time, it gave her another life learning experience of handling a much higher level of responsibility than most of her peers," adds Donna.

Although it's the kind of deal most parents could pull together with ease, Donna admits she may have found the prospect of buying an investment property with one of her kids a little easier because of the many creative investors she is surrounded with in her life.

Making a concerted effort to meet so many people in the real estate investment community "certainly helped my husband, Ron, and I create a portfolio that's given us a feeling of security far beyond what we could have imagined," notes Donna, who also runs a highly successful event-planning company from her home.

Real estate has not only been an added bonus to their lives, it also became a necessity that provides her with a sense of financial security. And security matters to Donna, precisely because she has experienced the flipside of that particular coin. In 1989, Ron was seriously injured in a motor vehicle accident. It would be four years before the highly skilled finishing carpenter would return to work. During this long period, no medical professional could predict his eventual recovery time line—and no one but Donna could make sure their family, including two daughters aged four and two (at the time), would be looked after financially. Looking for her personal truth in the midst of a situation she neither wanted nor expected, she knew she could "choose to be a victim, or step to the plate and make something happen." She stepped up and hit a home run.

That willingness to take charge of her own future led to the development of a seminar business that evolved into one of Edmonton's top event-planning firms. It also provided the impetus for her and Ron's decision to start buying properties in the early 1990s.

Looking back at those purchases, Donna says it "seemed from the get-go that my financial success came from purchasing properties with specific purposes. As a self-employed person with no pension or benefits, it was imperative that I have some assets in place to look after my future financial needs," she explains.

Her first purchase, a townhouse with her father as a joint venture partner, helped her get started in investment and helped her "support my father in getting a better rate of return on his money." Purchased for $52,000, that property is now valued at $250,000, "and we still hold it today for great positive cash flow."

Her second property "was purchased with the intention of having some cash available for when my daughters get married or take secondary education," notes Donna. Subsequent properties, including the Red Deer deal, were a result of the success she was having with previous purchases! Most are part of her retirement savings, while the Red Deer deal benefited Amanda, too.

Proving anything is possible with the right people and the right deal, Donna recalls a very rare deal coming to her where she paid just $1 to assume the mortgage on a rental condominium. She heard about it through the grapevine, once again, because of her willingness to surround herself with positive, successful and unselfish investors. In less than 36 months, that property put $100,000 in her pocket.

Running a successful business while investing in real estate also taught Donna the value of leveraging other people's time and resources. Buying properties in rental pools, for example, "makes it extremely easy to own revenue properties. This is a really good option for people who have no time to self-manage their investments."

Looking back, Donna says one of the most valuable lessons she's learned in life is that "'inner peace' isn't about the absence of conflict, but the ability to cope with it when it arrives." Ergo, while she admits a new venture (like starting your own company or investing in real estate) may seem a little daunting at first, following through on decisions like that is essential to taking charge of your life and future.

With their daughters now grown at 20 and 22, Donna admits, "All things considered, it seems like an awful lot of opportunities just kind of show up when we're surrounded by good things and great people."

———⊗⊗⊗———

Don Campbell's Observations

Donna's resilience and focus is legendary, and the results prove it. From nothing she has built a world-class event coordination business and a very strong real estate portfolio. It didn't happen overnight and she readily admits that, like all investors and business owners, mistakes have been made along the way, but when you see the foundation that she has laid for her family and her children, it has all been worth it.

The key lesson we can learn from Donna is to look at situations from many different angles. For instance, many Canadian families struggle to earn enough money to send their children to post-secondary institutions. When you add up the cost of the books, courses, rent or dorm fees and living expenses you can see why. So, rather than spend out-of-pocket for this important life step, Donna saw an opportunity to create an investment that would take care of all of these expenses, teach her daughter life lessons, and make a profit all at the same time.

The good news is there are many financing options available from banks and CMHC that are designed to support this worthy investment strategy, making it easy for you. This could work, if not for your own children, how about a grandchild, a niece or nephew or other important child in your life.

The process is simple. The adult investor puts up the down payment and co-signs the mortgage, and for this they receive 75% of the equity appreciation. In return the child learns the value of managing the property, looking after the ongoing expenses, collecting rent from the friends who are living with them and receives 25% of the equity appreciation. I have see situations where this 75-25 split is made after the school tuition is taken off the top of the profits, thus ensuring that the property does its job in providing free schooling. You can design the deal however you like; no matter how you do it the experience and the lack of student loans the child leaves with is priceless.

Donna also readily admits that this and the other successful deals she has completed have come to her because she is continually surrounded with positive-minded, successful people. There is one quote she used that truly gives us an insight into Donna's soul: "Choose to be a victim, or step to the plate and make something happen." That is how Donna, in one single sentence, goes out there and makes things happen. Those who know her are blessed to be surrounded with such drive and enthusiasm.

ACTION STEPS

1. Who do you know in your life who is planning on going to, or currently attending, post-secondary institution in a region with a strong real estate market?

   _____

   _____

   _____

   _____

   _____

2. Which ones would benefit the most from you becoming their business partner?

   _____

   _____

   _____

   _____

   _____

SUCCESS STORY #15
PUT ALL YOUR EGGS IN ONE BASKET, THEN WATCH THAT BASKET CLOSELY

Carla Smiley and Bill Smiley

I keep fighting the fear, because the cost of giving in is too high.

There was a brief time in their history when Carla and Bill Smiley thought they could rely on their Registered Retirement Savings Plans to carry them through their post-employment years. But life had other lessons to teach. First, they started their savings plan late. Then Carla left her social work position when their first daughter was born, further reducing the pie that was to feed them now and sustain them later. The next complication was even more problematic; in one of those stock-market drops nobody predicts and everybody feels, their already struggling account lost a quarter of its value.

Raised to save by "putting everything in one basket and then watching it real close," Carla was horrified. She was also enlightened. "We obviously weren't going to be RRSP people. But we did need to find a way to be really good stewards of what we had."

With the help of a good friend, who helped them build their log house in Nelson, B.C., the couple became homeowners in the 1990s. By 2002, the couple had developed a plan to secure their family's financial future with real estate investment, but their home's location was causing them grief. Even though they loved the community, its economic fundamentals were lousy. With a new government in the provincial capital, taxes rose and services were cut, leaving more people without jobs. Nelson had a great reputation as far as attracting renters, recalls Carla, but she and Bill knew "they weren't the kind of tenants we wanted."

She and Bill and their two girls relocated to Westlock, Alberta, a community of about 5,000 people. They bought a home. Bill worked in the community as a counselor. While Carla settled in with the girls, she joined REIN and went looking for investment property, soon buying a bungalow two blocks away from their new home. "We used the vendor-take-back [VTB] strategy, and because it was our first property and we had excellent credit, the bank let us put just 5% down even when we fully disclosed to them that it was a rental property. Our mortgage broker said he had never seen that bank agree to this for a rental property."

Five years later, the Smileys own five revenue properties, plus another six with joint venture partners. They've encountered some really sweet deals through that experience—like VTBs, in which the vendor asked for less interest than the Smileys were willing to pay, or properties that, at the very least, doubled in appreciation.

More importantly, Carla says self-employment taught her to take a more proactive approach to dealing with life's curve balls. Where she used to duck, she now gets out of the way—a strategy that provides fresh perspective on what could otherwise seem like insurmountable problems.

When traditional schools didn't offer the education their girls needed, she tried different options, then found home-schooling programs more suited to their daughters' needs. The end result? A more harmonious family life and the chance to make sure their girls are privy to the inner workings of the investment business. They've helped with yard and reno work and the oldest, 13, plays the adult version of the Cash Flow board game with her folks. She's also attended meetings with their corporate lawyer. "It's a way for us to educate them and to employ them," Carla explains.

Similarly, when Bill took a different job with a lengthy commute which cut into their family time, they put up with it for a while, then moved into the nearby city of Edmonton in 2007. Carla admits she prefers small-town life, but in the big scheme of things, what she needs most is to see her husband more!

Above all, real estate investment has taught Carla the basic wisdom of dealing with issues as they arise. "Problems don't go away," she says. Growing up in a family business where she "learned to be a great employee," Carla says the nitty-gritty of real estate investment was daunting at first, since she was responsible for all of the details. "Everything was new. I had never talked to a lawyer or an accountant before, and found out you needed both."

Her expectations of team members have been honed by experience. She provides feedback on issues and if changes aren't made, she cuts their ties. "This is critical to your success or failure," she says.

How does she measure success? In peace of mind, says Carla. "We live a modest life on one income, but we are also taking care of our future with our real estate. To Carla and Bill, that includes being able to pay for their children's post-secondary education and enjoy retirement—perhaps at the same time, given that Bill was in his mid-40s when their first child was born.

While she still thinks a quick prayer before a phone call is just plain good practice, Donna says "My confidence has increased a lot. I don't quake nearly as much."

—⁂—

Don Campbell's Observations

Bill and Carla are successful because they are doing the opposite of what the average Canadian would do. They feel the fear, but don't let it freeze them. Within the stories throughout this book you can read a subtext into each one: Most have fear around investing, yet they don't allow it to be a deterrent to their success. Only when they broke through the fear did they start to see their results accelerate.

Together they have built an amazing team while at the same time keeping their focus on what they want for themselves and their family. This is another important lesson for all of us to learn. Over the last 15 years we have witnessed investors sacrificing their family time to chase deals, justifying their actions by saying, "I'll soon have the time for my family and friends after I 'make it.'" This is a huge mistake and completely based in the fear of missing out. Relationships with family and friends should not be sacrificed because of a fear of missing a deal or two. If you have your system and you're working it, you'll find enough deals to help you achieve your goals.

There are many lonely yet financially successful people out there, because they made the choice that money was more important than life. These people went all out for years at the detriment of their relationships. Yes, they might have become wealthy, but at the same time they lost something even more important—relationships.

To avoid this scenario, you might want to use the Smileys' experience as a template; they've planned their investments around their family and friend priorities rather than the other way around, and therefore, when they do hit their goals, they'll have lots of people around them with whom to celebrate.

ACTION STEPS

1. What non-business relationships in your life may be suffering from not having enough attention on them?

   _____

   _____

   _____

   _____

   _____

2. What first steps, as uncomfortable as they might be, are you going to take to begin rectifying these important relationships?

   _____

   _____

   _____

   _____

   _____

SUCCESS STORY #16
HOW MAKING GOALS MEANS GIVING BACK

Betty Patterson and Gerry Patterson

Sure, there were some people who didn't understand what we were doing. But our real estate investments were never about where we were. They were about where we were going.

When you marry a soldier, you marry a soldier's life. So when Gerry Patterson was ordered to move to Edmonton from Winnipeg in 1971, he and his new wife, Betty, shipped out, carrying with them a few belongings—and the kernels of big dreams about what life would be like when Gerry's 20-year term in the armed forces ended in the late 1970s.

A registered nurse who easily found work in her new city, Betty felt like life was on track. Gerry left the army after 10 years and trained as a machinist, preparing for a new career in an energy industry encountering record highs and lows. "The timing was terrible," says Betty with hindsight. "The oil industry went caput just when he finished his course and he didn't have work for about a year and a half."

Gerry landed on his feet in a custodial job with a local school board that valued his mechanical training. "It wasn't what he really wanted to do," she says, "and the whole experience got us thinking. We figured that if we got into real estate, he would enjoy the work of renovating and maintaining the properties, and we could actually work towards doing something together."

Determined to boost their knowledge of how the investment business worked, Betty took a real estate seminar, then joined REIN in the mid-1990s. By then, their two children were through high school, and Betty says they were looking for a way to accumulate wealth. In line with their strong Christian values, they wanted money, at least in part, "so we could give it away to help others. We were never in this to lose money. We planned for it to be a full-time business and we started talking about both of us retiring when we turned 60."

In the early days, they bought properties in poor repair, then spent their evenings and weekends bringing them up to standard. Over time, they accumulated more than a dozen properties, most of them single-family homes.

They were creative investors. Their basement suites and even garages were rented separately, boosting cash flow. Following their own system, most of their properties were located in particular communities not far from their own home. That was especially important, as they were both working and handling their own property management.

Two years ago, they added a lakefront cottage to the mix. "It's an investment property, but not a tenant property," explains Betty. "It was a fixer-upper and it gave us a place to park our fifth-wheel travel trailer so we no longer had to rent a spot. Over the winter, we use it for a couple of days at a time, almost every other week."

About the same time as they bought the cottage, Betty and Gerry decided to hire a property management company. By then, both were retired and the move marked a major—and welcome—shift in their business model. "Last year, we did two major renovations and we chose to do that work because we can do it more cheaply than if we hired someone else," says Betty, 66. Still, it was nice to focus on the renovations without having to leave projects mid-stream to deal with property maintenance or management issues.

With Gerry managing the tenancy side of the business and property management and Betty doing the books, the Pattersons recently found themselves in an enviable position whereby they could start to reap the rewards of their portfolio by selling one property a year. That may not happen in 2007. "We took a second mortgage on the one we sold in 2006. We'll get that second mortgage money back this year, and may not need to sell another property."

Today, they're not in the market for more property. "But I'd never say never, either," says Betty with a laugh. They have talked about buying into an adult-only community. They wouldn't move there yet, but it could be an option down the road. For now, she enjoys the flexibility of a business that lets her provide part-time care for her first grandchild, a son born to her son and his wife, a lawyer/doctor duo, who now own the first revenue property his parents bought.

Their daughter is a missionary in Africa and her parents have journeyed there twice. Committed to her work, they also send her money she can use to help the people she's called to assist.

"Using what we have to help others has always been important to us," says Betty. Besides monetary donations, some of that aid now comes in the form of advice to others who need help buying properties. REIN's best lessons go beyond real estate. Betty says the network guided them to an understanding of why they were investing and taught them to continually set goals. They apply these lessons to every other aspect of their lives and it's a philosophy Betty shares with other women at personal retreats.

Beyond their personal financial security and the way it's helping others, Betty credits real estate investment for a stronger marriage. "Real estate was something we could do together. Gerry had the skill to handle renovations and maintenance and he's great with tenants. I liked being involved in the financial part, and feeling part of something we were building together."

People of faith, the Pattersons also thank God for guiding them and providing the health and strength they needed to build a business that could help others.

Ten years later, it may look like the Pattersons hold an impressive portfolio of revenue properties. But it feels like the kind of equity money can't buy. That's an equity based on financial freedom—and wrapped in happiness and strong relationships.

Don Campbell's Observations

It does not matter at what age you start investing—the key is to get started. It's never about age or what's happened in your past. You need to honestly ask yourself why you want to invest. You may initially think it is all about money, but you will quickly discover that chasing money is not very motivating ... and you never know when to quit. For the Pattersons, they're now able to help out many others. Sure, they could still be chasing money, but there's no need. They had a vision and now they've achieved it; it's time to enjoy the fruits of their labour.

In addition to being financially secure, they're able to support their daughter as she lives her dream as a missionary in Africa. So in essence their Canadian real estate is now dramatically affecting families in the heart of Africa.

You'll note the path of their investment careers. From an out of work machinist to a seasoned renovator and property manager, first out of necessity then out of choice. The real estate journey has brought the family closer together and now they are all reaping the rewards. It worked because Betty and Gerry brought different strengths to the business relationship.

As Betty and Gerry, along with their family, begin to enjoy the results of their 10 years of hard work, they can look back and be proud that they took action even when the going was tough. When they made the decision to grab control of their financial future and stay focused on their vision despite what others thought, they may not have even known the positive impact it would have on their family many years down the road. And the decision Gerry and Betty made back then is not just making their family comfortable, that decision is now helping to provide food and clothing to people in need halfway around the world. It doesn't get much better than that.

ACTION STEPS

1. Other than yourself, when you make your financial decisions, for whom else are you making these decisions?

   - _____

   - _____

   - _____

2. Whom do you know who, despite having obvious talent, may miss going to post-secondary school because they don't have the extra $25,000–$50,000 to pay for it?

   _____

3. Have you considered buying an investment property and using the profits to pay for this person's tuition so they don't miss out? You could even do it anonymously if you think the family may not want to take the charity.

SUCCESS STORY #17
AVOID SWINGING FOR THE HOMERUN—LOOK FOR GOOD, SOLID SINGLES AND DOUBLES

Darren Skovmose

Real estate investing takes time. So don't try to hit the home run right away. Get to first base, figure out what's working, duplicate it and move onto second base. Once your bases are loaded, you have runs coming in all the time.

Darren Skovmose likes starting new businesses. He also likes taking a tough look at those businesses and figuring out what he could do better. When he and his wife, Roseanne, owned a clothing business in their hometown of Medicine Hat, Alberta, they paid their staff more than the competition and stocked their shelves and store rooms with a greater variety of merchandise. In 1994, when Darren left his oilfield job, they sold the clothing enterprise and their sporting goods stores and started to focus on buying real estate—a major change in focus, which they made with relative ease.

A few months later, he and Roseanne took an introductory real estate seminar, then bought two properties that same weekend. Before long, they were buying fourplexes and duplexes for a $1 down payment on properties with positive cash flow.

"We rode up the price increase on residential housing," Darren recounts. "But we ended up buying properties scattered all over the province and the management side became more of an effort than I wanted." With his hands-on approach to residential property management, the distances between properties were problematic. Instead of managing, Darren was driving.

When his Alberta-based residential real estate portfolio hit 100 properties, he looked at the time he was spending on management, then consolidated and sold some of his assets so he could move into the commercial market. "I know it's not for everyone," he allows, "but for me, that's what made the most sense."

By the late 1990s, he was converting residential properties into commercial holdings. "The biggest roadblock, hands down, is dealing with the banks," says Darren "It's hard to find a banker that can say 'yes' even after you've presented a great project." On the plus side, he had little trouble getting his money partners to follow his move into commercial property, a fact Darren attributes to a fundamental business strategy that allows him to structure deals so he consistently beats expectations.

On the commercial side, as was the case with residential purchases, Darren pays a lot of attention to cash flow. He also pays close attention to the potential to build new relationships with every deal. When buying residential properties, for example, he typically stuck with the listing realtor and got the vendor's attention by offering full price—and a vendor-take-back option at 10% interest. Six months before that take-back was paid out, he'd send the vendor a letter and ask if he could use his money again. Having made every payment on time, most were pleased to stay involved, says Darren. "If you over-deliver and under-promise, you'll always find money for the next deal."

Darren and his partners owned about 10 commercial properties by mid-2007, including strip malls (his personal investment favourite) in Calgary, Edmonton and Medicine Hat. While still in the acquisition stage, he's also moved into land development. His first project, a 16-acre parcel of land alongside the Trans-Canada Highway just outside Medicine Hat, involved three other partners—and whet his appetite for more.

These days, he's completing a 1,000-acre development in the city itself. Assembled by buying out five owners, it will be one of Medicine Hat's primary retail and service power centres. Its first anchor tenant, Costco, opens its doors in late 2007. Darren is responsible for finding other tenants and for selling land. The process is consuming, but he loves the challenge.

He also loves to admit that he got to where he's at by learning from others. "Mentoring was critical in those early days," says Darren, who joined REIN soon after buying his first investment properties. Still a member nearly 10 years later, he still appreciates how that organization feeds his portfolio's success with sound economic data. Even though he works out his own numbers on each deal, he says that the unbiased information "gives our investors some assurance that what we are doing is correct because we have good economic and demographic information to back us up."

That assurance was important to Darren on a personal level, too. With only one reputation to protect and advance, Darren's never been big on taking unnecessary risks with other people's money. He's seen that done and, he notes, "I've seen novice investors get taken."

With two kids, ages 14 and 9, Darren is interested in protecting his own family's money as well. He is interested in what real estate investment offers his family in terms of future financial security—and current wealth. "Obviously, I'm still buying more property and I am interested in more land development, too. But I already have more flexibility with my time than I would if I was working for someone else. We've also reached the point where we can travel if we want—and we don't have to worry about where we stay. Does that feel good? Sure it does."

—— ∞ ——

Don Campbell's Observations

Darren Skovmose has turned his passion for real estate into a lifestyle filled with family time, real estate challenges and growth, all under the umbrella of never taking unnecessary risks. Many believe that you have to take risks if you want to progress from building an investment portfolio from two revenue properties to becoming a major land developer. And this is true. The key is not to take "unnecessary" risks. There are investors who look for real estate for the excitement in their lives and therefore take risks for risk's sake—following that path is the road to disaster. Sophisticated investors like Darren understand that you should look for excitement in other areas outside of your investments. Go skydiving for excitement and at the same time make your real estate portfolio as predictable as possible so it funds your excitement . . . not provides it.

The underlying theme in Darren's story is making sure his partners' money is well looked after. In the past he has said to me that he would never put anyone else's money into a deal he wouldn't be willing to put his own money into. That philosophy should be adopted by any investor who is using other people's money in a joint venture or RRSP second mortgage deal. In fact, I know most sophisticated investors complete more due diligence on a deal that includes someone else's money than they do on deals involving only their own money.

Darren follows the economic fundamentals, so he can share with his investors the latest market trends. And it's not about getting rich quick or hitting home runs. Home-run kings, those who try to milk every deal, are often the strike-out kings who end up chasing their dream for their whole life. Darren has created phenomenal success through real estate with one simple statement he shares with beginning investors whenever he can: "Find an economically strong area, buy property at market price, then when the time comes, sell it at market price." No need to squeeze every last dollar out of the deal when you buy, or when you sell. Hit enough of these single and doubles and you will be a real estate World Series winner.

ACTION STEPS

1. Be honest with yourself: do you have the tendency to try to achieve the "big deal" rather than take smaller and easier deals along the way?

    _____

    _____

    _____

    _____

2. In either case, are you happy with what this philosophy has brought to your life? Measure your progress from three perspectives: stress level, financial success and free time.

    _____

    _____

    _____

    _____

3. From what sources do you get most of your research on the real estate market?

    _____

    _____

    _____

    _____

4. Ask yourself, do you truly believe that this information is unbiased?

    _____

    _____

    _____

5. Where else can you start receiving unbiased research for yourself and your financial partners?

    _____

    _____

    _____

    _____

SUCCESS STORY #18
NOTHING LIKE A LITTLE BROTHERLY COMPETITION

Eric Gonneau and Mark Gonneau

We figured we'd pick up three classmates who'd rent rooms from us for the next three years. Instead, we had 10 tenants in three years. It turns out that this group of renters likes to change addresses—a lot.

Mark Gonneau is a successful Toronto-based chiropractor with three thriving clinics. He and his older brother, Eric, a professional engineer, are the brains and bucks behind an Ontario-based real estate portfolio that includes both highly positive cash-flow properties and properties purchased for their long-term capital appreciation.

But ask Mark about his very first real estate deal and his voice is tinged with the sting of a rejection that's almost 10 years old. Although Eric came to his rescue, Mark initially asked their dad to co-sign the loan. He was turned down flat. "Dad told me, 'If you can't afford it, you shouldn't buy it.' I really didn't expect that."

That conversation led to a phone call with Eric, who was working deep in the forests of Northern Ontario. Eric's remote location necessitated using a generator-powered fax machine and Mark's impending trip to the Bahamas complicated the deal. But Eric, Mark and Mark's roommate got the property.

Located 15 minutes from the University of Toronto, which Mark and his roommate attended, the house had a basement they renovated to add a two-bedroom apartment. Three rooms were also rented out on the main floor and the whole deal worked almost exactly as planned. The only complication? Tenant longevity. Whereas the three partners assumed their initial tenants would stay for the duration of their degree, that wasn't the case. They shared space with 10 roommates over three years. They also doubled their initial investment and took the money with a smile.

Within a year after the sale of their first house, Eric and his wife, Rita, both Canadians, moved to the United States as she pursued her career as a medical writer. He was gainfully unemployed and found it difficult to qualify for a work permit/visa in the angst of a post-9/11 environment. So, while Rita worked, Eric became a student of real estate investing. He read books, listened to audio tapes and attended seminars. In short, he started thinking like an investor.

One year later, Eric bought a two-building apartment complex in Trenton, Ontario. Mark actually found the deal, but, as he was expanding his practice, he couldn't invest. Eric bought the property—and soon realized his training had just begun! Books are one thing, concedes Eric, but real life teaches many more lessons.

The first night he owned it, a female tenant trashed a suite after she found her beau in bed with another woman. Eric laughs about it now, but the immediate aftermath of the event was very stressful.

Worse, the complex had terrible issues with cash flow and proved tough to fill with tenants. Complicating all of that, his two sets of investors weren't real estate savvy, but sat across the table from him at family gatherings. (His and his wife's parents were both involved!)

Eric's real estate agent advised him to go through the lengthy process of splitting title on the two buildings. He then sold each building independently. The end result was beneficial. Within two years, Eric had repaid his investors, including all interest due. He also doubled his initial investment.

"What can I say? That deal was a learning experience," he concludes. "More than anything, I learned to look for creative solutions to messy problems." He also learned the value of living up to his obligations to his investors. Painful as that first experience might have been, Eric managed to keep his investors happy—and both sets of parents continue to invest.

Eric and Mark had been business partners on a number of ventures since they were young boys, but their real estate ventures were providing fertile ground for new business connections. They follow an unwritten code whereby neither is formally obligated to participate in deals the other finds and they stick by a verbal agreement to always offer a new deal to their sibling first. As Mark says, "Even if my brother elects not to participate, it always helps to have an independent, unbiased, educated set of eyes evaluate the deal. He often sees things I miss."

By February 2005, Eric and Rita were back in Ontario and Eric joined REIN, an organization he'd learned about via another real estate investor. His brother had also heard about REIN from a different investor and, while business constraints meant Mark couldn't join until a year later, Eric signed up.

Three months later, Eric bought 14 townhouses in Orillia, with Mark partnering on three of the units. Eric held onto his units, but Mark's motives were short term and each respected the other's approach. "I think I doubled my money in six months," says Mark. Eric stayed in, and says his investment grew by another 20% over the next year.

Two years later, they share a real estate portfolio with an additional 14 properties, all of them professionally managed, a necessity given that both partners have full-time careers.

Six of their properties are within walking distance of Georgian College, located in Barrie, Ontario, where Eric and Rita live with two young sons. Working from a business model that puts tenant needs first, each of their student-housing properties was purchased only after it met a specific profile in terms of proximity to college, student-friendly fast food restaurants and banks. They've also set some basic standards regarding the number of refrigerators and bathrooms per student, have ensured there's sufficient kitchen cupboard space and even made sure each unit has the right number of towel bars per bathroom. "It's very specific, which allows us to charge premium rates. We really try to keep these units as nice as possible," says Eric.

Six other properties in their portfolio are brand new townhouses within walking distance of the new Barrie GO Train station. As the GO Train station wouldn't be built until late fall of 2007, the properties proved tougher to rent than expected. But the brothers aren't concerned. Looking ahead, the Gonneaus figure all six will be in high demand, especially since they bought lots that back onto a 10-acre conservation site.

"Let's face it. People move here because they work in Toronto and they want to feel like they've left the big city behind them. That protected environmental area will be a deal-maker," says Eric. In the meantime, they applied a value-added solution to the vacancy problem: "It turns out they rent faster—and for more money—if you include a washer and dryer," adds Eric. The two also own a property in a high-rise condo in Hamilton and a townhouse in the south end of Barrie.

"I'd say over the last five years, I've made more money in real estate than I've made in my engineering career," says Eric, 36, the voices of his sons vying for attention in the background. "But it has been a journey, and it still is a journey. I've made most of my money in capital gains, and capital gains doesn't put food on my table or gas in my tank. So I keep my career for a couple of good reasons: one to put food on my table and gas in my tank, but I also find that the engineering is a complementary career —[it] keeps me abreast of new changes in the industry."

But his real estate gains aren't all futuristic. Thanks to investments that offer some cash flow, Eric credits real estate with giving him the resources to help a young man he befriended five years ago through the Big Brother program. When the young man called because he was desperate, struggling with debt issues and about to be evicted, Eric gave him property maintenance work for a few weeks and helped him live up to his obligations.

Eric figures he or Rita will be able to leave their jobs in the next few years if that's what they choose to do (she continues to telecommute to a U.S. company). Between his clinic work and his investing, Mark admits his work days run long. Like Eric, however, he sees himself closing in on a time when he won't be working so hard. Indeed, "Freedom 35" looks like a possibility, says Mark, 34.

In the meantime, the brothers concede that without a blood connection, they would probably not have chosen each other as business partners, given their different outlooks and investing styles. Still, it's a connection they value, personally and professionally. It's also a connection they nurture with regular communication.

"Look at it this way," says Eric. "Mark, how often a day do we phone each other?"

The question is met by momentary silence. Then Mark smiles, "You mean, how many times a day do *you* call me?"

There is another silence, and the two brothers laugh. Who knows? Maybe this is the relationship their dad envisioned would develop on its own when he turned down Mark's first request for help to buy his first property.

Don Campbell's Observations

"It was the best of times, it was the worst of times." This opening sentence from Charles Dickens' *A Tale of Two Cities* also can describe what can happen when family members with differing philosophies decide to work together in a business or in real estate investing together.

Mark and Eric readily admit that they live their lives according to different philosophies; they have acknowledged this difference and have forged a real estate business that allows them both to exercise their strengths. They work together, but not exclusively, which helps to release the potential tension of disagreements.

They have worked very hard at building a team that supports where they want to go both as a team and independently. However, as with all family business relationships, clear communication is the key to success, as they have found out throughout the years of working together. Whenever there was a major dispute, it inevitably could be traced back to misinterpretation of poor communications. A great lesson for all of us in our business dealings is don't be afraid of getting clarification if you're not 100% sure of what was agreed to, and always get confirmation in writing, even if it is just a quick e-mail.

Family partnerships sound like a wonderful solution. Pooling resources and expertise with someone you know very well (often someone you've known for your whole life) to create a strong investment team with a single-minded goal. But along with the positives, there are often negatives that you wouldn't have to deal with if your partners were not close family. For instance, all the past family baggage and old "set-in-stone" family behavioural patterns come along for the ride.

ACTION STEPS

Family units investing together can create amazing results, as you'll hear in the many Family and Friends stories in this book. You're all working for the common good of the family legacy and wealth. The key to making a family-business relationship like this work is to set some very clear guidelines, for instance:

1. Acknowledge that difference in opinions will occur and that they need to be dealt with from a business only perspective.
2. Discussions of business should be during scheduled times, not every time you get together. For instance, birthdays, Thanksgiving dinners and other family gatherings are for family—not for business. Schedule regular business meetings to deal with the business issues. Just like the separation of church and state, you need to separate family from business.

3. All parties agree to work very hard to be "adults" and separate business disputes from family relationships. Remember, it is just a business deal, not life or death. Family *must* come first, before money.

4. Design a dispute resolution process for the inevitable impasse. Define who you will use as an outside source to help you reach an outcome.

5. Acknowledge that one party will always think they are doing more work than the other one (even if, in reality, they are not). Schedule a regular twice yearly meeting to solely discuss the division of labour and expertise.

6. Treat it like a business. All joint venture agreements, cash infusions, and division of responsibilities notes *must* be in writing and agreed to by all parties involved. No exceptions. Remember to deal with the inevitable situation in which one partner wants to buy a property and the other doesn't. Define whether the one who wants it can go and buy it on his own.

7. The older or more forceful sibling must agree not to lord over the younger or less forceful sibling, and the younger one cannot play the role of the "poor-me" victim.

8. Define exactly how you will break up the business joint venture if and when one of the parties wants to end it. Remember to address the key elements, such as property valuation; what the process is should the portfolio have to be liquidated; what the partner buy-out process is; and how the tax liability is going to be shared should one partner buy out the other. It is *much* easier to get these issues dealt with before there are large dollars on the table. Do it early.

If you treat the family-business relationship as a true business partnership and every party is clear on what your agreements are, working with a family member or two can be amazing. However, if you take this relationship more casually than you would a regular business relationship, you will have a recipe for disaster, and if there is a disaster in the business relationship, it can't help but ripple into the family. Don't let that happen: plan and discuss well in advance of starting the business and you will enjoy a business that will only enhance and strengthen family bonds.

SUCCESS STORY #19
Encouraging Their Renters to Become Owners Leads to Long-Term Tenants

Audrey Sloan and Cassandra Sloan

> *I encourage my student tenants to go scare up some money and buy real estate. This is not gambling. Real estate secures your future.*

A freshly minted diploma in human resources management was all Cassandra Sloan needed to land a great job in Edmonton's bustling energy sector. A few years into the job, however, the on-call shifts took their toll. The 24/7 connection to her employer's needs via a laptop and pager once felt kind of exciting. But those same demands now bound and chafed. The daughter of a forestry mill manager and teacher, Cassandra had nothing against hard work. She did, however, wonder why she worked so hard for someone else's bottom line.

A couple of years into that position, she got the kind of bonus earnest young employees dream of receiving. She also got some sage advice from her boss, who encouraged her to "go and buy a house." That got Cassandra thinking, but not because the idea was new; still in her early 20s, Cassandra already owned three properties.

Cassandra left her HR position in the fall of 2003 and joined her parents' real estate investment company full time. By then, her parents, Audrey and Doug Sloan, already owned a number of investment properties in Edmonton, about four hours south of their home in Grande Prairie.

Cassandra's mother had left teaching and, together, they incorporated a new enterprise. A cell phone still gives Cassandra 24/7 access to her business partner and their tenants, but the difference is palpable. "Now, when I answer that phone, I'm working for myself," says the business-savvy 29-year-old.

Audrey says she and Doug thought about buying revenue property for years before they moved back to Alberta from B.C. in 1999. Aware of REIN's reputation as a supportive network, Doug signed up soon after the relocation. Audrey, who was in a better position to attend meetings, assumed membership upon moving back.

That summer, they partnered with family to buy several properties in Edmonton. They were living in Drayton Valley, just over an hour's drive away, but they had no idea how long they'd be there, so Edmonton made the most sense. They had moved to Grande Prairie by 2004, but continued to buy in Edmonton.

Although she won't discuss the details of their portfolio, Audrey will say it secures a future already cushioned by pension plans. It also ensures they'll both be able to retire when she and Doug decide it's time. "We could have bought more property if we had done RRSP mortgages or pursued more joint ventures with others. But we stuck with family and friends and that kept it more manageable." Today, she oversees three separate portfolios: one with Doug, another with Cassandra; and a third with herself, Doug and JV partners.

With Cassandra on board, they handle all of their own property management, or buy property in a rental pool. "The biggest mistake I've made in real estate investment," says Audrey, "would be doing too much of the work myself for too long."

That's changed with time—and relationships. While she and Cassandra handle a lot of the minor repairs and maintenance themselves, all of the plumbing is farmed out. "We have a great plumber. We put a lockbox on the house, he does the work and sends us a bill," she explains.

"We also work very hard to make sure relationships like that stay strong." When others tell her they can't believe some tradespeople charge travel time, she waves off the criticism saying, "I need these people to run my business well."

They also nurture good relations with their tenants, some of whom send the Sloans Christmas cards or solicit advice from the teacher turned real estate investor. "I do talk to my tenants, especially the students, about why they should buy real estate," says Audrey. "One student-tenant actually ended up at a Quickstart weekend and started buying property."

As hands-on property managers, Audrey and Cassandra make sure their tenants understand that others are involved with decisions regarding the property and that there are rules to be observed. "Let's be honest. There are some 'professional' tenants out there who really know how to work the system. They've worked with landlords who don't know the system as well, and they take advantage of that."

The only thing Audrey and Cassandra Sloan want to take advantage of is their real estate portfolios. While Audrey may have a few regrets about not buying sooner and buying more, she readily admits to "not be-ing comfortable on the skinny branches. It's not money in the bank until it's sold. I'm really confident about the choices we've made and feel like we've managed the risk and work load really well. We didn't have the lux-ury of 20 or 25 years of investing, but that's that. I'm just glad we started when we did."

For now, the two keep busy managing their properties, with Cassandra on site in Edmonton and her mom a frequent working visitor. They also keep an eye out for properties to add to their portfolio.

Looking ahead, the mother of two kids in their 20s, Audrey figures she may eventually roll some of her properties into commercial real estate and take a big step back from daily management. Cassandra has her own ambitions, too. "I would eventually like to buy an apartment building, but will probably do that on my own." For now, she loves the life she's built. "Mom and I work really well as a team and I like that this is my own busi-ness."

⸺⸻⸺

Don Campbell's Observations

"Regrets, I've had a few," sang Frank Sinatra, a tune that many inves-tors could sing throughout their investing career. Should we have bought more when the market was slower? Sure. Should we have sold more when the market was hot? Sure. But the lesson that Cassandra and Audrey have learned is that you can't live in the past, you can only shape your future. Regrets are only excuses to hide your fear of taking action. I recommend you immediately remove the phrase "if only" from your vocabulary, as Cassandra and Audrey have.

They've also learned the very important lesson that you don't have to do everything yourself. Having a strong team around you can make life much easier, and real estate investing more fun and profitable. Relationships are such a priority for them that they clearly state "they work hard to keep those connections strong." Your time, as an investor, is worth much more per hour than you may initially think. When you register this book at www.realestateinvestingincanada.com, I am going to provide you with a unique interactive exercise that will help you define exactly what you are worth per hour. The result might just shock you into looking at delegation from a different point of view.

When it comes to relationships, oftentimes as landlords we can forget the importance of everyone on the team. It's easy to identify the obvious repairmen and banker relationships; however, often lost in the busyness of day-to-day life is the tenant relationships. Many unsophisticated investors believe that tenants are a necessary hassle in the real estate game when, in fact, tenants are the cornerstone of your investments, and you should treat them that way. They pay your mortgage; they cover all of your operating expenses; many even maintain your property, and all they ask in return is a nice place to live—no financial compensation required.

Audrey and Cassandra take this relationship to the extreme by treating their tenants so well that they hope the tenant eventually ends up as home buyers. This strategy will seem quite counterintuitive to most investors, when in fact it makes sound sense. When 99% of tenants feel that you are treating them well, and have their best interests in mind, they will reciprocate and treat you and your property well. If you enter a tenant relationship on a typical confrontational basis, you can expect the same in return.

As a team Audrey and Cassandra have identified their risk profile; they've identified their goals; and they've identified under which philosophy they want to run their business, then set out to build their business with these three foundations. What we've learned from them is you can still be very successful while keeping a humanitarian outlook in your business. Sometimes all it takes is being counterintuitive and going against what the average person believes to be true.

"Do what you can, when you can do it. Don't look back" would be a perfect title to this story. Audrey and Cassandra live that philosophy and have built a strong financial foundation for themselves and their families.

ACTION STEPS

1. How much do you believe you are worth per hour? How much would you be happy earning?

    $ _____

2. Register this book at www.realestateinvestingincanada.com and download the interactive "What Am I Truly Worth?" exercise.

3. Complete this exercise twice—once when you include your investment portfolio goals and once without it.

4. Observe how valuable your time really is. What three things in your life can you delegate knowing your true hourly worth from the above exercise?

    - _____

    - _____

    - _____

SUCCESS STORY #20
Partnership with Mother-in-Law Sparks Growth

Colleen McGinnis and Ryan Chernesky

People who don't understand real estate investment talk about how risky it is. I think the biggest risk is being someone who goes through life waiting for the weekend.

You can park the mother-in-law jokes at the door. When Ryan Chernesky decided to expand his real estate investment holdings, the full-time dentist headed straight for his wife's mother, Colleen McGinnis. A native of Calgary, Ryan bought a fourplex in Lethbridge in 2002. A year later, he was a long way from transitioning out of dentistry. But he saw what was happening in Alberta's real estate market—and he wanted in. He also wanted a partner at his side and figured Colleen was the ticket.

A former registered nurse who was conducting microbiology research, Colleen liked Ryan's ideas. By late 2003, they were brainstorming a strategy and she jumped in full-time the next January. "Ryan, bless his heart, would say, 'Just go and make some mistakes.'" Colleen recollects. "I just followed every lead we came across. It wasn't so much that I knew what I was doing, but I sure wanted to learn."

Three years later, RCM Homes Ltd. owns 30 residential properties and is comfortably nestled in what Colleen and Ryan agree is a holding phase. Big on leveraging time as well as money, the business partners have always farmed out property management and maintenance and repair work. "As a dentist, I have two hands and that limits me in terms of the amount of work I can do and the amount of money I can make," says Ryan. "It's the same principle with buying real estate. If I want to buy property, I need time to do that. On the plus side, once I have that property, it works for me."

Building a portfolio as the Alberta market took flight, Ryan and Colleen paid close attention to equity. "I learned there's really no such thing as cash flow in this kind of market," notes Colleen. "Instead, we aimed for cash-neutral properties, and even that was hard to do!"

Sticking to specific criteria helped. Properties near urban transit stations appreciated 25 percent more than similar properties without that aspect of their location. Determined to optimize rents, they also updated all of their purchases before moving in tenants.

"The plan was to buy for future growth in equity," adds Ryan. "Once there was equity in a property, we refinanced and bought more. In this way, debt was like our biggest friend because we used it to buy appreciating assets." Working with joint ventures and RRSP investors, he figures they were able to turn each of their houses into four or five more properties.

Less than four years into their partnership, Colleen, 55, is nearing her own Personal Belize. No longer looking at buying more properties for RCM's collection, the young grandmother of three is looking for a place to live on the West Coast, where she grew up. "I'd like to keep my hand in the business," she says, "but I could be here for a week a month and spend the rest of the time on the coast."

Ryan, on the other hand, is just getting started. Recently having sold his practice, the 35-year-old is throwing his hat into an investment ring where deals start in the millions of dollars. He's part of a high-rise apartment reconstruction project in downtown Calgary and a major redevelopment project southwest of Edmonton. And he's loving every minute of it. "That development near Edmonton includes mixed light industrial and high-density residential and single-family residential. What we're building will provide housing for 400 families. Now that's exciting!" enthuses Ryan.

"People who don't understand real estate investment," he adds, "talk about how risky it is. I think the biggest risk is being someone who goes through life waiting for the weekend."

Colleen agrees. She enjoys working in an area that took her right out of her comfort zone. "I learned how to deal with everyone from real estate agents to lawyers and investors, and I got to develop a lot of relationships with good people I met along the way. For me, that's been one of the biggest benefits I didn't anticipate."

———— ᴓᴓᴓ ————

Don Campbell's Observations

Colleen and Ryan's partnership is obviously quite unique. They have different timelines and different goals and, to top it all off, they're in-laws. Even with these differences the partnership works because of clear and constant communications of the partners' expectations.

We can learn a lot from their story; however, the main message is find a system that works, divvy up the tasks so that each partner is focusing on their strengths and make adjustments as you go. You can already witness that Colleen, in just three short years, is starting to see that her ultimate goal is right around the corner and therefore won't be playing as much of a role in their company as she had done in the past. This is occurring right when Ryan is just getting started and diving into new and larger projects. It is the perfect transition period where both partners have come out on the winning side. Colleen provided Ryan with what he needed while he was busy in his practice (someone with some time to pursue properties), and in return Ryan provided Colleen with knowledge, backing and business experience. Both found what they needed by forming this partnership.

The final lesson is all about mistakes. They were not afraid of making mistakes; they acknowledged that mistakes would happen and would be a part of moving forward. Most people are so afraid of making mistakes in their life that they are frozen out of taking any action. They are judgmental, so they assume others will judge them. Once you figure out that people making mistakes are the ones who are moving forward, just like Ryan and Colleen, you quickly begin to care less if others judge your mistakes.

A final interesting observation in this story is Ryan's perspective of risk. He agrees with most sophisticated investors when he shakes his head when people say that real estate is risky, when they're 100% comfortable throwing money at the volatile stock market.

Imagine an investment:

- Where you can research exactly what long-term demand for your product will be based on over 100 years of historic data, based solely on the macro movement of people and jobs.
- That does not collapse in one day based on a rumour or a bomb going off halfway around the world. Real estate values take time

to move upwards and take time to move down, allowing you to sleep well at night and not have to react to every headline you read.

- Where you have a direct impact on the increase in value of that investment and the income it produces, providing you with the opportunity to directly affect the investment, not hoping that some boardroom decision is designed to help your value.

- Where long-term trends drive values and demand, so minor fluctuations in the market can be ignored. While others panic, you sit back knowing you've done your research.

- Where automatic computer-based trading can't shave 20% off the value of your investment based on some algorithm designed in someone's tech lab.

- Where major banks will provide you three extra dollars for every one dollar you invest, providing you with strong leverage.

These six points above define what real estate can provide you with. Compare that to many other investments out there in which you receive a piece of paper representing your investment, a board of directors controls all of the decisions on your investment, you cannot use your expertise to help the value of your portfolio, and you sit and wonder what the next "world crisis" will be that will drive your investment value down substantially. You're always on the edge, watching the latest news report, trying not to be the last one to know. Not having control, now that's risky. Whom do you prefer to look after you? Yourself, or some faceless and nameless group of corporate board members?

ACTION STEPS

1. Take a look at your risk profile. What level of risk do you accept in your investments?
   ❏ Low   ❏ Medium   ❏ High

2. Define risk in your life. Are you more comfortable having someone else's opinion control your financial future, or do you believe that you would look after your own interests the best? (Be honest with yourself.)

3. What investment vehicles provide you with the best combination of the two?

    _____

    _____

    _____

    _____

SUCCESS STORY #21
TRUE RESULTS TAKE TIME

Tiffany Young and Corey Young

How do you learn to grow flowers if you never get your hands dirty?

Tiffany Young was afraid. Married at 19, she was afraid of the future she and her husband, Corey, were building with a small business that sold indoor air systems, provided cleaning services and kept them running from one sale to the next. She was afraid for her parents' health and the fact they didn't have the financial freedom she thought they deserved after decades of labour. She was afraid for her young nephew, Rio, a boy she and Corey have helped raise since he was less than a year old. Were they teaching him what he needs to know to be financially successful in life? Could unconditional love ever be enough?

"Fear is a good motivator, but it's a miserable boss," says Tiffany, who was 24 years old when she attended her first real estate investment seminar in search of a smarter way to make a living. Others followed. "You name it, I took it. If it was in the paper, or on the radio, I signed up and went." She understood that not all of it was going to help her, but one new idea that supported her vision would make it worthwhile.

She and Corey figure that education cost them about $10,000. It wasn't all for naught, but the information they took home always stopped short. "You never really learned what you needed to know to take the next step so you could actually be a real estate investor," is how Tiffany sums up the experience.

Fast-forward six years and you find her and Corey planning what they hope to be a five-month journey to Mexico beginning in the fall of 2007. There, they and Rio will volunteer their time to help the Mexican people. They spent two months there the year before. "It was the best two months we've had since we got married," says Tiffany.

Their real estate portfolio will be working while they're away from their acreage helping others less fortunate. Valued at $9 million by mid-2007, their portfolio is a hybrid combination of nearly 40 single-family homes, including condos and half-duplexes.

"Real estate investment has changed everything for us," says Tiffany.

"We can retire and never have to work again. For me, I think the biggest thing has been being able to show my dad that I can work with my brain and not my back. That's what he used to tell us kids. I also like knowing that he also owns 10 properties—and I helped make that happen!"

To Tiffany, real success began for her and Corey after they joined the Real Estate Investment Network in 2005. They and her parents already owned a condo together. "But we bought that before we really knew what we were doing. In hindsight, that property really didn't meet all of the economic fundamentals I've since learned. But we still own it, and I think it's fair to say it's been a good teacher."

More than anything, REIN helps the Youngs approach the investment business with an ever-higher level of sophistication. "I've learned you never need to fear not having a tenant. The cost of an extra month of vacancy is much better than renting it to the wrong tenant." To her, patience is the key.

Hers is the voice of experience. "I once accepted half a damage deposit from one tenant. That was a huge mistake as you can't get that money later."

Experience has also proven the value of working with tenants when things aren't going well. When an accident meant one tenant couldn't make his rent, Tiffany struck a deal whereby he would help with everything from snow removal to picking up the mail. That gave her more time to focus on a deal to sell that property. It went for $100,000 above what they'd paid six months earlier. "I knew I was going to be okay and that gave me the freedom to help this tenant out. It was a good deal for both of us."

From the start, the Youngs used joint venture money. They bought one property with her parents, then bought one on their own. After that, they sought JV partners who had experience in real estate. "These people understand investing," says Corey. "We don't have to educate them about the economic fundamentals. We don't have to help them lose their fear."

These days, Corey spends his days looking for properties, often with Rio in tow. "We've walked into places where Rio has told me, 'Oh Uncle, no one is going to want to live here.' That always makes me smile, because I know he's learning the business!"

That business is focused on revenue properties that attract what

Tiffany calls "an executive tenant. These people won't bounce a cheque and they'll pick up the phone and call a plumber if they need one. That works for me, because I self-manage the properties and I like it when tenants help out." They treat these tenants with respect and in return they treat the Youngs and the property with respect.

The Youngs, who've bought about 100 properties since March 2005, admit that properties don't always come with that kind of tenant in place. One of their biggest investments includes 40 units in a development with a reputation for unemployed tenants, many with substance abuse issues.

"We started taking units as they became available and, in less than a year, 35 of the development's 60 units are rented by quality tenants," says Tiffany. "There's also a new property manager at work and the profile of that building is really changing. It takes time, but we're part of a move to offer better-quality homes to people who need it."

Increased financial freedom means they could retire and never work again. "Before, we made money if we were physically working. Now our money does the work," says Corey.

That's a side benefit to the real advantages of their success with real estate investment. More importantly, the business gives them time to do the things they really want to do, whether at home or elsewhere. "Being able to be there when mom needs chicken soup or Rio goes on a field trip, when friends and family need help . . . that's what it's all about," says Tiffany.

As for the fear that first motivated her foray into real estate investment? It's gone, says Tiffany. "Now, it's all about the economics for me. It's like a science. I take the numbers seriously and, in return, I am not afraid."

Don Campbell's Observations

Although Corey and Tiffany have built a portfolio of over 100 properties in a very short time, they will be the first to say that true results take time. Many get into real estate expecting to create wealth and cash flow instantly. Sophisticated investors know that a property portfolio doesn't really start to perform until you've owned it for at least three years. It is at that time that you will have built up a nice equity base and you should be receiving regular positive cash flow every month.

Investors should not expect much from their property investments in the first three years, a period we call normalization. This is the period in which you are completing your renovations, often changing tenants, increasing the revenues and spending money to decrease the operating costs. It is also the time where the majority of your mortgage payments are made up of interest rather than principal. Because the Youngs have built their portfolio in economically strong and stable regions, their 100 properties should provide them and their joint venture partners with a large equity gain and strong positive cash flow in just three short years. Patience is a virtue that exists in both of them.

Corey and Tiffany's story can teach us many other lessons. Fear played a part in their lives at the start of their investment career; they just learned to turn this fear into a motivator. They quickly discovered that economic fundamentals help decrease the confusion in the market, which in turn helped reduce their fear of taking action.

The Youngs are definitely not sitting back waiting for "retirement"; they're living their life now. Traveling internationally, finding ways to give back to those in need and becoming true inspirational leaders. With their recent experiences, they're now able to provide financial leadership to their immediate family and friends, an obvious priority for them. Tiffany sums it all up best when she states that having the ability to be there when your family or friends need you makes all of the hard work worthwhile. Real estate is not about money and wealth; it's about the freedom it provides you to do what you want, with whom you choose.

ACTION STEPS

1. What date do you want to retire?

   _____

   _____

   _____

2. What will you do when that time comes?

   _____

   _____

   _____

3. What's stopping you from doing more of that starting today?
    Think hard on this one—is your answer a roadblock that is beyond
    your control, or is it one of your own making?

    _____

    _____

    _____

SUCCESS STORY #22
DON'T LET YOUR UNIVERSITY DEGREE GET IN YOUR WAY

Navaz Murji

It's not enough to know real estate investment is the key to long-term financial security. You need a plan that's based on good information— and you need a way to tap into the good experiences of others.

Navaz Murji thought he knew what he was doing when he urged his parents to buy a home in Edmonton soon after the family emigrated from the East African country of Tanzania in 1979. A couple of years later, Navaz, the fifth of sixth children, found himself helping his dad make payments as interest rates skyrocketed. "I was on the hook. I'd talked him into it and my dad was working minimum-wage jobs," recalls Navaz, who was in his early 20s at the time. Worrisome as the situation was, he watched his father pay off that property by the early 1990s and move into his retirement years with relative ease. "There was a time in my life when I said I'd never buy residential property again," Navaz reflects. "But then I saw what it helped my parents do and I knew real estate investment was important to long-term wealth."

That lesson was driven home by the people Navaz was meeting through his work as a certified general accountant. "My dad always told me to go to school, work hard and you'll do well. I did that, but I was meeting clients who didn't have much in terms of formal education, but had a ton of money through real estate."

If that was Lesson One, then Lesson Two was learning the difference between knowing what you want to do and doing it well. "I bought my first real estate investment property in 1997," says Navaz. Now a certified general accountant living in Burnaby, B.C., he bought a single-family dwelling in nearby Surrey. "I didn't have a plan. I didn't understand the market and I sure didn't understand how the type of property affected cash flow."

Still possessed by a vision of successful real estate investment, he started reading more about the business and took his first formal real estate investment course. By early 2000, Navaz owned a 25-unit multi-family building and started buying properties in Prince George, Vancouver and Kamloops, eventually building a portfolio of 20 single-family properties.

Through all of the acquisitions, however, it didn't seem like the vision of success was any closer, says Navaz. When he and his wife Rozmin sold their own home to buy a multi-family property, their three children were still living at home. In addition to the hassles of finding themselves back in the rental housing market, property management issues on the single-family front cost him hours in travel time as the property was located in another province. Through all of this, he also had to balance the demands of building a busy accounting practice.

Seeking a new direction, a better plan and an unbiased view of the real estate market Navaz joined REIN in late 2005. By then, he'd sold the multi-family building so he and Rozmin could buy another primary residence. Now focused on consolidating his workload and creating more free time, he divested most of the properties in Vancouver, Kamloops and Prince George and set a fresh course.

By February 2006, he'd bought his first multi-family building in Edmonton and added three more in less than four months. When his father took ill that same year, Navaz backed off the acquisitions to spend more time with his family. He's back looking now and will buy properties as they come his way. "It's at the point where I don't need more," he confides. "But if a decent deal comes through, I'll be looking."

Unlike his past approach, Navaz now targets a single geographic market. "Because my single-family homes were so spread out, it was tough to find good help with property management. That just added to the frustration."

His advice to those thinking about real estate investment comes quick and blunt:

1. Educate yourself.
2. Let income and capital profit drive your investment decisions (not income tax avoidance!).
3. Don't get caught up in analysis paralysis.
4. Find people who can help you do what you want to do. Build a team.

"The biggest stumbling block for me was my own mindset," he says. "At first, I spent too much time thinking about what could go wrong. And then when I did take action, I complicated things with some kind of bad choices."

On the upside, he affirms, "I didn't quit. I found ways to stay the course. And boy, am I ever glad now."

Don Campbell's Observations

As a professionally trained accountant, in order to achieve his goals Navaz had to get out of his own way. This occurs with many investors who professionally trained (such as accountants and engineers). The good news is, once you break through this mental trap, professionals can become amazing investors, as you have witnessed in many of the stories in this book.

Real estate investing is not a black and white science; there are often variables that can't be totally accounted for, and this can lead to analysis paralysis among professionals and non-professionals alike. In today's society, we are trained to look for reasons *not* to do something rather than to find a way in which to make it work. Let's be brutally honest—if you look hard enough, you can find a reason not to do anything, no matter how low the risk. So that's a mindset that has to change if you want to move forward.

As soon as Navaz decided to find a way in which to use his professional training to help him become a better investor, his portfolio began to grow the way he dreamed it could. And now, a few short years later, his portfolio is allowing him more time for the things he loves including his family and playing golf. Now his analysis paralysis can be used only on the putting green.

ACTION STEPS

1. Do you get caught in analysis paralysis when considering an investment or any major decision?
   Yes ❑   No ❑

2. Rate the following on a scale of 1 to 7 in order of importance to your decision-making process (1 being most important):

- ❏ Level of risk
- ❏ Fear of making a mistake
- ❏ Having enough information
- ❏ Having done it before
- ❏ Not knowing what you're doing
- ❏ Afraid to look bad in front of others
- ❏ Fear of losing money

Analysis paralysis is based mostly in fear. Many investors love the act of analysis—they can sit in front of their computer analyzing properties and think they're making progress; however, they're not moving forward until they take real action by getting out into the market and making offers.

Analysis paralysis can happen no matter how deep an investor's experience. From fear of success, to fear of making mistakes, it can be pervasive and become a paralyzing force—if you allow it. That's the bad side of fear, but there is a good side as well.

Learning to use the good side of fear is one of the major strategies successful investors use to rise above the crowd. This elite group all admit that fear exists, but they've learned the habits of turning this fear into a positive motivator. And how they do this is the message of Navaz Murji's story.

> *"Fear always lurks behind perfectionism. Confronting your fears and allowing yourself the right to be human can, paradoxically, make you a far happier and more productive person."*
>
> —Dr. David M. Burns

Following are the most common fears that real estate investors encounter and the strategies to break through them.

FEAR OF TAKING ACTION—
The Ultimate Way to Defeat Success

The ability to take action is the number-one difference between successful real estate investors and wannabe investors. Having the confidence and motivation required to move boldly forward is the one single thing every one of these overachievers has rated as their most important attribute.

Our study revealed the one characteristic that holds back investors from taking more action is *fear*! This fear of taking action reveals itself in many different ways, but you can immediately identify it as the basis of the "web of excuses."

You would be shocked to hear the many different excuses we've heard from investors explaining why they can't act right now. This web of excuses includes, but is definitely not limited to, making excuses about their lack of knowledge, lack of time, lack of financing, lack of good deals, all the way through to the ultimate excuse of blaming others for the investor's lack of action. I believe in the last 15 years we've heard them all—and each and every one is based in fear.

So, if this fear of action is ever present, how come it doesn't stop the successful investor? Well, the first lesson to be learned from the successful is their ability to turn these fears into action . . . instead of excuses.

TAKE ACTION—Don't Make Excuses

There are a number of different strategies to achieve this, but one of the most effective ways comes from one of our most successful REIN members. It is called the "Positive Spin Strategy" and is something you can start using in your life immediately. Here's how it works: every time an excuse-based fear pops into your head, follow these three steps:

1. Stop whatever you are doing and write it down on a piece of paper.
2. Physically cross it out with your pen.
3. Then write out the Positive Spin version of the excuse and state it out loud.

For example:

The Excuse: "I don't have any more money to buy real estate."

Positive Spin Version: "I have access to all the money I need—I just have to ask the right questions of the right people!"

Those who use this strategy commit to doing it no matter what . . . and the changes they see are immediate! The key difference you will see is this: **It keeps you focused on what your positive options are**.

Successful investors know that if they allow excuses to impact them, they will stop you in your tracks. With the Positive Spin Strategy, you literally eliminate the excuse (by crossing it out) and then turn it into a positive motivator. This strategy is brilliant, and when you see the results these people are getting, it obviously works.

Take the fear and excuses in your life and turn them around. Commit to use her strategy for just one month and watch what happens . . . you'll be amazed. And so will many others around you!

THE FEAR OF MAKING MISTAKES—
Where Wrong Is Right and Right Is Right!

This is the second most prevalent fear for investors—the dreaded fear of making a mistake. This fear has been trained into us through years of schooling and upbringing, and if not taken control of, can stop you from taking action.

Throughout our lives, we are taught that mistakes are bad and wrong (remember the big red X in school), when in reality they're not. The difference is in how we handle the results they bring, and in most cases we can turn mistakes into very positive experiences.

What truly successful real estate investors understand is that mistakes are going to happen, no matter how much knowledge investors have, or how careful they think they're being. The key is to minimize (not avoid) your mistakes by learning from the mistakes and successes of others. Talk to investors, surround yourself with them, and never be afraid of asking a question. Share your results and ask them to share theirs. If the group is good, you will discover just how to leverage your knowledge with that of others. This will greatly decrease the mistakes you make.

Successful real estate investors follow these steps in order to minimize their mistakes:

- **they follow a proven system** that takes them through the complete buying process—from finding the properties to managing the properties.
- **they don't skip any steps in the system**.
- **at least once per year they review their system** from top to bottom. This is much like an athlete's annual training camp. They review and practise the basics so when the time comes to use their talents, the steps become automatic, thus minimizing their mistakes.

Successful investors don't wait until they know it all because they are acutely aware that they will never "know it all," and if they try to wait until they do, the market will pass them by. I recommend that you adopt this philosophy.

THE FEAR OF MAKING OFFERS—When Either YES or NO Makes You Nervous.

Although it is a well-known fact that the more offers you make, the more real estate you'll buy, our research shows that average investors make significantly fewer offers than the super-successful.

Successful real estate investors are continually making offers, whether formally through realtors or informally on napkins while sitting at a vendor's kitchen table. They understand that most of these offers will not be accepted, but the mindset of success is with each NO they hear, they just moved a step closer to receiving a YES! You see, it really is a numbers game—the more offers you place, the more offers will be accepted.

Through our research, we've discovered that the main reason why some investors don't make offers is a rather unique type of fear. We call it a double-edged fear. It encompasses both the fear of rejection and fear of acceptance!

This sounds like a rather bizarre mindset to be in, but this double-edged fear traps more investors than all the others combined. Here's how it works:

Up until the time of the offer, finding properties can be a lot of fun (due diligence, talking with realtors, even number crunching), but as soon as it becomes offer time, the whole process becomes actual. It is time for the buyer to step up and take action, and that's where the fear kicks in.

So what do the super-successful do to deal with this special double-edged fear? Well, as with the majority of effective strategies, this one is also very simple. Here's what our research has revealed:

Successful real estate investors acknowledge their fear of placing offers. They admit that it exists at two levels (rejection and acceptance). Then, they use a tried and true strategy to turn this fear around by asking themselves, "What's the worst that can happen by placing this offer?" And there are very simple answers. The following are the potential outcomes, along with the no-risk solutions to each:

The offer is rejected: If the offer is rejected outright, then you know you haven't found the motivated vendor you're looking for. And as described in the real estate Money Funnel in the REIN Quickstart program, successful investors understand that they must be dealing with motivated vendors! The successful investors understand that the vendor is rejecting their offer, not them personally. Remember, this is a business not a popularity contest.

The offer is countered: Now you have the power back in your court, you can do whatever you like at this point. You have just been handed three options, all of which put you soundly in the power position:

1. You can reject the counter-offer outright, and move on to another piece of real estate, releasing you of any obligations on this property.

2. You can make a counter-offer to their counter-offer. At this point, if you are following a proven system (as we discussed earlier), you have completed a major portion of your due diligence. You already know what you can pay for the property and what terms you need to make it fit your system. You set the price and terms and send it back.

3. You can accept their counter-offer. If they counter-offer at a price and terms that fit your system, you can just accept their offer knowing that you've bought a property that works in your portfolio. And because you have structured the offer properly (with the proper clauses), even if the remainder of your due diligence reveals any surprises, you can still walk away from the deal. A truly no lose situation!

The offer is accepted: Because you are following a proven system, you can celebrate because you've just identified and received an accepted offer on a property that you wanted. Once again, because you've structured the offer using a proven system, you can still walk away if necessary should you be unable to close, or if your additional due diligence reveals a surprise. But, in reality, you have just found another property to add to your portfolio!

In other words, no matter what the vendor says about your offer, you still win. And you'll note that in every option above, you are always in the power position, meaning you decide whether to move forward or not.

Successful real estate investors understand that they are the ones who hold all the cards when they are buying—and so should you. This one change in your mindset will give you a huge advantage in the marketplace: While others fret and worry before placing an offer, you will have already jumped into first place by stepping up to the plate and placing your offer. You'll have acknowledged the fear and understand that there is never any downside to placing a properly structured offer (as detailed in the REIN Quickstart Program available at www.reincanada.com).

Here's a truth in this business: You have to make offers to make money! If you aren't making offers, you've stopped before you've started. Never be afraid of making an offer after you have done your initial due diligence. If the property seems to fit your system, place an offer. Use a "sophisticated investor" clause such as "Subject to buyer's lawyer's approval," just to ensure you have a safety valve.

The worst thing that can happen is the vendor doesn't accept your offer and you must move on to another property. The best thing is you end up owning a property that fits your system. You will be shocked at the success that comes to you, seemingly out of the blue, when you place offers.

Your Ultimate Advantage

The bottom line is, you can give yourself an amazing advantage in the marketplace just by using these simple strategies and acknowledging that fear exists. Now that you are aware of the power that fear can have—listen and watch carefully to others around you. Watch how it manifests itself through their excuses to justify a lack of action.

By using the above tools to turn fear into a positive motivator, you follow the footsteps of some of the most successful real estate investors in North America. And while others will be stuck in fear, you will be moving forward, making offers, buying properties and creating whatever level of success you want.

Move boldly forward, acknowledge the fear and let it propel you to greatness! Make a commitment to yourself to place an offer this week!

Courage is resistance to fear, mastery of fear—not absence of fear.

—Mark Twain (1835–1910)

SUCCESS STORY #23
DON'T BE AFRAID TO ASK—THEY MIGHT SURPRISE YOU AND SAY YES

Winnielee Chuus

Real estate investment is about relationships. I try to serve others first, and my business is stronger for it.

Things got pretty cold in Edmonton in March of 2006, but the economy was running hotter than ever before. Real estate investor Winnielee Chuus of Vancouver was excited about accompanying one of her partners, Michael Wong, to Edmonton. He'd never been to Alberta's capital city, and she and her brother, also her investment partner, Paul Chu, wanted Michael to understand that all the investment hype and excitement was real.

Then the storm blew in, literally. "It was freezing cold and there was so much snow that some roads were closed," Winnielee recalls. "Others were impassable. But somehow, our real estate agent got us to the properties we wanted to see. I think we got one of the houses because another guy from Australia, who was just along for the ride, befriended a homeowner. They struck up this conversation about Australia and I think it won the vendor over."

The end result: $103,000 for a three-bedroom townhouse valued at more than $240,000 a year later. "And," adds Winnielee, "we weren't even the first offer in."

Winnielee, an accountant who still works full-time in Vancouver, and Paul, a web marketing specialist (who stuck with the traditional spelling of the family name), started investing in 2003, when they both bought one unit in a townhouse condominium in Surrey, B.C.

She remembers the early excitement of that first deal and being inspired by the Quickstart recordings, which she listened to while walking on her lunch hour. "Inspired, but not enough to take any action."

That changed when she took her first live Quickstart course later the same year. "Since then, I'm all about taking action," she says with a quick laugh. And she has the portfolio to prove it.

By July 2007, she and her partners, plus Wayne Wong, a joint venture partner living in the Eastern United States, ran a portfolio of 65 properties valued at $18 million. All are in Edmonton or nearby communities and, while most are townhouses, the partners also own two single-family homes and a number of condominiums.

Their portfolio's quick growth is a testament to the relationships they've built within the investment community. One of their joint venture partners is involved in almost one-third of their properties. Another has money in five of their deals. She figures their star property manager in Edmonton has found 70% of the units they control.

By contrast, a different side of property management takes centre stage when Winnielee talks about her biggest investment error. It didn't take her long to realize their first property manager wasn't working out. Even though demand outstripped supply, some of their properties took longer than necessary to fill. Other places had maintenance issues, including one that cost the company several thousand dollars. "There was some water damage and she rented dryers to speed up the process. It turns out it would have been faster and cheaper to just rip out that drywall and do it over," says Winnielee.

To make matters worse, she later learned that a more diligent property manager would have caught what was really a simple problem with a laundry drain long before any water damage occurred.

Not one to mince words, Winnielee knows the buck stops with her. "I was too cheap to buy out that manager's contract, even though I knew the relationship wasn't working. It would have been worth every penny of the two-month penalty, versus about $5,000 in damages."

A commitment to relationships is behind the partners' decision to make communication a key priority. They set up regular conference calls with all four present and, at least twice a month, she, Paul and Michael talk specifically about what they're doing—and about what they could be doing better.

Most of their joint venture partners now contribute at least $100,000 per deal, up from $65,000 a few years ago. JVs hold about 50% of the total portfolio, all of which is managed as revenue property for buy-and-hold appreciation.

When Paul and Michael wound down a successful web marketing venture, Winnielee was relieved. "There is no way I could have created this kind of wealth if I'd just been working a full-time job. Right now, I am still working. It helps that Paul and Mike have more time to focus on the investment business. That's how things get done."

For Paul, that now means regular trips to Edmonton, where he assists the property manager. "We face the same issue as every other employer in that market. It's tough to find people to do the job—and we're fussy about doing it right," explains Winnielee.

Still in the buying phase of their portfolio development, "doing it right" includes finding investors who share their vision to hold properties for three to five years. It also means "being able to use the business to help other people," notes Winnielee. When one investor lost a significant amount of money in an investment not related to real estate, Winnielee let her out of one of their longer-term investments "so she could get her hands on some cash. It felt good to help out."

A self-confessed fan of the give-and-take associated with negotiating a deal, Winnielee admits real estate investment has changed her life. "I take a lot of personal development programs because I am interested in learning what I can do to be a better person." She recently took a three-week trip to India with people she knew from one personal development course. "I loved it. It cost a lot of money, and I could afford it because of my investing."

A take-charge personality makes it hard for Winnielee to identify any real roadblocks on her path to success. "Okay, my parents used to wonder what I was doing going to Edmonton all of the time, especially when I started taking my brother along!"

Three years later, her other brother helped her parents get the line of credit they needed to start investing with Winnielee, Paul and their partners. Her parents are now partners in four properties and Winnielee recognizes that investment for what it really is: A vote of confidence in the market—and in their real-estate-savvy kids.

———— ∞∞∞ ————

Don Campbell's Observations

When you meet the team of Winnielee and Paul, you immediately know why they are so successful—their enthusiasm and tenacious attention to detail are really second to none. Once they have a goal, large or small, there is no doubt that they will achieve it.

One of the key lessons we can learn from them is their lack of fear around asking for what they want. Many investors, and people in general, are afraid to politely ask for what they really want: They dance around the issue rather than getting to the point. This fear is often based in a fear of rejection. What Paul and Winnielee have discovered is that the worst that can happen is the other person will say no, and the best that can happen is they'll say yes, and there is always the midpoint between the two: "I can't do that, but I can do something else for you."

With this philosophy, they are purchasing properties that other investors don't even know are for sale, which means no competitive bidding and low purchasing prices. One of the most powerful questions any investor can ask is: "Do you know anyone who is thinking of selling their property?"

I know of many investors who use this question in conversations no matter where they are—at a party, a family gathering, a sporting event, anywhere a conversation is struck up. Obviously they don't lead the conversation with this enquiry—they just work it in at some point. It also provides a good opportunity to pass on their business card with a simple "Well, if you do hear of anyone, please don't hesitate to call me. I'm a serious buyer."

This question should be asked of any vendor you're purchasing a property from. Change it a bit: "Do you or anyone you know have any other properties for sale? I'm still looking for a couple more." Winnielee obviously asked this of their property manager, and that opened up the floodgate of unlisted properties.

Make sure that everyone you know, or come across, is aware that you are a real estate investor looking for good properties. This is the second lesson we can learn from Paul and Winnielee. You never know who will want to be a joint venture partner, or who may have information you might not have including properties that are about to be listed for sale.

Now, beginning with Winnielee's leadership, her whole family is able to take advantage of the real estate market's strength. The leadership that Winnielee and Paul have shown to their family is now crossing over to friends and fellow investors. Their enthusiasm for the deal is infectious, and that's a virus you want to catch.

ACTION STEPS

1. Who in your life does not know you are a real estate investor? (It might be a long list!) Each of these people may represent a potential property, and even if only 1 in 10 lead to some piece of knowledge you didn't have, spreading the word was well worth it.

   _____

   _____

   _____

   _____

2. Make sure you have professional-looking business cards listing your contact information and with "Real Estate Buyer" as your title. Have them professionally designed and printed, and always carry them with you. Like you, your card should make a good impression.

3. What three professionals are you going to ask, "Do you know of any-one who is thinking of selling a property?"

   - _____
   - _____
   - _____

SUCCESS STORY #24
"You're Not the Babysitter, You're the Parent!"

Claudio Gambetti

I tell people that owning property is like being responsible for a baby. Real estate agents, lawyers, accountants and property managers are all critically important, but they are like babysitters. You are still responsible for the growth of your child. It's your property.

When Claudio Gambetti sits down at the dinner table, he faces the primary three reasons he's glad he got into real estate investment. They're also the three primary reasons why success is the only option. No, make that four. Besides his kids (aged 15, 12 and 8), there's his wife Mary. Mary was a stay-home mom until a few years back when she rolled up her sleeves and got involved in the family business after the couple had to fire the property management firm for their first building, a sixplex that was about to take them down!

Claudio, whose own father died when he was just 3 years old, sings the praises of Canada, the country his widowed mother brought him and two siblings to when he was 15. They were to stay a year, hone their English skills and move back to Italy. Instead, the family immigrated to Canada (his mother fell in love and married a Canadian and added a baby sister to the family). Claudio pursued post-secondary education in engineering, followed by a long-term career in the telecommunications industry clustered in the Ottawa–Carleton region.

A fan of self-help books, Claudio went looking for an opportunity to build long-term wealth for his growing family, eventually settling on real estate and joining REIN in the summer of 2003, when he was 38 years old. "I went to two meetings," he says, "before I knew I was ready to buy."

Using knowledge harvested from books and especially from REIN programs and contacts, Claudio uncovered a sweet deal and secured direct communication with the vendor. He and Mary put 10% down on a $525,000 deal, with an additional 5% through an agreement with the vendor, and became the proud owners of a sixplex.

Then life hit the fan. Less than a year into the new venture, Claudio fired the property management firm, having discovered straight-out fraud and incompetence. They were thousands of dollars in the hole, with three of the six units vacant and two more tenants having given notice to leave because of the incompetent management. The Gambettis were told that problems with the building's electrical system would cost a whopping $7,000 to fix. Compounding everything, Claudio then lost his job. "All of this happened in the space of about two weeks," says Claudio with a sigh. "I was sure the property was a good one, but we had to focus on making it work."

That's when Mary stepped in and assumed a key role on the sixplex front. In six weeks, all six units were full, helped by the fact the two tenants who planned to move stayed when they saw the changes. Concerned by the estimate they'd been given regarding the electrical work, Claudio used his engineering background and sought new information. The problem was fixed for about $500.

Those early problems aside, Claudio figures that the sixplex has enriched their lives in many ways. While cash flow is limited due to the planned leveraging, the potential is rapidly building. Better yet, Claudio and Mary's kids get to see their parents working together, and treating their tenants and the people they call to help with maintenance or repairs with dignity and respect. "Even when things go wrong, we act professionally," says Claudio. "We're showing the kids how to look for solutions and how to avoid creating bigger problems, and mostly how to maintain integrity."

The kids have also learned the complexities of running your own business. Claudio admits that some entrepreneurs don't like to talk about problems they've encountered, but he thinks that such discussion can be educational for others, especially since he learned so much in the process.

Careful screening of tenants has created a mix of university students, young families and working adults. "We now have amazing tenants," says Claudio. "If they're moving within the city, they actually ask us if we have another building they can move into because they like dealing with us. Another tenant, who worked in the window industry, used his contacts to help replace four windows and a door. He did all the work, with amazing quality, and asked for only $1,500. It was great."

This kind of relationship is nurtured by Claudio and Mary, who host an annual barbecue for tenants. In 2006, they called it "Under the Tuscan Sun" and Mary prepared a five-course meal. "We just stepped back and let the tenants get to know each other better," Claudio recalls. "We offered some fun prizes and the person who won the DVD player traded it with another tenant for a giant package of toilet paper because she already had a DVD player. Another volunteered to start babysitting for a young couple who was just being introduced to the group. It was pretty cool—and exciting."

Recently, they started buying property on the other side of the country, with Claudio using vacation days to travel west. Their distant five-property portfolio already includes three properties where they are the money partners, and two where their joint venture partner put up the funds. Still feeling the pain of their first experience, Claudio's insisted on two separate property management companies, hedging his bets should one not perform to expectation.

Claudio and Mary's success has also inspired his two siblings and parents to invest. "I like that. I feel like I am giving back time and knowledge to people who've made a difference in my life."

Another blip in the telecom industry left Claudio out of a full-time job again in early 2007. It's a shift he was ready to embrace. Now able to focus on the family investments full time, Claudio believes his own kids will become real estate investors. "I don't think it's a matter of 'if' they'll buy, it's 'when.' I figure we can help them be financially free before they leave high school. Imagine having your university paid for!"

With the acquisition phase of his business still picking up steam, Claudio knows regular trips to economically strong regions of the country—and away from his family—are a fact of life. On the upside, he no longer has to use up his vacation days to make the investment business work, and he loves the way his personal and business lives are so well-connected.

Now that he's reaping the benefits of real estate investment, Claudio wouldn't have it any other way.

Don Campbell's Observations

Although Claudio is a serious businessman who truly treats his investments like a business rather than a hobby, it really is always about what's good for his family in the long run. In fact, in his story, you can see this commitment to the future of his family finances. This is always an interesting subject when speaking with investors. Many selfishly believe they are making decisions on their own behalf, when in fact they are making decisions for their current family as well as future generations of their family that may not even exist yet.

The wealth that investors create today can and will make a financial difference for decades after they pass. Imagine what life would have been like in your family if your grandfather and grandmother (or mother and father) had created an extra $2,000,000 of net worth before they passed on. In what positive ways could that have affected your life, your schooling, your career paths and your long-term goals? Quite dramatically, in many cases. Sophisticated investors understand that they can create a financial legacy for their family and/or their favourite charity or church just by taking small, yet immediate, action today.

This all being said, the biggest lesson we can call learn from Claudio's story is the same lesson we all heard in kindergarten "Treat others as you would like to be treated." Many of us know this in the back of our minds, but few live it as fully as Claudio and his family. They are building communities and having a positive impact on the many lives they touch.

ACTION STEPS

1. For whom, or for what charity, do you want to create a financial legacy? In other words, for whom are you making your financial decisions today?

   _____

   _____

   _____

2. Do you honestly treat others the way you wish to be treated? If yes, *congratulations*, you are one of a minority. If no, make a short list of

important people in your life whom you will try to do this with on a more consistent basis.

_____

_____

_____

_____

SUCCESS STORY #25
LEAVE SOMETHING ON THE TABLE FOR THE NEXT PERSON

Patricia Scanlon and Ricardo Melendro

Once you start to learn about real estate investment, you see properties differently. You also start to realize that some properties aren't such a "great deal" after all.

Patricia Scanlon rises early for her 30-minute commute to her job teaching French and Spanish to high school students in the nearby community of Bayside. A resident of Brighton, Ontario, she likes the work, but readily admits she would prefer to enjoy her days at home with her husband, Ricardo Melendro, and their one-year-old son, Daniel.

Then again, the sacrifice is nominal when you think of how it nourishes a life dream that includes two full-time parents for Daniel and the financial freedom to fund schoolchildren living in Colombia's Alta Guajira region. That's the impoverished and remote desert area where she and Ricardo met, fell in love and started planning a future that included an active search for ways to make the world a better place.

An experienced teacher who spent four years teaching in Colombia, Patricia knew real estate investing could provide the kind of passive income she needed to support a growing desire to help the people of the Alta Guajira.

By February 2003, she was back in Ontario teaching and the newly emigrated Ricardo was plying his environmental engineering experience with a Kingston-based company more than an hour's drive from their home. Daunted by the lengthy commute and the prospect of his having to rent a room, the couple bought a two-bedroom condo in Kingston, then secured a renter to cover the mortgage. "Over the three years, I had two roommates and they were excellent," recalls Ricardo. "In fact, I barely saw them as we worked all week and I left for home on weekends."

Buoyed by that experience, they bought a semi-detached house in Brighton that April. "We found tenant-buyers for it, and drew up a lease option contract," says Patricia. "Our return would be over 100% in 18 months. We were pumped!"

Their appetite for investment was whetted. Patricia kept her eye on local real estate information and eventually ended up at an auction where three townhouses were up for grabs. "Their starting price was $27,500 apiece. I knew they were in dire need of repair, but I thought to myself, 'How bad could it be?'"

With her brother Mark as their partner, Patricia and Ricardo bought the three townhouses, embarking on what could be described as the steepest learning curve of their investment careers. Under Plan A, they would hold and rent the units, whereas with Plan B they would sell the units. They decided to go with Plan B when they encountered contractor problems and concerns over wet crawl spaces. They sold the three units to another investor.

As that deal was progressing, Patricia joined REIN on the advice of another brother, John. It meant lengthy trips to Toronto for meetings, but it spelled a turning point in their investment strategy.

Fast-forward a couple of years and they own a fourplex, triplex and duplex in Ontario and several properties outside of their home province. Working with colleagues they know from their work abroad, their JVs include Australians and Colombians as well as Canadians.

They now walk into—and out of—deals with people they do or don't trust, having learned what happens when you don't ask enough questions. "We're also big on leaving something on the table for the next person," says Ricardo. "We want to work with people, not compete against them."

Determined to work to live, not live to work, they've farmed out property management from the start. "If all we had to do was collect cheques, it would have been fine," says Patricia. "But we know there's a lot more to hands-on property management and we weren't prepared to give up that much time to learn and then do it well. The whole idea of investing was to provide us with freedom, not tie us down." They do screen their own tenants, part of a due diligence strategy that acknowledges exactly how each party contributes to the upkeep of the property.

That same focus on excellence guides their growing commitment to the Alta Guajira. Having been exposed to extreme poverty, decisions like foregoing cable television and giving up a full-time income from Ricardo's professional career are easy to make, since they are willing to make sacrifices now in their quest for future financial independence.

But theirs is not a life of hardship. Ricardo spends his days with their son, and Patricia loves knowing Daniel is in good hands while she works.

They've also bought two horses, one more than the steed Patricia promised herself when she first envisioned what she could do with long-term wealth based on passive income.

They're also building a list of JV partners to carry their business forward. And Patricia likes knowing their JV deals are structured to take care of their partners' interests first. "We can look at people and honestly tell them that we don't make money unless they make money."

That same win-win approach will be at work as they move into larger commercial buildings, says Ricardo.

With the business entering a period of growth, Patricia and Ricardo move closer to establishing their fund for schoolchildren in the Alta Guajira. Slipping her educator's hat back into place, Patricia is excited about the possibilities. In a place like Colombia, education is a key force in the fight against poverty "and who knows what brilliance lies within the mind of a child too poor to attend school."

Don Campbell's Observations

Society needs more people like Patricia and Ricardo. They truly make a difference at home and abroad. The personal philosophy of leaving something on the table for the next person sounds very altruistic, and in fact can be. But, from a pure investment strategy point of view, it works like magic.

If you enter all transactions with this philosophy you will:

1. Never hang on too long to your investments just to squeeze the last few thousand dollars out of a deal. If you aim for the peak, invariably you miss it. If you decide early that you will let someone else take some profit, not only does the other person have a great chance of winning, but so do you. It is the incessant drive to maximize profit that creates inevitable losses.

2. You will gain a reputation for being fair, yet firm. Vendors, realtors, mortgage brokers, joint venture partners and tenants will all want to work with you over and over again. They know you understand that you're not the only one who has to win in the deal,

and by dealing with you they have the opportunity to win (profit) as well.

3. You won't lose a great deal because you dug your heals in over $1,000. I have witnessed many investors who had to "win the negotiations at all costs" rather than see how good the deal in their hands really was. These investors believed that negotiations are all about winning and losing, and they were going to take every penny off that table no matter the cost. Sadly, many of these deals never closed, sacrificed for such a small amount of money that down the road would have profited the investor tens of thousands of dollars.

To ensure you are focusing on the big picture, make the goal to win the whole game, not just the first inning.

The second lesson we can glean from Patricia and Ricardo is that your tenants are your partners in the business; they know that the kind of relationship they have with their tenants is significant to their success. That is why, even though they have delegated their property management to a professional company, they still keep the critical responsibility of approving the tenants themselves.

Veteran investor Tim Johnson created the best description of a tenant and the partnership they have with investor landlords:

A tenant is your "partner in business who will open up the shop each morning and lock it up at night. They will look after security and inform you of potential problems in the business. They will cut the grass, rake the leaves, shovel the snow, and pay all the utilities. They will even pay all of your mortgage payments and taxes. Then, in the end, they will relinquish all monetary interest in the business and walk away, leaving you with the profits." In return you provide them [with] exactly what they need, a safe and clean place to live.

By designing their business on these two key philosophies, Patricia and Ricardo are well on their way to making a major difference in lives across Canada as well as the schoolchildren in Colombia. However, it is important to note that not only do others win when they come in contact with this very special couple, Patricia and Ricardo also win by living the lifestyle they choose while making a profit, with no compromises.

ACTION STEPS

1. Your tenants make your business possible and should be acknowl-
    edged. What surprise thank-you gift are you going to send to each of
    your tenants in the next three months?

    _____

    _____

    _____

    _____

SUCCESS STORY #26
GET IT DONE . . . BUT DO IT RIGHT

Paul Falkowski and Bob Holm

We spend a lot of time checking numbers and double-checking numbers to make sure we can honour our word and meet our obligations. When you work with other people's money, you take care of other people's money.

They laugh about it now, but Bob Holm and Paul Falkowski's first attempt to build an office for their growing real estate investment company left them victims of their own success. Construction started in late 2006. Ten months, 10 bays and 16,000 square feet later, they sold every one of the condo-ized units. "And we still didn't have an office," says Bob.

They won't make that mistake again.

In December 2006, they broke ground on another development in St. Albert, just outside of Edmonton. By mid-year 2007, 11 of the 13 bays on their new 25,500-square-foot condo-ized warehouse were sold, including one they'd kept for themselves.

The warehouse developments personify the "Get It Done" approach Bob and Paul apply to their investment business, New Dimension Investments. That shared approach is the reason they're full-time business partners, having clicked at a professional level even though their personal lives have taken remarkably different courses.

Bob, 44, has a wife and three kids and spent 15 years working for a local equipment dealer. By the time he was offered the chance to run his own dealership, he owned his own home and had already banked some experience buying properties to renovate and resell.

Paul, 34, married in April 2007. He'd been thinking about real estate investment since 1999. But when he bought his first house in June 2000, a joint venture partner provided the down payment. It turns out Paul, a bank employee, was helping clients get residential loans, but had trouble qualifying for one on his own. Armed with a growing awareness of what it takes to build equity, Paul's first home was delivered alongside a serious debt-reduction plan. "When I bought that first house, I lived in the basement suite and rented out the main floor and the garage. I needed to reduce my expenses and it was a good experience."

Before long, says Paul, "I started looking for investment deals during my lunch breaks and after work." With the help of a partner who had money and no time, Paul set up Takita Properties and bought 18 bungalows and townhouse units in the Edmonton area. He left the bank in July 2001 and worked full time on Takita, where he managed all of the properties himself.

Paul and Bob met each other at REIN meetings. By then, Bob managed 13 single-family homes in his own portfolio. When they joined forces in May 2003, property acquisitions were the priority and they soon boasted a joint portfolio of 23 houses. Determined to grow the business, they hired Bob's brother Dan to manage the properties (he now owns five of his own) and went looking for more.

Their current portfolio features 50 houses, plus a 20-unit apartment building with an onsite manager. All are held for long-term capital appreciation. While positive cash flow is still the ideal, both admit it's darn tough to achieve given the hard-to-budget demands of regular maintenance coupled with the unexpected demands of repairs to everything from roofs to furnaces.

Their partnership's success comes from a shared work ethic likely honed, at least in part, by childhood experiences. Bob grew up in a single-parent home where "we learned to value the dollar." Paul's family lived in subsidized housing and "expenses always outstripped income."

Bob says their partnership is based on a "get it done philosophy that aims to run an honest business and treat people right. We're not after the money. We're after buying time to spend with family and friends." His wife, Lori, left a 25-year career with Air Canada to join their company as bookkeeper about two years ago. Two of their kids, now teenagers, still live at home. The oldest lives in one of their St. Albert properties and is getting ready to buy his first place. Bob loves knowing that his work as a real estate investor means he can be with his family when they need him, without answering to a corporate boss.

Paul's wife, Adrina, works full time but often goes with him when he's renting properties or handling maintenance. They moved into their own home in St. Albert in July 2007 and Paul, thanks to real estate, looks forward to a lifestyle that balances family and work.

Four years into their business partnership, Paul and Bob expect they've got another 6 to 10 years to build their portfolio. They figure they spend one-third of their working life checking market fundamentals to ensure their investors will get paid and all the economic fundamentals are still pointing strongly upwards.

"We've been hearing rumours of that 'bubble' for years," says Bob. "Well, the fundamentals behind the market show that there is no bubble. This market's success is based on economic strength, not speculation."

Don Campbell's Observations

Paul and Bob have built their business on a worthy business philosophy: "Get it done, do it well and treat people well along the way." I must point out a quote from their story, "We're not after the money. We're after buying time to spend with family and friends."

This quote may sound trite coming from someone else, but when you hear Bob and Paul speak you know that this is exactly how they live their lives. Real estate, and the profits it brings for them, are just vehicles to provide them with a desired lifestyle. Doubtless many others share this philosophy, but it is too rare an outlook.

Money seems to drive the majority of people's decisions; they believe that money is the end game. Truly sophisticated investors, like Bob and Paul, understand that money is just a scorecard. It can provide you the freedom to pursue your other passions, but money and the chase of it has many addictive qualities that must be subdued.

Chasing the next dollar, or the next big deal, is exciting, and if you have been doing it for many years, it can become a habit. However, this habit can be destructive if it is not kept under control. Whole industries of the next "get-rich-quick scheme" have been developed to feed this insatiable thirst for the mighty dollar. You see the ads everyday in the newspapers and on late-night TV. "Secrets Revealed about . . ." or "14 Speakers in One Weekend that Will Change Your Life Forever . . ." Sadly, many of these types of programs are designed to keep you in what Robert Kiyosaki calls the rat race, despite what their marketing may say. The longer you stay in the rat race chasing the next big deal, the more money the promoters make. It's really as simple as that. Bob and Paul have the answer to this addictive cycle: stay off it. They focus on one pursuit—in their case, profitable real estate—and allow themselves time so the system can work from start to finish. No chasing 10 rabbits for these guys—they're mastering the one thing that all sophisticated investors need, and that is "focus."

Either consciously or unconsciously, by focusing on the end goal (or what we call their Personal Belize), Bob and Paul have completely undermined the potential money-chasing-habit. They know their end goal and when they get there all of the options in the world open up to them. They can continue in real estate development; they can relax and follow other passions; they can spend valuable time with their friends and family. But most importantly of all they'll know that they don't have to go and chase the next big deal just for the sake of staying in the race.

Another insight that they share is how their business is based on knowledge. They devote a full 33% of their time during the year to studying market fundamentals and proven systems. They take the time to reflect, to refocus and to ensure they are making knowledge-based decisions. There are many people who call themselves investors who don't spend any real time studying the economics behind the market, and those people aren't investors, they're speculators. The knowledge that Bob and Paul glean during these focus times has given them the confidence and knowledge to move their business from buying single-family homes to completing major commercial developments.

As Bob and Paul clearly state, money is designed to buy you time, and soon these two investors and their family will have all the time in the world.

ACTION STEPS

1. If you had one affirming quote or personal philosophy that you would like to build your business upon, what would it be?

   _____

   _____

   _____

   _____

SUCCESS STORY #27
You Can Always Get What You Want

Catherine Brooker and Mindy Lamont

The biggest lesson for me has been that I can dream big—and bigger when I surround myself with like-minded people.

As an emergency room nurse in one of Edmonton's busy hospitals, Catherine Brooker is on the frontlines of the essential services that are feeling some pain related to the rapid influx of people providing the brains and brawn behind Alberta's economic boom. Originally from small-town Saskatchewan, Catherine loves her job. But there's a lot more to her than meets the eye. Beneath the scrubs of a woman in a traditional "helping" profession beats the heart of a real estate investor.

Catherine's interest in real estate investing was sparked by one of Robert Kiyosaki's books, *Retire Young, Retire Rich*. An American author, businessman and self-help guru, he introduced Catherine to the notions of the passive income and leverage available through real estate investment. She is unequivocal about the impact of the book she chose as her "summer vacation fluff read while reclining on a deck chair soaking up some sun. It changed my life."

Her interest piqued, she spent the rest of 2002 reading more books, taking courses and talking to people connected to real estate investment, eventually finding herself at a REIN meeting. Now part of a group of people doing what she dreamed of doing, Catherine bought her first revenue property in January 2003 at the age of 41. A renter herself, she admits to having been remarkably naive. She knew little about landlording and even less about home maintenance. None of that really mattered because her ignorance paled alongside her determination to use knowledge and money to build a source of passive income!

"Over the next two years, I gradually acquired nine properties," recalls Catherine. Then she hit a wall. Working full time and handling her own property management, she had used up her savings, borrowed other people's RSPs as second mortgages, and was tapped out in terms of finances and time. But she wasn't disappointed. "Nine properties is good enough," she told herself, content in the knowledge that their increase in equity would eventually provide her with a comfortable retirement.

That strategy changed dramatically when she met Mindy Lamont at a REIN meeting in 2005. It was one of Mindy's first meetings and she listened intently when Catherine made an announcement at the microphone. "She talked about how she got rid of a long-time boyfriend who didn't understand real estate and kept telling her she would lose money," Mindy recalls. "Catherine stressed how you should surround yourself with people who support what you're doing. I was already serious about real estate investing and her story impressed me."

Mindy had been looking for someone she could partner with and, by August 2005, a few months after their first meeting, the two were full-time business partners. They leased office space, established Momentum Real Estate Investments Inc. and forged ahead with a strategic plan focused on acquisition and long-term holds. Catherine cut back her nursing hours when she and Mindy launched Momentum. While a lot of investors don't open a separate office, the new partners decided to do so. "We needed an office outside of our homes where we could meet and take our business seriously, especially since we wanted to attract more joint venture partners and get creative about using other people's money to buy more property," says Catherine.

Capitalizing on their individual strengths, Mindy handled finances and office management while Catherine focused on property purchase, renovations and tenant relations. The business flourished. By the summer of 2007, they held 38 rental units, most of them single-family houses. To run it all, they have two office staff and a full-time renovation crew that includes Eric Meadus, who is now Catherine's live-in boyfriend.

"Eric has taught me how houses work and I am now able to inspect houses and quote renovation jobs on my own," says Catherine. "Having a partner who understands my passion for real estate and is equally enthused about it, too, enables me to become better at what I do. Eric's support helps me be a more courageous business owner."

That courage is infectious. It begets the professional and personal contentment that Mindy Lamont now cherishes. With two young kids at home, ages 8 and 11, Mindy says, "I proudly tell people that I work banker's hours. I work very hard, but I have the ultimate flexibility in when I do what I do. It's great." A graphic artist who used to juggle contracts with motherhood, she and her husband, Steve Godreau, like the way real estate investment secures their family's future. "I really had no idea this would turn into such a passion for me. I really like what I do and what Catherine and I are building. That's a real bonus."

Catherine admits it's tough to say exactly what their company's goals are for the future, "since we keep raising the bar." For now, she likes being a full-time investor and enjoys part-time shifts at the hospital, where she often talks to other medical staff about real estate investing. "I am very gentle when I share what I know about real estate investing and the overall market. But let's be honest. If I could help one nurse buy a rental property and it went up $100,000 in value, what a difference that would make to her retirement!"

Future financial security aside, Catherine insists the biggest bonus she's collected from real estate investing has little to do with ledger notes and bottom lines. "The biggest lesson for me has been that I can dream big and bigger when I surround myself with like-minded people."

Don Campbell's Observations

Serendipity played a major role in the meeting of Catherine and Mindy. A chance word at a meeting by Catherine that struck a chord with Mindy is all it took. What many do not understand is that serendipity can be managed through awareness.

Throughout life we are presented with these opportunities and it is only in paying attention to them that we start to accelerate our life's momentum. There were over 300 people in that room when Catherine stood up at that microphone, yet only a few were really listening and only Mindy took the opportunity to move forward. And look what paying attention has done for these amazing women.

At the time, it may have seemed like a coincidence that they met, but it wasn't. Catherine made a declaration of change; Mindy was in the real estate market and looking to build a support team.

Life is all about paying attention. A vast majority of the successful people you meet will also prove to be some of the most aware people you've ever met. They will focus on you when you engage them in conversation; they'll make you feel like you are the only one in the room, even if there are hundreds of others surrounding you. These are also the people who often have a group of people around them at meetings; people are drawn to people who pay attention. In other words, they get more attention on themselves by paying more attention to other people.

Many believe that, in order to bring attention to yourself, you must carry your own spotlight. These are the people who always turn a conversation back on themselves. What they don't see is how this quickly turns people off, and it becomes a self-defeating process. Self-promotion is necessary, but only to a point.

Often times people are so focused on what they are going to do or say next, they forget to listen to the conversation they're in. They become so focused on themselves that they completely miss key opportunities that are presented to them every day. You see them in grocery stores and parking lots all the time, not paying attention to anyone else, cutting people off, leaving carts blocking the aisle. This is a symptom of not paying attention to their surroundings. And these people wonder why they struggle more in life, when the answer is really quite simple: they're not aware of everything that goes on around them.

One way to expand your awareness is, while you are going about your day-to-day business, to pretend you are watching yourself from afar. It will be a revelation; you'll see how your interactions with people make a huge difference in how you are perceived in the world, and you'll see how much chaos you are capable of leaving in your wake. You might be quite amused at what you see when you expand your awareness.

Another strategy that many very successful people follow is to enter every meeting or gathering with a purpose or goal. Many people attend workshops, seminars and local meetings with a only a very vague idea of what they would like to take away from the event. Successful people go in fully primed and fully focused on a specific outcome. For instance, "I want to meet someone who has in-depth knowledge on condominiums," has much more clarity of purpose than "I wonder if condos are a good investment."

Having a clear goal, even if you don't fully achieve it at that meeting, gives the whole event a purpose for you. Every event, gathering or meeting has potential to provide you with one great idea; you just have to be clear and make it happen, rather than have it handed to you.

Catherine and Mindy make things happen. They don't hang around waiting and hoping something happens. Catherine made a clear choice to change the people she had in her life and declared it publicly. I'm sure she didn't have the goal of attracting a new business partner by doing so; however, she replaced a negative influence in her life and attracted two people with very supportive and positive outlooks.

Catherine and Mindy have become leaders in their real estate investment community, and people are drawn to them because of their focus, drive and ability to take action. They have a passion for what they do, and it is directing this passion that they will continue to do so well.

ACTION STEPS

1. What are the next three gatherings, meetings or events you will be attending where you can interact with others?

   _____

   _____

   _____

   _____

2. What is the single specific goal that you want to achieve at each of these events?

   _____

   _____

   _____

   _____

JUMPING OFF THE PROVERBIAL CLIFF

SUCCESS STORY #28
WHEN YOU'RE IN A HOLE, QUIT DIGGING!

Troy Sirett and Bonnie Sirett

Warning: Successful real estate investment can change your life, secure your future—and, umm, make you parents!

Troy and Bonnie Sirett had it all according to conventional society. They were young, in love and held great-paying jobs in a booming industry. They were also smart enough to realize they were building an entirely unsustainable lifestyle heavily subsidized by borrowed money. "Between credit cards and lines of credit, we were about $65,000 in debt," says Troy. "Once we realized what we wanted in life, and saw how far we were from getting it, we knew we were on a train that was headed for a major wreck."

Living in an agricultural community of about 5,000 people in Central Alberta, the Siretts got married in July 2003. During their Christmas honeymoon they reflected on the life they were living and looked ahead to the life they wanted. They were in the habit of spending money before they had it and now had wedding expenses to pay off, including flying in a band for the post-nuptial party. They knew they had to make some changes.

Although their shared income tallied more than $100,000, Troy and Bonnie had to admit they were highly dependent on their jobs, with no chance of getting ahead. The new plan was simple. "What's the first thing you do when you realize you're in a hole? Stop digging," says Troy, now 40.

They cut up credit cards, tackled high-interest debt, cut their expenses—and, unfortunately, lost some friends who liked the lifestyle, along the way. "Some people looked at what we did for a living [operating an oil and gas consulting firm] and figured it was odd for us to cut back because we had high incomes," recalls Bonnie, 36.

Reality was a little tougher. Determined to change their lives forever, the Siretts began to follow a strict budget. Bonnie laughs as she recalls going so far as to return unnecessary grocery items. One of her most vivid memories of that period of their lives occurred when they had $18 left for their monthly food budget, even though it was only day 24 of the month. Adamant about sticking to their self-imposed food budget, she chose to buy a few fresh food items then turned to creative ways to get them through the next seven days.

This intense frugality was applied to all areas of their life, from heating bills to long-distance phone charges and even unnecessary insurance. Gradually, their ship began to change course.

"Some people couldn't figure out why we thought we had a problem," says Troy. "In the early days, we thought the way to get rich was to be really tight with our money. Looking back, that was definitely the first step, and then eventually, we had to find balance. But when we were in the thick of debt reduction, our focus was pretty intense."

It was also darned effective. They gave themselves a year to conquer their debt, but were debt-free and saving in just seven months. The next step in the process was to begin to grow money for long-term wealth. They investigated several other business options, and even ventured down a few "wrong" paths, before joining REIN in late 2004. In the end, they liked the mentorship approach.

They bought their first property in April 2005 and have since built a portfolio of single-family houses, apartment-style condos, townhouses and duplexes that numbers 52 properties. They've bought and sold a few properties, but prefer to buy and hold. "When people hear you make $30,000 on a deal you turned around in a few weeks or months, they think it sounds like great money, but it's amazing how many people get a piece of that pie," says Troy.

Troy and Bonnie's skill sets dovetail beautifully. Troy's strengths are finding properties and structuring the deal that best suits their partners' portfolios. Bonnie handles the myriad of finances and works closely with their property manager. With joint venture partners and a finely honed purchasing system, the Siretts have created long-term wealth for themselves and their JV partners. "We are very fortunate to have this small, close-knit group of committed investors, who we love to work with, and whose company we equally enjoy," notes Troy.

The two recently journeyed to the African nation of Ghana and spent several weeks working with the agency running a local orphanage. The idea of spending several weeks abroad doing charitable work came from an abiding sense of gratitude for all that they have, explains Troy. "And really, do you know what happens to our investments when we're away? They keep going up in value!"

Troy and Bonnie thoroughly discussed the purpose of the trip. They would volunteer, play with children, then come home and plan the next journey. For a couple who's found such success in setting a plan and then sticking to it, "the need to be clear about our expectations" was entirely natural.

What happened next defied their expectations. Five months after that first trip, Troy and Bonnie Sirett returned to Ghana to finalize the adoption of two young sisters they'd met several months before. By early June 2007, the adoption was approved and the new family was getting to know each other on an extended African holiday that included their daughters' first exposures to warm water showers and swimming pools, as well as time spent on school work, under their "new mom's" supervision.

"Our adoption order has, as one of its conditions, that we will return to Ghana this December 2007 to meet again with the judge and the social welfare representative to review that the children are being cared for appropriately," writes Troy via an e-mail from Africa. He and Bonnie "welcome this review and are excited to show all parties how well the children are doing in all areas of life."

Don Campbell's Observations

Troy and Bonnie discovered a sad but true fact about change. No matter how positive the change you make is, you will have people trying to steal your dream and discount your actions. You may have experienced this sad state of affairs yourself. You decide to grab control of your future and change your obviously destructive pathway, and those who are on that pathway do everything in their power to dissuade you.

You may know of people like this; the key is to understand that their comments are really a reflection of their fear and their inferiority complex, not a comment on your commitment. So, if you must, listen quietly and then get back to living your life. It is best not to try to defend yourself or your actions to them, as that discussion will only lead to frustration. You can't convert someone who is too lazy or too afraid to make changes in their own life.

Troy and Bonnie are to be applauded for their ability to cut through this noise and stick to their new path. Sure they lost people from their life, but these are the people who would have held them back from achieving the amazing results they have.

Their true success story is just beginning as they have just started to see the rewards of the financial decisions they made just a few years ago. The stage that they have crossed to is a great place to review the most pertinent facts. And those facts are pretty awesome: To Troy and Bonnie Sirett, real estate investment offered the chance to stay out of debt, build long-term wealth and finance a lifestyle that included regular charitable works abroad. To 10-year-old Fati and her 5-year-old sister, Lamisi, real estate investment meant finding a family and living a life they didn't even know existed.

Imagine, it only took seven months to get themselves out of the financial hole they had dug. Was it easy? Probably not, but was it worth it? Absolutely. Just ask the two beautiful children they've adopted to see if their decisions have made a difference. As Troy and Bonnie discovered, there are many unintended consequences from the decisions we make in our lives.

By making the decision to change their financial lives, they have been able to have a major impact on an orphanage halfway around the world. When they started the new financial journey, that wasn't the reason, but look at where it has led them. Unintended consequences work both ways; you don't always immediately see the impact of a negative or positive decision. Often times the results come many years hence. That is why having a long-term outlook, rather than a get-rich-quick mentality, is so important.

Patience is key. You cannot change 20 years of negative financial habits overnight. It takes time. You have to first eliminate the old habits, then replace them with new and more productive ones. However, the effort is well worth the reward. Once Troy and Bonnie filled in their financial hole, they were able to build a very solid financial foundation, which is starting to provide them with a brand new lifestyle.

Imagine the unintended consequences that would have occurred if they had listened to all of the naysayers who were trying to hold them back. The orphanage wouldn't have the Siretts' support, their two children wouldn't have a new life, and their joint venture partners wouldn't be enjoying the fruits of their labours. For Bonnie and Troy, they should put up a sign in their office stating: "No Dream Stealers Allowed!" because they've seen the unintended positive consequences that change can bring to life.

It will continue to get better and better for Troy and Bonnie as they stay on their chosen path, and all it took was simply some introspection, a determination not to listen to those who discouraged them and an undying love for each other. We all can't wait to hear what other amazing results they create in the world.

ACTION STEPS

1. Lesson in observation. For the next 30 days listen carefully to the conversations you enter or hear around you. Count the number of times you hear others, or yourself, putting someone down for the decisions they've made or the actions they've taken. When this happens, ask yourself if it is a productive line of discussion or a justification to make someone feel superior.

2. If you are drawn into a conversation such as this, try using the line: "Sorry, I am not comfortable talking about someone else's decisions/life/action without knowing their side of the story." You will be surprised at how often you have to use this line in an average month.

_____

_____

_____

_____

3. Whom, in your past, have you strongly criticized for an action you thought wasn't right, even if your opinion wasn't requested? How trusting is this relationship today?

_____

_____

_____

_____

4. Who, in your past or present, consistently questions your actions and decisions? When you analyze these comments, can you see where it was all about them, not you?

_____

_____

_____

_____

5. If you honestly analyzed them, what financial or personal habits do you have that are holding you back from achieving your ultimate life goals?

_____

_____

_____

_____

6. Is the inconvenience of changing these habits not worth the end result in your life?

_____

_____

_____

_____

SUCCESS STORY #29
PERFECTIONISM IS DEFINITELY NOT PERFECT

Arden Dalik

Live your own dreams, not someone else's.

At the peak of a successful career in human resources management, Arden Dalik had a closet stuffed with toys. Forever on the road for her job, Arden took comfort in knowing that her only child had such a close relationship with her grandparents. They cared for Arden's daughter, Kelby, while the newly divorced mother travelled the continent in a lead role with the Canadian office of an international firm. "I actually told people how lucky she was," says Arden. "And because I didn't have the time to really shop for a special gift every time I was on the road, I cleverly 'shopped ahead.' I really did have a closet full of toys and I would sneak one into my suitcase so Kelby would think I had bought her something special."

Forget about skeletons. It was that closet full of toys that helped push Arden to an epiphany that climaxed with a diagnosis of depression and a doctor-ordered leave of absence from a job she thought she loved. Some people thought she'd lost it all. They were wrong.

Arden had been in love with life. A University of Calgary business grad, she worked in Toronto before setting up the Calgary office of an international human resources management firm. Before long, she was named principal of the firm's Canadian compensation practice, a position that made her responsible for dozens of employees across the nation. She was proud of the way she moved through the world. "I pushed myself hard and fast and I thought everything was the way it was meant to be." For necessary R & R, she would travel to Hawaii to windsurf.

In 2001, her toy closet epiphany brought that world to a crashing conclusion. After taking some time off to recover, Arden realized, "I was living someone else's dream. I was a willing participant in a rat race I had never deliberately chosen to be part of." Building on HRM contacts, Arden started a consulting company. "Starting my own company from scratch meant a huge drop in income initially, but I felt more in control of life than I'd ever been."

She also recognized that she no longer had the luxury of the "automatic saving for the future" that she'd enjoyed with big company pension and savings plans. Looking for a way to create "future wealth," she followed up on a contact who'd introduced her to the idea of real estate investment. That led to a Quickstart program, a REIN membership—and to a decision that she would no longer work in a building she did not own herself!

Her first purchase didn't work out exactly as planned. While her consulting practice eventually moved into a small house owned by her business partners, her first property experience was a life lesson illustrating the chasm between property ownership and complete control over that ownership. In this case, Arden wisely chose a small home in a residential neighbourhood on the edge of gentrification. That's the process by which an older neighbourhood, often feeling the pains of age and wear, is rediscovered by a new demographic of buyers. The community of Ramsay, near downtown Calgary, met so many of the qualifications, but, as gentrification wasn't really in full gear, the zoning changes that were so obvious to her proved impossible to get passed.

Today, that home is part of Arden's buy-and-hold portfolio. She loves the lessons its ownership has taught her, including what to do when tenants can't (or won't) pay and how to evict them if you're sure (but have no legal proof) they're dealing drugs. "I wouldn't trade those tough times for anything. They are invaluable in giving me the confidence to face tomorrow's challenges."

As for gentrification, Arden learned she and her partners didn't want to be the first ones in an investment neighbourhood. "We're not the pioneers," she learned. "We're the settlers."

Her second purchase, more solidly based on market fundamentals, appreciated by $235,000 in just two years. This time she bought a small home in a neighbourhood where a subtle form of gentriciation was already underway. Zoned commercial, she used it for office space. That investment soared after the provincial government, determined to cut costs, literally imploded the hospital across the street.

Arden knew the property was located in a community with a future. She could not predict what was to come. The following week a major announcement that the old General Hospital site would be home to a multi-family residential and commercial development called The Bridges was made. Property values in Bridgeland soared.

When she and her partners sold that building two years later, they bought commercial space in Calgary on 12 Avenue, S.W. Located in what's known as the Design District, it's another property with a future. Arden likes what the long-term appreciation will mean over time. She also likes knowing this property is about 20 minutes closer to home and to her daughter's school, where Arden is president of the school board and is a regular fan at sporting events.

Today, she owns and shares that space with three other investors whom she brought into the deal. But her HRM consulting days are over. In 2006, she and Shamim Rajan of Richmond Hill, Ontario, formed Wealth Launch Investments. They own about 40 doors between them; "doors" being investor jargon that lets investors track leases [renters] versus properties, since some properties have more than one tenant. Their portfolio of 40 doors includes a collection of single-family homes, four-plexes and multi-family units located in Edmonton, Red Deer, Sylvan Lake, High River and Innisfail, the latter being the proposed site of North America's largest biofuels refinery. Construction of the $400-million plant began in the summer of 2007 and Wealth Launch's research indicates that those construction workers, followed by plant employees, will need places to live.

But Wealth Launch isn't restricted to Arden and a single business partner. They've already got more than 15 joint venture partners and they plan to match even more investors with real estate deals involving multi-family residence apartment buildings and townhouse-style condominiums, as well as single- and multi-family homes and commercial properties.

Their partners are what investors call "time poor," says Arden. "They have money to invest, but no time to become real estate experts in growth areas, acquisitions, management, tenanting, etc. That's where we come in."

Given the size of the projects Wealth Launch pursues, the joint venture partners put up a minimum of $75,000. Arden lays out business plans and particular deals after investors come on board. "But I never talk anyone into investing. If there is any discomfort, I walk away. I'm not here to convince someone they should do this."

That conviction comes from having learned that efforts to attain personal dreams should make you feel good, not frightened or defeated. An avid horsewoman, she spent years "walking around with the dream of the perfect horse in my mind." It would be a Hanoverian, bred to excel in equestrian events like jumping and dressage.

After years of waiting, she realized she'd let that ideal image keep her from taking action based on where her life was at right now. "My dream was so perfect it was keeping me from purchasing a horse," says Arden, shaking her head. Never one to sit idly by, she and Kelby have just bought a new jumping horse and a second "rescue horse."

"There was no reason to wait! I had to remind myself that, although we have a huge focus on the future, the future starts today!"

From where she now sits, real estate investment has let Arden Dalik take control of her life.

While she still jets to Maui to windsurf, it's because she wants to, not because she needs to. Nor does she have a closet of toys to assuage her guilt. Instead, she enjoys a more seamless approach to her work and personal life.

She has also learned to smile nicely at those who tell her how lucky she is to have found success so easily.

Arden Dalik doesn't believe in luck any more than she ever really believed a closet full of toys made her a good mother. "I am big on personal accountability and I am big on gratitude. I like working with other people, so I surround myself with people I like to work with. I want to lead a life that makes me happy, so I find ways to add happiness to my life and to the lives of others. I am grateful when that happens, but it's not a coincidence."

<hr />

Don Campbell's Observations

Perfectionism is a blessing and a curse. A blessing because it forces you to look at all of the little details; a curse because it often leads to analysis paralysis. Arden, with her perfectionism now under control, is all about processes and systems. Her whole business is driven by checklists and spreadsheets. That may sound like a lot of work; however, in truth these systems automate her investment life, leaving her more time for her family, her horses and whatever other exciting projects she wishes to take on.

The old "work-life balance" debate was created by people who believe that life is divided between work-related and non–work related activities.

This may be true for those who don't love what they do for a living. In reality, life is life; when you are doing what you love, with those you enjoy, your whole life is in balance whether you're at work or not. Sadly many are spending their working hours surrounded with people they don't like, doing a job they don't like, just waiting for the weekend. For those who choose to fool themselves into believing that they are caught in that treadmill, there never will be a work-life balance no matter how many courses they take or books they read. In those cases, work is so bad that their time off will never be able to compensate for it. That's why there is a whole industry that has sprung up around finding a balanced life. This search for work-life balance is also another reason why so many people carry so much guilt around working long and hard hours at what they love. No one seems to gripe when a musician or an artist practises or creates for long days, weeks on end . . . but as soon as this work ethic is transferred into the white- or blue-collar world, suddenly it is a bad habit. What if you love what you do for a living? Why should you feel guilty about doing it?

Arden teaches us a lesson that life is one big experience that we can manage. She designed her business and investments to be integrated into her life, rather than to be a separate piece that had to be compensated for through free time. You'll notice in her story that her hobby of windsurfing is no longer an escape from work: it is just another enjoyable experience in her life.

ACTION STEPS

1. What checklists and systems do you use to free up your life?

   _____

   _____

   _____

   _____

2. If you could spend the majority of your time following one income-producing pursuit, what would it be?

   _____

   _____

   _____

   _____

3. If you knew you could do the above, full time, beginning in five years, would you be happy with that?

   _____

4. Follow in the footsteps of many who have gone before you. Use real estate investments today, so that in five years or less you won't be worried about work-life balance . . . you'll be living your life full on!

SUCCESS STORY #30
Saw the Diamonds in the Rough

Marnie Griffiths and Ryan Griffiths

If it doesn't kill you, it teaches you—but you've got to be willing to learn the lesson.

There is a boat in Marnie and Ryan Griffiths' future. It's tied to a dock in Snug Cove, Bowen Island, where they also have a modest but comfortable home. It's a fair isle retreat where the locals expect rain almost any day of the year. Ryan's fine with that. A native of British Columbia's often cloudy skies, his favourite memories and most cherished dreams involve the waters between Vancouver Island and the mainland. He likes knowing he will be able to take a ferry from Bowen Island and be at Vancouver's Horseshoe Bay in just 15 minutes. Not that Ryan will need the ferry, given that he'll have his own boat.

And not just any boat. The boat of his dreams is a 136-foot Grand Banks: a trawler that moves through the water at just 11 knots. For those who travel by land, that factors out to a mere 20.36 km/hr. That's slow for some, but Ryan figures it's the perfect speed at which to enjoy life.

"I'd buy a pleasure boat because I'm not in a hurry," says the 38-year-old seafaring wannabe.

His wife, Marnie, 35, giggles and nods her head in agreement. She figures Ryan will have that boat. But it won't be the only tangible thing bought and paid for by Insumo's Property Solutions Ltd., the couple's real estate investment firm.

Marnie would like to see their investment dollars help make the world a better place. She figures the money will buy them back the time they spent working full-time for other people. She'll use that time, and at least some of the money, to support charitable projects. She also wants to role-model the difference between money and wealth, and live a less ordinary life, for the couple's numerous nieces and nephews.

In the meantime, she and Ryan are living a more immediate dream. This one involves life as successful real estate investors—and they couldn't be happier, nor could they be more certain their Big Dream is within reach.

Ryan began working as a Ford mechanic in 1987. He and Marnie were married in B.C. in 1998. Life was good, or so they thought. By 2002, the couple was less enamoured with the path they were on, mostly because it seemed their days were entirely predictable (get up, go to work, eat, sleep, repeat). Interestingly enough, the raw sameness of each day obscured their end goals.

An administrative assistant with BC Hydro, Marnie left that job to experiment, albeit briefly, with organic farming. They then spent some time on the family acreage after Ryan's dad died, helping out and living in a camper to save money. They also started reading about real estate investment and taking a few courses.

They figure they spent $11,000 on seminars and programs, a financial pinch that left them more hungry than hurting. Every one of those courses provided at least some valuable information, recalls Ryan, but they inevitably failed to tell the whole story. "It was kind of like hearing, 'Hey, we'll tell you more of what you need to know—just as soon as you give us another $3,000,'" mimics Ryan with a wry smile.

But the experience wasn't all for naught. One of the programs they entered offered a mentorship component and, from the Griffiths' point of view, their mentor did two things right. First, she knew what she was doing and led them into their first revenue property investment. Second, she suggested they join REIN.

By the fall of 2003, Ryan and Marnie were REIN members. By May of the next year, they had assumed the mortgage on a two-year-old single-family home located in Airdrie, minutes north of Calgary. Using contacts offered through their mentor, it was a sweet deal for neophyte investors, recalls Marnie. "For $20,000, we assumed the mortgage on a home built in 2002." Their mentor helped them secure rent-to-own tenants, and their investment portfolio got its first asset.

Before long, a mere $8,000 let them assume the mortgage on another single-family home just down the street. Ryan smiles, admitting it was a "Who-You-Know" kind of deal. That second place was appraised at $188,000. By early 2007, its value hit $330,000.

So. It turns out real estate investment is a virtual walk in the park, right?

Hardly, say Marnie and Ryan. They have no regrets about the business venture they credit for all of the positive changes in their lives. But success takes work. And the learning curve is steep.

With Marnie acting as their hands-on property manager, the couple moved to Calgary in early 2005. Ryan got a job with a local Ford dealership, a position he left in February 2007, by which time their growing portfolio demanded more of his attention.

They owned seven properties and planned to end 2007 with another five purchases. Their business, financed by joint venture partners from B.C., is focused on the single-family market, but includes townhouses, a duplex and a triplex.

Information gleaned from REIN research helps them find and screen tenants, but Marnie admits they inherited a few lemons along the way. On the upside, she's learned how to deal with those who don't make the connection between the fact they have a quality place to live—and what the Griffiths do for a living.

Marnie, who handles everything from prospective tenant checks to bankers, says most tenants appreciate being appreciated. She and Ryan send gift baskets when new renters move in. They send thank-you notes when they notice what renters have done to maintain a property's value.

When tenants don't live up to their contracted obligations, she takes a different sort of action. "Yes, I've used bailiffs to serve eviction notices," confides Marnie, "and I've done my homework to make sure I understand certain legal issues. This is our business. Our tenants are our clients, but this is a mutual relationship."

Marnie and Ryan (who handles purchase negotiations) say they're always looking for the next deal, but they're not in a hurry to find it. "We haven't hit the stage where there is 'no stress' in making a deal work, but I do get excited when we find opportunities or when opportunities find us," says Ryan.

Those opportunities aren't always pretty. And some stink, literally. One of their revenue properties joined their portfolio in a disastrous state. There were holes in the wall and cat urine vied with cigarette smoke for putrid supremacy. "The owner at the time just wanted out of that building. We knew it was going to take some work and we knew we'd have to do it ourselves, but we saw a gem in the rough," notes Marnie. "It just needed a little TLC."

One of their favourite deals began with a For Sale by Owner sign parked on the lawn of a home not far from another revenue property they already own. They never got that house. But it spurred them to focus on that neighbourhood and they ended up getting a triplex kitty-corner from it, and that triplex never went for sale on the formal market. "That deal made me feel like an investment 'insider,'" jokes Ryan.

How their world has changed: Now he's uncovering inside information on a $15-million, six-acre piece of land just south of Calgary. In the short term, he suspects the parcel will deliver cash flow through something relatively simple, like RV storage. Down the road, it's apt to be a multi-residential development. "It's exciting to think we're on the ground floor of a deal like that."

Looking ahead, he and Marnie say their success owes much to surrounding themselves with like-minded, positive-focused people. By doing so, they do not need to reinvent the investment wheel and can save themselves inordinate amounts of time, energy and money by leveraging the knowledge they gain from these new found colleagues. Ryan and Marnie attend meetings with more regularity, now that Ryan's not torn between property maintenance and that full-time job. They know that's the best way to build their network of mentors and investors, and they genuinely like being around people who share their passion for the nuts and bolts of real estate investment.

To Marnie, networking with other successful investors is the difference between thinking like investors and acting like investors. "That move towards real action is one of the biggest hurdles new investors encounter." They keep the Griffiths moving forward.

For now, Insumo Property Solutions is all about action. The Griffiths want to keep buying property for a few more years, eventually building a private portfolio valued at $5 million. If Plan A involved working for others, Plan B is all about building long-term wealth. After that, it's all about Plan C. Add a nautical twist, and you can call it "Plan Sea."

Don Campbell's Observations

I meet thousands of investors a year in my travels across the country, yet I can still remember one key day when I ran into the Griffiths at a workshop I was presenting in Vancouver. Like many beginners they had a ton of enthusiasm, which every investor needs, but they also had something else—an obvious commitment to where they were going. Many investors have enthusiasm; however, within one minute of speaking with them it becomes quite apparent that there's a lot of fluff and talk but not a lot of substance to their plan.

With Ryan and Marnie it was different. At that point they didn't know exactly how they were going to get to where they are now, but they knew, in no uncertain terms, that they were going to make it happen. It goes back to the early observation I made in this book: Once you become very clear on what you want to achieve, the world begins to conspire to help you make it happen. Sure, sometimes sacrifices need to be made in order to achieve your dream. That's why even though Marnie and Ryan's dream involves a boat on the west coast, they decided to pick up and move to the prairies in order to make their fortune. They followed the economic fundamentals so that their money could work harder and help them reach their goal more quickly. Once they got there, they surrounded themselves with others who had moved there from all across the country and who were also focused on making their dream come true. With that type of commitment, support and enthusiasm, there is no doubt that they'll achieve whatever they want in the coming years.

ACTION STEPS

1. Be honest and ask yourself: "Am I willing to do whatever it takes, morally and ethically, to make my dream a reality, or do I prefer the safety of just dreaming about it?"

---

2. When I meet others and tell them of my dream, does it come across that I believe it and am committed to it or do I come across as a vacant-eyed, get-rich-quick dreamer? (If you don't know the answer to this, ask a few people you trust to be honest with you. They want to conspire to help you achieve more, but only once you are committed to the pathway.)

SUCCESS STORY #31
SAW THE FUTURE 20 YEARS AHEAD—
AND IT WASN'T PRETTY

Dan Heon

I like using my experience to help others. And why wouldn't I, since I owe an awful lot to other people for my success?

Dan Heon is good with his hands. Weeks into his new job building train engines on the same shop floor where he'd completed his apprenticeship as a heavy-duty diesel mechanic, he realized he was also pretty darn good with his mind. And therein lay the problem. Surrounded by what he calls a union mentality, Dan realized he was making the same money as the guy across the work bench. Only the other guy had been there 20 years. No wonder he thought night shifts included a little nap time on the company payroll!

"It took me about four years to apprentice and people kept telling me that 'once you put your foot in the door, you're set for life.'" Now safely on the inside, Dan didn't much like the view.

So he did what made more sense. Keeping his night job (it takes seniority to get a day shift), Dan started using his free time during the day to buy property. He joined REIN in 1996, bought eight properties the first year and was earning enough cash flow to pack up his tools. Twenty-six years old with few expenses, he recalls, "I was relatively financially free."

Then he hit the wall. Two years into professional real estate investment, Dan was challenged to get financing for his next deal. He was assuming mortgages, but with $200,000 due in the next six months, he needed a secure way to replace vendor money with investor money. The time was ripe. By 1997, Calgary was experiencing the start of an economic boom thanks to growing awareness of Alberta as a great place to do business. As awareness of what the Alberta government liked to call "The Alberta Advantage" picked up steam, the tech market bubble burst. Those investors were looking for a place to park their money and Dan, by then well-plugged into economic fundamentals, had an idea of where that money could go.

"I became a mortgage broker," he says. "The whole plan came from knowing that investors like me needed more creative ways to finance their real estate purchases."

That was in 2002. By the time 2007 rolled around, the mechanic-turned-banker had a successful brokerage business and a personal portfolio of 40 single-family properties. He was also working other deals on the side. In December 2006, he bought and sold 24 townhouses. The next year, he and a partner teamed up on a project to build 99 town homes just west of Edmonton. That project tallies a $30-million investment "and that amazes even me," jokes Dan, an affable man who laughs when he overhears people at investment gatherings tell others they need to talk to Dan Heon, "that tall bald guy over there."

It's not like his chosen path has always been easy. The town home project, for example, was one that he says he tried to do on his own, "but it was too complicated. I needed someone who knew more about getting things done; there are contracts and zoning issues, the sheer logistics are overwhelming."

Earlier in his investing career, he also learned what it was like to not have a job and lose track of your cash-flow income. And, of course, there were weeks of angst when he realized he was on the hook for $200,000—with no way to pay it back.

All of which has reinforced for him what he terms, "the power of the group." The "group," for him, is REIN. These days people seek his advice and his mortgage company's support brokering deals. It's a role Dan plays with pleasure, in no small part because he's encountered the same problems—and has benefited from the wisdom of veteran investors he surrounded himself with. "It's almost like, when you're ready for the lesson, the teacher shows up!"

While his condo properties are all managed professionally, he still looks after some of his other properties. It's work he enjoys. "I hire a company to rent them out, but I collect the cheques and do maintenance."

When his own business coach says he should be charging people for the advice he gives on portfolio management, Dan laughs. "I know it's valuable information, but I see it as part of giving back to the investment community that helped me."

Dan Heon's company is now partnered with a mortgage firm in Vancouver, and he feels his real estate star is still rising. But his optimism is tempered by a keen sense of where he has been, or could have stayed. This past winter, Dan took his wife and two of their kids (married in 1999, they have a blended family) to Costa Rica. When his wife told him it was the best holiday she'd ever been on, Dan was thrilled; he was also filled with an abiding sense of satisfaction about where his life was heading.

And it turns out his mentoring isn't only valued at home. Dan and Rebecca plan to return to Costa Rica. The next time they go, however, it will likely be to do work with its disadvantaged people, thus giving back to a country that offered them such peace.

It's the kind of thing you do when your business is a fortress of relationships where each individual (lawyer, bookkeeper, property manager, and so the list goes!) contributes to a stronger whole. More importantly, it's the kind of thing you do, says Dan, "when you know your success owes an awful lot to others."

Don Campbell's Observations

Now that Dan has achieved his "Personal Belize," he's helping beginner investors to see the pathway he took. In fact, Dan has lived the "help others, help yourself" philosophy his whole investing career.

As Dan progressed as an investor, he made mistakes and hit roadblocks. Each time he met one of these, he saw it as an opportunity to provide a solution to investors who would be coming along the path behind him. That is one of the reasons why he became a mortgage professional: he realized that financing issues were the most common problem, and if he could solve this problem, ethically and morally, he could help himself while he helped others.

Dan was not born with a silver spoon in his mouth. He was a talented heavy-duty mechanic who saw the future, through the eyes of his veteran co-workers, and didn't like what he saw. It was a great paying job, with wonderful benefits . . . the proverbial golden handcuffs. But for Dan that wasn't enough, so he arranged his work life so he could focus on his financial future and his investment real estate. This was his first smart move—keeping his job while starting his investment portfolio. He understood that banks love it when an investor has a full-time job. They like the security it provides. So lesson number one: before you quit your job to do real estate full-time, think of the direct consequences this will have on your ability to get approval for mortgages, because, without bank financing, your portfolio will not grow very quickly.

Dan made a plan, started taking action with one house and over the following 10 years has grown his portfolio so that his family now can enjoy life and work as little or as much as they want, all the while making a difference in other people's lives. For Dan, and many others like him, life doesn't get much better than that.

ACTION STEPS

1. What can you do with your current job so you can find a few extra hours a week to focus on your investment real estate? (Take longer shifts over a few days, make better use of lunch hours, become a contractor to the company, etc.)

   _____

   _____

   _____

   _____

2. Whom do you know who is on the same path as you (whether in your job, your investment world or your personal life) that you could provide guidance to?

   _____

   _____

   _____

   _____

   By what date will you contact that person?

   _____

If you wish to learn how veteran investors free up enough time to build their portfolios, while having time for their families and their jobs, visit www.realestateinvestingincanada.com and read about the Time Management for Real Estate Investors Program.

SUCCESS STORY #32
The Treadmill Leading to Nowhere

Russell Westcott

Real estate investment is like hockey. If you want to play, you've got to learn to skate and handle the puck.

Russell Westcott had it all. A university graduate with a degree in commerce, he held what looked to be a great job in Vancouver, the Western Canadian headquarters of a global dairy business. Canadians gauge success by how far they've come from where they started; Russell knew he was doing well because he was living two provinces away from his roots in the rural Saskatchewan community of Lanigan, a small town whose Internet profile boasts of its location on the Yellowhead Highway and a grass landing strip that caters to light aircraft.

But Russell had a problem. During a trip home for Christmas 2001, he put pencil to paper and came face to face with the fact that he was spending more money than he was making. "Worse yet," he says, "when I crunched the numbers, it looked like the road I was on offered no chance to get turned around."

That Christmas he resolved to make significant life changes. He began by writing a Seven-Year Life Plan that included financial goals and long-term vision. A new awareness of his economic circumstances also prompted a meeting with an investment fund salesman. But it was his personal reading about real estate investment that really caught his attention—and his imagination.

Russell knew some people read the same books he was reading and jumped aboard the real estate bandwagon because they thought it was headed for quick riches. He saw something different: an opportunity for long-term wealth; an opportunity to really be the guy in control of his own life.

In late 2002, Russell flew to Edmonton to take one of REIN's Quickstart programs. He bought his first property, 12719-122 Street, Edmonton, early the next year. Determined to buy one property a month, he spent his days working at his job—and another 20-plus hours a week learning, building his real estate investor network and buying properties. Most of those properties were in areas, says Russell, "where the market fundamentals were really strong." Looking back, he figures he was working 60 hours a week and getting smarter all the time.

In December 2004, Russell left his national marketing position to immerse himself in real estate full-time, investing and teaching others how to invest. He had close to two years' experience with his investment systems by then. More importantly, he was taking action. "I had this hockey coach," he reminisces, "who used to tell us, 'You've got to shoot the puck.' Real estate investing is the same thing. Once you've learned what to do, you've got to go out and do it."

Russell was buying about two properties a month, all townhouse-style condominiums, by early 2007. One hundred percent of them were in economically strong Western Canadian regions.

Russell makes sure his properties have at least two bedrooms, comparable market rents and are in good complexes with good tenant profiles and good condo boards. Having built on what he knows about his market, he will write an offer without seeing a property, especially if it's in his target area, which is near a new ring road project that promises short-term construction jobs and long-term housing for commuters. "I like my tenants to have good jobs," says Russell with a smile.

That willingness to write an offer site-unseen is a testament to his relationship with a real estate agent who specializes in investment property—and knows what Russell wants. But that high level of mutual trust doesn't compromise due diligence; Russell always stipulates a conditional time frame that gives him the opportunity to get from Vancouver to wherever the property is located. "This is a business decision," he insists, "and my system stipulates due diligence."

By mid-2007, his portfolio tallied $13-plus million (starting from zero in 2002), with Russell owning 58% and the rest shared among 17 joint venture partners. The portfolio is sustainable with a break-even cash flow and he anticipates hanging on to most of the properties for at least another five to seven years.

All of the properties are professionally managed. "That's absolutely a lifestyle choice based on the fact I have a full life," explains Russell, "and don't make any money managing properties on a day-to-day basis. I want to focus on the investment side, plain and simple."

He also wants to focus on the "life" side of the Seven-Year Life Plan he started back in 2001. The most up-to-date version spans 77 pages and although his business is still in acquisition mode, Russell is using his assets to shape a bright, secure future.

Three years ago, he gave his niece a share in his investment business. Under that deal, she gets 25% of the first property he bought after Christmas for three years in a row. She's now 12 and has her own joint venture portfolio.

Russell bought his parents a retirement home in Arizona in 2006. "When I started out, they helped me with loans on my second and third properties," he says, "and that really helped me get started."

He's also using his investment knowledge to help others. With Russell's guidance, his girlfriend has purchased two investment properties, plus her personal residence. Russell says she's done so "with the goal of buying one investment property for each of her three beautiful children." Cash flow from those properties meant she could quit her job to spend more time with those children, a move that freed her parents, who'd been helping with childcare for seven years. It's trickle-down economics, family style.

His top tips:

1. Surround yourself with good people.
2. Take risks you can live with.
3. Don't get caught up in the positive or negative hype that surrounds a real estate marketplace.

And what does Russell tell people who think they may want to invest in real estate? "Start at the beginning and pick up a good book like *Real Estate Investing in Canada*. For a $35 investment, you can figure yourself in or out. If you're in, then take the next obvious steps, as clearly described in that book. It is not any more difficult than that to get started."

Thinking ahead is important precisely because wise real estate investment, based on market fundamentals, is no get-rich-quick scheme. "You'll need to do the homework and then you'll need to take action. Shoot the puck!"

Don Campbell's Observations

Russell is like many Canadians in that he was on a treadmill that was eventually going to lead him nowhere. The one thing that makes Russ different than most is that he recognized his lifestyle was shortchanging him. He was brutally honest with himself and then he made a change. In his case it was a drastic change; he literally "jumped off the cliff" by leaving a burgeoning career, one that he had trained for through university, to start fresh in a whole new life. He knew that change was inevitable, so he forced the issue himself, he made life happen rather than had life happen to him. I'm sure it wasn't a simple decision, nor was it a simple transition; however, the results of this change have been quite spectacular.

As you go through life, you will have the opportunity to change course, perhaps many times, and like Russell, despite what many believe, you are not stuck where you are. You will read in other stories in this section how people have made serious career course changes even though they had a growing family or other financial obligations. A person starts to really live their life once a clear direction is established. Change is scary, but the only way to get through fear is to analyze it and see the truth behind it. Russell may still have done okay in his real estate investing if he stayed at his old job, but would he be as happy? The good news is that Russ doesn't have to find out, now that he is following his passion. What about you?

ACTION STEPS

1. Be honest and ask yourself: "Do I feel I am doing what I love to do?"

   _____

   _____

   _____

   _____

2. If not, list the real alternatives. Be creative. It doesn't mean that you will do everything that you list; this question is just designed to make you think. I'll start you out with one:

   a. Win the lottery

   b. _____

   _____

c. _____

_____

3. What is the best thing that could happen if you stay on your current pathway?

_____

_____

4. What is the worst thing that will happen if you stay on your current pathway?

_____

_____

5. Are you willing to accept these outcomes?

_____

_____

SUCCESS STORY #33
FLEXIBILITY IS CRITICAL IN SPORTS AND REAL ESTATE INVESTING

Krista Hope and Jared Hope

It's not about material things. It's about being able to spend time with my family and not be stressed about money.

Jared Hope had it all. At 18, he was drafted by the Toronto Maple Leafs and was secure in the knowledge that his professional hockey career was powered by a winning mix of skill and ambition. Originally from Edmonton, he'd been playing in Spokane, Washington, since he was 16 and the Leafs training camp was the stuff of dreams. He felt good. He skated great. And then he got hurt.

Between 1995 and 1996, Jared's brain bore the career-stopping brunt of three major concussions. Worse than the raw physical pain was the convalescence. There were days when he was barely allowed out of bed and weeks when he wasn't allowed to drive. There were days of confusion and sorrow as his brain slowly healed while his colleagues tied their skates to hit the ice and do what he had worked towards his entire life.

"I remember a counsellor telling me I was experiencing a mid-life crisis. She said the depression was normal." Jared didn't feel normal.

Determined to build a new life, Jared moved back to Edmonton and enrolled in a community college to study marketing. Post-graduation, he spent 18 months in sales before he knew he wasn't finished with the ice. He hired a personal trainer, a nutritionist and a psychologist and took a year to get his mind and body back in shape for pro hockey tryouts.

What happened next defied the odds. When the Edmonton Oilers picked him up and sent him to its farm team in Hamilton, he'd been gone from the game for five years and now he'd made the pros. "No one has ever done that before," he says Yet, somehow, it no longer was enough. By then, Jared nurtured a different dream.

Heading back to Edmonton in 2002, he went to school to become a personal trainer, eventually becoming a popular trainer at one of the city's upscale training facilities. Behind the scenes, a new enterprise was taking shape.

When he and his bride-to-be, Krista, needed a place to live, they bought a $140,000 home in Edmonton's Capilano district, subsidizing the mortgage payment with a basement suite that rented for $525 a month. Upstairs, a roommate paid $300. "I'm a numbers guy," Jared declares, "so it didn't take me long to see we were onto something good. Our mortgage payment was $850, taxes were $170 and insurance was around $30. We were looking at just over $1,000 in payments—and we were bringing in $825."

Two years later, Krista signed them both up for REIN. She wanted to learn more about how to make money in real estate. Jared was annoyed. Still, he went to the meetings, listened and learned. By the end of their first year, they owned four properties, including that first property and a new principal residence they'd built themselves.

"When I do something, I don't just dabble," says Jared. "But all of this stuff we have is really because of Krista, my wife. After she went to an all-day workshop, she signed us up. I wasn't really keen." As his enthusiasm grew, Jared secured a niche in finding properties and making deals while Krista handled the accounting side.

Some days, Jared spent 10 hours at the gym, then worked long past midnight on their real estate business. It was exhausting, but a plan was taking shape. His skills as a trainer were in demand and real estate was something they'd do on the side. "I figured we'd buy five houses between 2004 and 2009," he says.

Today, the two hold about $18 million in real estate. Most of their 90 doors are in Grande Prairie, Krista's hometown, with a few in the Edmonton area.

Jared self-manages the properties but has two assistants and two maintenance guys he calls on. "I understand why people hire outside property managers. But right now, I feel like I need to be in control. I don't feel right about a third-party manager when I'm using investors' money."

His biggest challenge for 2007 was finding more of that money. Having bought 60 doors in 2006, he had secured some good cash-flowing properties.

Jared's not done buying, but he is done with the gym. He left his training job on May 31, 2007. He and Krista are now in a position to focus on their real estate business. Jared moved the office out of the family home and started transforming the information he's carried in his head into "systems" others can help him run. He also hired a bookkeeper to free up more time.

"For me, the flexibility is key," says Krista, when asked about how real estate has changed their lives. "We'll be able to spend more time raising our kids together and not be stressed about money. Material things don't really factor into my vision of the future, but I definitely want time with my family."

That's a vision Jared shares and he spends an increasing amount of time thinking about an exit strategy. "I'm only 29 right now, so there will be something else for me, another challenge to take on down the road." He envisions a time when he and Krista are the money behind future deals someone else manages.

In the meantime, he and Krista have a new baby and a busy little two-year-old girl whose first house was bought the day she was born. That deal came to Jared via one of the three trusted real estate agents he works with in Grande Prairie. "We have a really good working relationship. They know what I'm looking for and what I don't have time for. Honestly, it's at the point where if they call me, I know I'm buying a property."

A lot of people tell Jared he's lucky. Jared shrugs. He admits he still feels good about what he managed to do in hockey and he's grateful he and Krista started investing in real estate when they did. But it's not like his athletic or real estate success came without effort—and he's weathered the challenges, from the physical pain and financial cost associated with getting back in shape for pro hockey to tenant hassles and a for-sale-by-owner deal where he had to call in a lawyer. "Nothing has 'fallen' into my lap."

Having experienced how others can help you be better, his current team includes real estate professionals (from lenders to lawyers, accountants and mentors), a personal development coach and a speech coach. Jared Hope doesn't have to be the best. But he wants to be his best. "My goal is financial security, with very little risk, and I'm making that happen."

Don Campbell's Observations

Sometimes a dream is not what you expected it would be once it comes true. Jared had achieved what many Canadian men dream of—he'd been drafted into the NHL and offered a contract. Once he'd made it, he was confident enough to step back and say, "Is this really what I want for me and my future?" And the answer was no.

Even though he had to overcome a lot of adversity and had to sacrifice a lot to achieve this dream, he was aware enough to know that at the end of it all, it wasn't what he really wanted. Most people, when they achieve a career goal in their job (finally got the corner office) forget to take the time to look at their new position to see if it is all they hoped it would be. And even if they do, and find that it is not, they feel they've worked too hard to get there to give it up. Jared showed tremendous courage when he changed his direction after such an accomplishment.

This courage and ability to step back and analyze his direction has served him very well in building his real estate portfolio.

Jared and Krista are committed to building their dream together, and they are helping many joint venture partners build their own net worth. You can see that they honour their partners and focus on treating the partners' money better than they would their own. They know that it is an honour to be entrusted with someone's financial dream.

In Jared's story, as in many of the others in this book, he is called "lucky." He was called lucky when he was drafted to the NHL, he was called lucky when he made the team five years later after a serious injury and now, once again, he's lucky that his real estate portfolio is doing so well. What most people don't see is the drive, determination and honesty that has led him to where he is today. It is quite obvious to anyone who knows him that he will be a success in any endeavour he throws himself into fully.

He's learned that adversity is just a part of life; the difference is in how you deal with it. Successful investors use it as a motivator, pushing them forward. . . . Those who sit back and call him lucky are missing the point. Jared is blessed with a growing and happy family, and he is willing to do whatever it takes to provide for them as best he can.

Adversity is just a bump in the road. Accept it, deal with it, then move on, as Jared and Krista have on their road to financial independence.

SUCCESS STORY #34
TOYS ARE FUN, BUT THEY KEEP YOU ON THE TREADMILL

Jason Mattern

If I can do it, anyone can do it.

There was a time when Jason Mattern was all about the toys. We're talking two trucks, a new boat, a snowmobile and a mortgage. But what looked good in the driveway looked bad on paper. Really bad.

"I moved to Edmonton from a small town called Vermilion," he recalls. "By the time I realized I was drowning myself in bad debt, I was working as a sales rep for an import company and was operating paycheque to paycheque. I was going financially nowhere, really fast."

Now 32 and married with a brand new baby girl, Jason is a real estate agent, a real estate investor and owns a real estate brokerage including 12 full-time agents and support staff. The brokerage's property management division has grown to 200 properties under management in just over a year. The brokerage, which specializes in investment real estate, provides residual income while he grows his portfolio. Like his revenue properties, he also expects the firm to become more valuable over time. "It's the kind of business someone will eventually buy," he asserts, "because of its revenues and its systems."

Jason bought his first revenue property in 2001. To do this, he sold his first principal residence, unloaded all of the toys (bad debt!) and moved into a one-bedroom condo. It wasn't his ideal home, but he was starting to understand that it was the kind of purchase that would help him move towards the proverbial dream home and lifestyle.

His foray into investment led to getting his real estate licence in 2001, when Realty Corp Inc. was born. "It was another way to look for deals to build my portfolio and stay self-employed with more control over my personal life," says Jason.

Before a year had passed, he met Russell Westcott. Russell was REIN Canada's general manager and an investor already sold on Edmonton's real estate investment market. They hit it off. Before long, each saw the other as an invaluable member of their investment team, with Jason finding properties and Russell finding money. The rest, as they say, is history.

Jason's personal portfolio hit 77 properties in June 2007, with 20 single-family units and the rest in multi-family units.

"Oh, I've had deals go wrong," he admits. "But when they cost you thousands of dollars, you don't make the same mistake twice. In the early days, I definitely sweated the details. Now I do my due diligence and I make things work. But if I lose a deal, I move on. I used to think a lost deal meant I had to work harder, right now. Now, it's an excuse to go home early. I know there'll be another deal another day."

Is there any advice he can share with those contemplating real estate investment? "Surround yourself with smart people." He recently hired a university-educated general manager and he's bringing in agents who, like him, have a knack for finding the kind of properties their investing clientele want to buy.

"There is a lot to learn in this business. But there are people who will teach you. Learn to listen."

Don Campbell's Observations

Jason was lucky that he caught himself early on the path of financial destruction. Since then he has learned a critical lesson on good debt vs. bad debt. It's true, toys, gadgets and vehicles are all great fun—until they become a financial burden. Today's society is geared to make us want to have these distractions before we can afford them. In fact, many are now sold to the consumer based solely on a monthly payment. This is what would be called bad debt designed to keep you on the treadmill, running at full speed but not getting anywhere.

Good debt, on the other hand, helps you get off the treadmill. Good debt is any debt that you can use to help increase your cash flow or net worth. For instance, if Jason took those monthly payments for the toys he used to have and set them towards a property's mortgage, he would be creating equity in that property. Even more significantly, if he used that money to buy a property and had the tenant pay the mortgage, he'd be building equity even more intelligently.

We all need to live our lives; life is supposed to be fun. I'm not saying that all toys are bad and you must focus 100% on money. What I am saying is that it is important to be self-aware enough so that you're not just accumulating things just to accumulate them.

A great lesson we learn from Jason is to take a giant step back and look at our lives with an objective perspective. Let's be honest; it's easy to justify buying any toy or vehicle we want. However, in order to get ahead of the masses we must be honest with ourselves by saying that we're willing to wait a couple of years to have the toy. And if you do invest correctly, it really takes only a few short years, as Jason found out.

ACTION STEPS

1. Make a list of items you have in your life that may be considered "bad debt" type items. (It doesn't mean the items are bad or useless, it's just an exercise in awareness.)

_____

_____

_____

_____

2. Total up the cash you have locked up in them:

_____

_____

_____

_____

3. Total up the monthly cash flow they eat up in payments:

_____

_____

_____

_____

Knowing what you know about your dream of getting off the treadmill, analyze the above figures and determine if this is the best use of your money while you are trying to build a financial foundation.

SUCCESS STORY #35
SURROUND YOURSELF WITH ACTION-TAKERS

Brad McDonald

If you surround yourself with others who are also investing in real estate, you'll invest in real estate. If you don't build that kind of support, you'll talk yourself out of doing it.

Brad McDonald's real estate investment portfolio defies a lot of stereotypes. Then again, so does Brad McDonald, a dentist-turned-real-estate investor who moved his practice to Alberta in 2004 precisely because he wanted to invest in residential real estate.

Attracted by a strong economy, low personal income tax rates and assumable mortgages, Brad figured Edmonton was the place to invest and Calgary was the place to live. "I wasn't even thinking about the oil," he says, "nor predicting what was going to happen in 2006. I was just thinking this is the place a lot of companies will be moving to in the future. In the end, I got lazy and bought properties in Calgary instead of Edmonton. But that's the thing about real estate. If you take the time to learn about your market, you should be able to invest anywhere and make it work."

His portfolio is different from many in that 9 of the 11 single-family homes he owned and managed by mid-2007 are located in upscale neighbourhoods in suburban Calgary. His renters, typically economic migrants to Calgary, tend to hold professional jobs and take pretty good care of the property while staying put at least a year. They also pay premium rents and give at least six months' notice before moving. "Not because I ask," he stresses, "but because that's just the kind of people they are."

In return for all of this, their one demand is that Brad take his responsibilities just as seriously. So when taps leak or toilets are plugged, they want immediate action. He figures he's replaced at least five dishwashers since he entered the revenue property market in 2004. On the upside, the new units are a higher quality than the previous models, so Brad figures that's a cost he won't face again any time soon.

One of his other properties is a single-family home located in a relatively new suburb, but in a neighbourhood more commonly associated with life-time renters. Brad manages this and the other nine properties himself and he enjoys the process. "These are good properties and I take care of my tenants. The kind of people I'm renting to just aren't complainers, so we work together if there's an issue."

The 11th property is a different story. Located in a Calgary neighbourhood with a notorious reputation for social problems ranging from crack houses to street prostitution, it's the one property Brad won't self-manage. He tried, but found his efforts emotionally draining, since the early days with that property included experiences with a backyard squatter who refused to move (and, believe it or not, used the lawn as a toilet).

"It's a good thing I had some money to back me up, because that property was an expensive proposition at first," concedes Brad. But the bigger lesson rests in his awareness of the risks associated with letting his emotions override business. "Without a property manager, I probably would have sold that house in Forest Lawn after 18 months. That would have been an emotional decision—and a bad business decision. Even when other property values in this city started levelling off in 2006, property values in that neighbourhood kept rising. With higher property values came higher rents—and a different kind of tenant," says Brad.

When he and his wife, Teresa, first moved to Calgary, they put 5% down and bought a home in the city's northwest quadrant. Before that, Brad practised dentistry in Ontario for a couple of years. During that time, he joined REIN's Ontario chapter, making six-hour round trips to meetings in Toronto and reading everything he could about real estate investment and what it takes to be a sophisticated investor. "As soon as I got around other people doing that kind of thing," he reports. "I was hooked."

Brad bought his Calgary practice in March 2004 and took it over that July. In the meantime, he started buying properties that fit an investment model based on long-term capital appreciation. By sticking to what he admits are "really nice neighbourhoods," he's able to go after a specific kind of tenant, most of whom he first connects with via the Internet.

The plan is working. Brad figures his net worth went from negative $250,000 to $2 million in two years.

More importantly, he learned something about himself. Aware that he enjoys investing more than dentistry, Brad cut his clinic hours to under two days a week and started spending more time on his investment business—in particular the search for joint venture partners. Make no mistake, Brad knows he's running a business. "I'm going to take real good care of my tenants, but we're not going to play games. Honestly, that part of it is a no-brainer."

Although strict about things like paying rent on time, Brad likes working with tenants so they can identify and meet mutual needs. One tenant, for example, had credit issues linked to having declared bankruptcy after 9/11. He wasn't in a position to buy a home, but Brad helped the guy stay in the kind of home and neighbourhood he was used to while he rebuilt his business. Another tenant had some collection issues related to a recent divorce. Brad saw through the paper trail and got to the real person behind the numbers. He found a woman who was serious about making her payments. She also got to rent one of his places.

He takes the same straightforward approach to his current efforts to build relationships with JV partners. Determined to grow his own business, Brad says it's time he helped others leverage their time and money, too.

A receptionist from his clinic helps manage the real estate books and takes calls related to property management, freeing him to focus on real estate or his family, which now includes three preschool-aged children. Exactly who will handle those duties may change when he sells his practice completely, but one thing's for sure: Brad knows he doesn't have the time to do it all himself.

And time is what it's all about, says Brad. With Teresa's family still in Mexico, they will likely spend more time there to ensure their kids appreciate their Canadian-Mexican heritage. He may eventually work as a locum dentist, travelling to offices for short-term assignments when other dentists are away. If he works in Mexico, it will likely be at free clinics.

As for real estate, that's a business he'll be in for a while. His own portfolio has reached the point where it looks like he may be buying multi-family and commercial real estate. "Sure, I'll go farther. I have a net worth I'm comfortable with right now, but I'll do more because I want to teach my kids about real estate investment, too. I keep looking for a better way to build long-term wealth, but I still haven't found anything better."

Don Campbell's Observations

As a dentist, patients were very important in Brad's practice. Now, as a real estate investor, a different type of patience is just as important. You can see from his story that he understands that results in real estate take time. Not a whole lot of time, but it's not about overnight riches.

Many busy professionals (lawyers, doctors, dentists, etc.) often do not find the time to get into the real estate market on their own, often playing the role of the financier to the deals in a joint venture role. Brad's proven ability to build a strong portfolio and his contacts with his fellow professionals will prove to be a great combination for future deals, allowing him to progress into the areas he wants to focus on, larger commercial and multi-family properties.

The niche that Brad has focused on so far is an underserved area of renters. The mistaken belief among unsophisticated investors is that all renters live lower-income lifestyles. Brad has disproved this myth, like many others that surround the real estate market. It takes more cash to get into these properties with higher down payments yet, when the math is done, he's receiving large returns on these investments. Brad currently has properties in all socio-economic areas of his target city, but no matter where his tenants live, or what their income level, he treats them all the same, which is a great lesson.

You could call Brad's landlording strategy fair but firm. He is fair with his tenants, yet he doesn't let them take advantage of his nice side. Most tenants respect this style of landlord–tenant relationship. All expectations are clearly communicated in both directions. Tenants pay their rent on time and treat the property well, and in return Brad provides them with a good place to live and acts quickly if the property has a maintenance issue, always under-promising and over-delivering.

You can see by the stories about the tenants to whom he has given a break that his heart is in the right place, proving once again that there is no need to be ruthless to be successful. This philosophy flows over to the rest of his business relationships. Clear expectations are voiced and, if not met, everyone knows the consequences.

Brad's next steps should become quite obvious to anyone reading this: work with his fellow professionals to allow them to profit in the real estate market by leveraging Brad's experience and proven system.

Brad and Teresa are on the exact path to making a huge difference in many people's lives and to think it started with the simple act of buying that first revenue property, even though it was uncomfortable.

ACTION STEPS

1. Is there room in your landlording system for exceptions to your rules?

   _____
   _____
   _____
   _____

2. If so, and you give a break to someone and they take advantage of you, how are you honestly going to feel? Will this stop you from giving others a break every once in a while? Be honest!

   _____
   _____
   _____
   _____

SUCCESS STORY #36
WORK HARD TODAY, LET YOUR MONEY WORK HARD TOMORROW

Jayson Sidhu

With my first investments, I wasted some money and I wasted some time. Now I understand that I really didn't know what "due diligence" or a "real estate system" meant. I was naive, so I let myself be talked into deals I should not have made.

Jayson Sidhu was living what many believe is "the dream." Unhappy with his way-too-safe but steady progression through a credit union that was paying for his training as a certified management accountant, the young Vancouverite earned a spot at the prestigious Vancouver Film School. It's a post-secondary entertainment arts school that offers an intensive, production-oriented educational experience and boasts a reputation as "the studio that teaches." And Jayson was there to learn. In an industry where the top 5% of graduates find jobs in the field, Jayson graduated number two in his class before landing a great position as an animator with a Burnaby, B.C.-based video game company vying for the electronic attention of the world's gamers. Few would have guessed he'd stay for four years then strike out on his own in the world of real estate investment.

Two years into that position, he started investing in real estate. Before long, it was like he had two jobs. "By the time I left, I was already spending a lot of my work day on the phone lining up deals or making arrangements to go see property," Jayson recalls. "I knew I wanted to be in real estate investment, but it was all a little complicated seeing as my job was in B.C. and several of my new investments were in Alberta."

His first deal came in 2004, when he used gaming company stock options to buy a condo in Abbotsford for $55,000. Just over six months later, that property sold for a $30,000 profit. Jayson's feet were wet—and he couldn't wait to jump in deeper.

When he couldn't attend a nearby book signing that featured Don Campbell, Jayson sent his wife, Kelly, a finance administrator with the Canadian Armed Forces. She was impressed. Jayson called REIN, then soon after joined the group. "It was a no-brainer," he says. "I had a couple of dogs in my portfolio thanks to some earlier investing with other associations. Here, I saw about 40 people, 5 groups of 8 people, all helping each other out. There wasn't anyone at the back of the room selling property, and I liked that."

By the time he left his job in animation, Jayson was already buying property and building an investment team in Edmonton. He was also earning his real estate licence, a move that would secure a position with an Edmonton-based brokerage that specializes in investment deals.

Working alone and with JV partners, Jayson acquired B.C. property including a fourplex in Merritt, two residential homes in Abbotsford and bare land in Quesnel. In Alberta, he owns a fourplex in Wetaskiwin and a house in St. Albert. He rents out the basement suite of the bungalow and lives upstairs when working in the Edmonton region. He and his dad also own 25 acres of bare land in the state of Washington.

Jayson is committed to the idea that his time is worth money, so all of his property is professionally managed, freeing his time for investing and his real estate clientele. He's also got his eye on a bigger investment pond: residential and commercial development. "I like what I'm doing now," he says, "but I obviously like change—and challenge."

Jayson has a plan to make that happen. To build the capital he needs for development projects, he explains, "I will sell pieces of my portfolio to buy more doors." He figures he and one partner will share $300,000 in profit when the Wetaskiwin fourplex sells, and that's money he'll pump back into capital investments.

Overall, Jayson likes where real estate is taking him, even though it often means he's a province away from Kelly and from his own family, including two younger brothers to whom he is very close. "That's tough, but I understand there's a long-term plan in place and I will stick to the vision," says Jayson, whose specific long-term goals include building a dream house in West Vancouver, a Ferrari, a membership on a great private golf course and season's tickets to the Vancouver Canucks. "It's a sacrifice now," he admits, "but it'll be worth it."

Don Campbell's Observations

Jayson is another brave soul who was not afraid of changing course in mid-stream despite spending time, money and effort in education for his old path. Many believed he was living his dream, when in fact he was living other people's idea of a dream lifestyle.

His one foray into real estate showed him just how financially effective investing could be; he just needed a system to follow. Now that he has one, there's no holding him back.

Giving up on a career choice is fraught with many potential landmines, most of which are based in emotions. Friends and family call you crazy; your current employer will think you've lost it; even strangers will shake their head if you tell them the story. However, you'll be the one who ends up laughing in the end . . . when they change their tune and start calling you lucky.

Jayson also learned the lesson of having a strong team surrounding him and treating his investments like a business. You'll note that he has put his capital to work not in his backyard but in an area where he believes his money will work the most hard for him. Many Canadian investors do get caught in the trap of investing only in their own province. This is a very unique trend to Canadians. Most European, American and Asian investors look to areas where their money will work hard, while Canadians seem to be trapped in some biased view of the rest of their country. While that trend is slowly beginning to change, it is still very prevalent. There are opportunities all across this country of ours, as the investors around the world are discovering. They are coming here by the planeload to grab investment property in Canada, while Canadians sit back and watch.

When you compare the economic fundamentals of Canada's market to most places around the world, our market looks very good. We'll be witnessing an increasing number of investors, both large and small coming to Canada as a safe haven. Our job as Canadian investors is to take off our blinders and start looking around at what we have here. The perfect investment may not be in your backyard, but it sure is in many areas of the country.

Jayson and Kelly know that their financial future is based on their money working hard for them, rather than they working hard for their money. We should all learn from this.

ACTION STEPS

1. What specific towns or cities of Canada do you believe to be strong real estate investment areas?
    a. _____
    b. _____
    c. _____

2. Get some unbiased research to discover other areas. For instance, order a copy of the research report *The Top 10 Towns to Invest In* available on www.realestateinvestingincanada.com.

    _____
    _____
    _____
    _____

3. Arrange to take a trip to at least one of the Top Investment Cities or Towns that you haven't visited in the last three or more years. Take the Goldmine Scorecard (see the Appendix) with you so you can check it out. Make it a fun trip, stay overnight, bring the family. This first trip is just designed to open the blinders so you can see where opportunity lies.
    By what date will you take this trip?

    _____

SUCCESS STORY #37
LOSING MY JOB WAS THE BEST THING THAT EVER HAPPENED TO ME

Ken Wilson

Systems, relationships, follow-through. I love those things. That's the essence of life, whether you're talking about real estate or something completely different.

Ken Wilson was excited about his first Quickstart meeting in Toronto. It was the fall of 2004 and he was looking for ways to boost his latest business venture. He'd invested in real estate before, but always alongside the comfort of a relatively secure job as an engineer in the high-tech industry. Now, laid off by a stumbling high-tech sector after 32 years in the business, he wanted to make real estate investment his full-time occupation. "It was like I took a look in the mirror and realized I wanted to do something different," he says. "I felt free."

He also felt like bumping up the risk factor. "Part of my success, from the very start, is due to my marketing. I try to do everything against the crowd," says Ken. "I was in Ontario to meet people and I knew I needed to do something different to attract their interest, so I took a step outside my comfort zone."

Knowing he was in prime Maple Leafs territory, with a few Senators and Habs fans most likely thrown into the mix, Ken donned his Calgary Flames jersey. A fashion anomaly in a room of suits and dress shirts, the jersey raised a few eyebrows at the Friday night session. He wore a Leafs jersey the next day. On Day 3, he pulled on a colourful T-shirt that reads like his business card. "The biggest roadblock to getting started as an investor can be meeting people. By Sunday, I had 15 people around me and I knew I was onto something good."

Three years later, Ken and his wife, Linda, a real estate agent in Calgary, own 43 doors, including a quartet of fourplexes in Calgary and revenue properties in Edmonton and Grande Prairie. They have about 10 JV partners, some with a couple of properties, and Ken is still excited about his new business, especially since he's learned from earlier errors.

Their first purchase in 2003 is a case in point. They'd bought a bungalow with an eye to suiting the basement, then learned that contravened zoning restrictions. "We got a quote, but we didn't want to have the work done and then have to remove it down the road." Sticking within the law compromised cash flow, but the lesson was in the bank. Avoiding shortcuts and "grey area" transactions always pays off in the long run.

One of his favourite buys shows his new wisdom at work. Two attached bungalows on an oversized lot in a working-class neighbourhood popular with renters, the properties will eventually be replaced with four infills. "As [veteran investor and REIN mentor] Tim Johnson used to say, 'Buy by the yard and sell by the foot,'" says Ken.

When it comes to buying property, he's also learned to optimize his investment by sticking to communities where pride of ownership is strong. He likes it when infills are already present, since that's a sign of an older community's transition towards renewal. Access to transportation, including major highways, is another plus for Ken's market. "If these things are present, the property offers several strategies. It will work for investors, homeowners and revenue property."

A stickler for details, Ken admits he's a master of the spreadsheet tool. He uses one spreadsheet to track business transactions and another to update JV partners on how their particular property is doing. Another version tracks tenant data, noting everything from their phone numbers to rent, the last rent increase, any problems related to that property—and even down to the kind of filter used on the furnace. Noting details like that can save a lot of time.

He colour-codes the tenant spreadsheets. "You do not want to be in the red zone," says Ken, who keeps careful records of any problems related to issues like rent, noise or property damage. "I'm firm but very fair, and our tenants know that if they stay the course, we won't raise rents." He delivers gifts of appreciation, from flower arrangements to turkeys and special event tickets when tenants help him out. He sent one a gift certificate for $100 after their unit experienced some problems related to a broken tap. "It wasn't your fault," insisted the tenant. Ken agreed, "but it wasn't her fault either and I appreciated her attitude."

"Systems, relationships, follow-through. I love those things. That's the essence of life, whether you're talking about real estate or something completely different," notes Ken.

On the relationship front, he uses a healthy bottom line to nurture relationships with JV partners.

"I tell my JV partners not to expect cash flow for the first 6 to 10 months until we have a reserve equal to 2 to 3 months of gross rent. Each property has its own separate savings account to hold this money in the event you need to replace the roof, furnace, etc., and this prevents a significant cash call on your personal pocket book. This is just another part of good project management."

The great thing about really liking what you do for a living is that your contentment on the professional side spills over into the rest of your life, says Ken, 57. Because he gets so much pleasure from his daily work, he can't envision a time when he's not working on some part of a real estate deal. "For some people, retirement means you quit working. I think it means you stop working at the place you think you have to work at and start doing what you enjoy."

The people you work *with* also matter. "If I hadn't joined REIN, I wouldn't have had the tools or, more importantly, the friends that have helped me keep focused and on track. Many of them have helped me with sharing in the deals I wouldn't have found myself."

Increasingly playing the role of a mentor, Ken offers the same sage advice to investment newcomers as he'd offer to his and Linda's six adult kids: Learn from the mistakes of others. "I would say the big lesson is that you have to create a business plan, have a mentor check it with you and then stick with it. If you've got a good mentor, you'll be on the right track."

Don Campbell's Observations

In many cases a traumatic life experience can be used as a catalyst to change directions for the better. A major accident, a health scare or, as in Ken's case, losing a long-term job after 32 years often makes us look at our life from a different perspective. The key is to deal with the reality of the situation and look for ways in which to turn them into opportunities for renewal. Ken is a great example of turning lemons into lemonade.

He felt fear, probably some anger and a little bit of excitement all at the same time. Ken then used these three components to build a new life for himself. Where many others would have focused on the anger and turned themselves into victims, Ken focused on the excitement and built from there.

Ken surrounded himself with like-minded, positive-focused investors who could show him the shortest path to the results he wanted. He provided value and received value in return, all of which kept him on track during this change in his life. Now, many years on, he continues to hang out with and give back to this group because he knows that the real estate markets are always changing and any professional investor knows that knowledge is the key to making sound decisions.

I still remember when Ken walked into that Toronto workshop in his Calgary Flames jersey. The thought that went through my head was, "Here's a guy willing to make things happen." From past experience it is the investor who's willing to be a little different, to stand out in a crowd who eventually attracts the most joint venture money. Ken surely stood out and the long-term results from taking a chance like that are quite astonishing.

Unlike Ken, many investors are often afraid to tell people what they do. They are also often the people who struggle with building their business. Real estate investing is just like any other business. In order to make business easier and more profitable, you need to stand out in your target crowd. If you are trying to attract joint venture money, tell people what you do and that you work with joint venture partners. They might not be interested, but they may know someone who is. Build a solid reputation so that any time someone thinks of investment real estate they think of you first.

The same goes for attracting tenants. If you want to attract quality tenants, even in a high-vacancy area, it's really rather simple. Stand out from the crowd; make your advertisements unique; find out what the tenants really want and figure out a way to provide it for them. Quality tenants are the lifeblood of your business. The product you offer is rental property; tenants are your number-one customers, so treat them that way.

Always think of what can you do to attract more customers to your business. By standing out and thinking a little differently, you create results. Just as Ken has done by standing out in all aspects of his business.

ACTION STEPS

1. If a traumatic event occurred in your life (i.e., you lost your current job), what would you do differently as you rebuilt your life?

    _____

    _____

    _____

    _____

2. Time to be brutally honest with yourself again. Rate the following six aspects of your life in order of importance (1 being most important, 6 being least important). Pretend no one will ever see your answers and no one will judge you. Rate them according to what's real for you, not what you believe society tells you must be real.

    ___ Wealth

    ___Family

    ___Friends

    ___Job results

    ___Health

    ___Joy

3. Now a little tougher question. Rate the following seven values in your life in order of importance (1 being most important, 7 being least important). Take your time, read them all first. Pretend no one will ever see your answers and no one will judge you. Rate them according to what's real for you, not what you believe society tells you must be real.

    ___Personal achievement

    ___Avoiding embarrassment

    ___What people think of me

    ___Not making mistakes

    ___Being wealthy

    ___Being healthy

    ___Having prestige

4. Now look at the answers you provided to the above two questions. Are you living your life today with a true focus on your values and what you rate as important, or are you living someone else's version of your life?

_____

_____

_____

_____

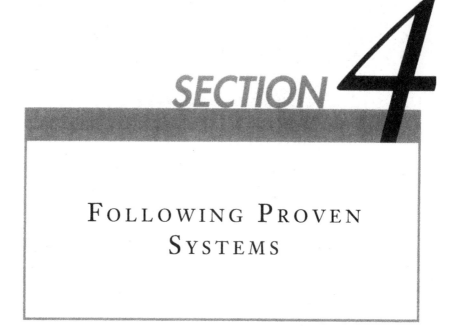

SECTION 4

FOLLOWING PROVEN SYSTEMS

SUCCESS STORY #38
HE NOT ONLY FOUND A NICHE—HE CREATED ONE FROM SCRATCH

Valden Palm

You learn as you go and you will make mistakes. But if you're not making any mistakes, you're not doing anything.

Every once in a while, the guy a lot of Canadian real estate investors call Mister Home Buyer or Mister RRSP answers his phone and hears the voice of a banker concerned about the size of his account balance. "I see there's $300,000 just sitting in your bank account," they say, "and I'm wondering if we could help." Valden Palm loves these calls. It's been a long time since he's really had to take the advice of a banker, but he gets a kick from knowing some of them worry he might not know how to put his money to work!

If necessity is the mother of invention, then desperation must be her ugly sister. Valden Palm has met them both and lived to tell a successful tale. In the late 1990s, he and his wife, Chaturi, and their four kids moved back to Edmonton from Vancouver, B.C., where he worked as an architectural technologist and had started to invest in real estate. Valden had grown up in Edmonton, and he moved back to work with investors who needed his expertise managing their growing portfolio. That relationship soured, devastating Valden emotionally and financially. "They were in control of my income and because I was living in one of their places, they were in charge of where I lived, too. I tried to buy that place so my family had a place to live, but that didn't work out either. I was moving back to Alberta in two days, but now it was with no job and no place for my family to live! Would my family still come? It was a dark time."

Valden regrouped. He got a job in the architectural field, found a place for his family to live and set to work buying property.

His first purchase was a unit in the same townhouse condominium complex where he'd been living in the property owned by his former business partners. Using a loan from his in-laws for a down payment, he bought and renovated the unit, eventually buying another one, too. He paid only $71,000 for each of the two units he still owns in that complex.

One unit in the complex sold for $290,000 in 2007. Another went on the market for $330,000. Valden's not selling due to his belief in long-term fundamentals. But he definitely is smiling now.

Valden's plan to make real estate investment his primary focus included re-joining REIN (he had a membership in B.C.) as soon as he could. "I started with zero cash," he recollects, "and my spouse and my family weren't very keen on the whole real estate thing. Some friends thought you bought rental property so you could be a kind of slum landlord." These folks equated making money in real estate to feeding off the misfortune of others. They had no sense that an investor may be trying to help people out of a bad situation by giving them a quality place to live. "I had to wrestle with some of my own fears, doubts and bad habits, too, and I learned to see my mistakes as lessons. What matters is that you learn the lesson—and move forward!"

To Valden, that meant focusing on the Edmonton market, "not investing for the pure sake of investing. I decided I'm an Edmonton guy, and this is where I'll concentrate." That focus translated into 45 properties valued at more than $2 million in equity alone by mid-2007. He self-manages them all, with Chaturi now on board as bookkeeper. Valden expects at least one of their children to follow him into the business.

That business is undergoing significant change. Valden's current portfolio is a mix of townhouses, apartment condos, single-family homes and houses with suites, but he's turning his attention to larger, multi-family complexes and even land development. To get there, he'll keep buying one property at a time, using his reputation as Mister Home Buyer to find and secure deals.

As Mister Home Buyer, Valden cuts to the chase and advertises himself as a private real estate investor who wants to buy or lease homes. A lot of his deals come through referrals from what he calls "the secondary real estate market, a.k.a. the For-Sale–by-Owner market." Today's environment is more complicated given the dramatic rise in Edmonton prices. "But honestly," says Valden, "you can buy in any market. You just buy differently." Excuses are not allowed.

A few years back, he took that same model and introduced a sister company, Mister RRSP. He got into that business after hearing how investors can use their mutual fund and stock-based RRSP portfolios to invest in mortgages. "I heard about this strategy at a REIN meeting, and when I looked around the room, it was like everyone had this "deer in the head-lights" glaze in their eyes. No one really seemed to know how to do this or understood the power of this program. So I decided I would crack the code on this RRSP financing system." The potential of a system that allows real estate investors to tap into the vast stores of RRSP funds that Canadian hold was enormous, and Valden was the only one in Canada to see this at that time. He created his own investment niche.

Having studied, tested and mastered the RRSP in real estate strategy, he now teaches other investors how to do it, too. That kind of "giving back" is a fundamental tenet of Valden's life philosophy.

Now 48 and seasoned as much by fire as success, Valden credits "workable systems" for his business's steady development. Once you learn how to do something right, compromises no longer make any sense, whether you're talking about due diligence with tenant screening or specific property purchases.

He's also a realist expecting positive results, but always having a Plan B ready just in case. He reminds investors, "Not every property works and you learn when to cut your losses. I've dusted properties that were a pain to manage. Some of them have really appreciated in price since I sold them, but I don't care, it was the right decision at the time. If it's costing me money, time and frustration, I sell it and move on to a property that is more hassle-free. It's important not to get too emotionally attached to any one property. If you can fix a problem, fix it. If not, then cut it loose with no regrets."

But make no mistake. When Valden moves on, it's with the people he loves most at his side. And for that he is grateful, since some of his hardest life lessons have been dealt by people he thought he could trust. "I've learned to surround myself with people who have a positive attitude and avoid naysayers and dream stealers at all cost. It's easy to be negative. But it will destroy you."

Real estate investment has also taught Valden that his most valuable resource is himself, and his greatest gift, his time. "You only have one day to spend. Be careful who you allow to take those time coins, because you can't get them back."

He values the way real estate investing gives him time with his family and friends, and time to help others be as successful. "Honestly, my Personal Belize is all about doing what I want, for who I want, when I want. I honestly can't ever see myself retiring. I'll always be tinkering with some deal, although in the future that may mean I'm the banker, or I'm helping investors find more interesting ways to do new deals."

∞∞∞

Don Campbell's Observations

Anyone who has met Mr. RRSP (Valden Palm) knows that life for him is all about helping others become better at anything they want. From his humble beginnings in a business relationship that left him devastated (with nowhere for his family to live) right through to him becoming one of the most respected investors and real estate investment trainers in the country, he has kept his heart on his sleeve and his engineering brain in full gear.

His story could have fit in many different categories in this book. He's obviously overcome a lot of personal adversity (he left his great job and moved cities to pursue his dream—even with a family of five to look after); he obviously has a focus on helping his family and friends. However, he is in this Following Proven Systems section because the biggest lesson his story can teach us involves the importance of creating automated systems for our real estate investments.

Valden is the first to admit that having systems for every part of his business makes life so much easier; it clears the lines of communications and it sets expectations for every business relationship. He is continually improving his system as he learns new lessons in his business.

For instance, every dealing with his tenants is systemized. If they have a pet, he has a system to deal with *all* the problems this could create; if they bounce a cheque, he just hauls out the appropriate system and follows it along (including the exact wording of the letters he sends); when they provide notice, he grabs his "move-out" system and works through it. Each system is a simple checklist and each system was developed out of past experiences. Life becomes simple because he doesn't even have to run the system: he can just hand it off to an assistant and they will do just the same as what Valden would have done.

The added benefit to having all of these simple systems in place is that it frees up brain space to be creative and to uncover more real estate deals. With systems you don't have to remember everything; the systems do that hard work for you. I have witnessed hundreds of investors become completely overwhelmed after owning only few investment properties all because they don't have systems with built-in reminders. Valden's 75 purchases would never have happened if he had to keep all the details in his head and he had to start from scratch each time he considered a property or moved in a new tenant.

The system he is known for across Canada covers the complex subject of how to use RRSP money to invest in the real estate market (without having to cash the money out). He first published his "RRSP Secrets" program back in 2002 (see the "tools and research" section of www. realestateinvestingincanada.com for more details on his program). Since then, there have been many pretenders trying to duplicate his system, but there is really only one true Canadian expert in this niche.

In a few very short years, he moved from owning one single investment townhouse to owning multiple properties and a multi-family building, and it was made possible because of his unwavering focus on building systems that helped him create the financial dream he held for his family.

ACTION STEPS

1. What two components of your real estate investment business are the largest user of your time or give you the most frustration?

    _____

    _____

    _____

    _____

2. Take a few minutes to outline the steps that you take whenever these situations occur (you may need a separate piece of paper for each one).

    _____

    _____

    _____

Systems don't need to be computer based, nor do they need to be formal. Just use the outline above to make a checklist of the steps you take in the situations. I feel much more confident when flying with a veteran pilot who still uses a checklist every time he hops into the cockpit. These simple real estate checklists will start to build your confidence in your real estate investments.

3. Review these outlines. Notice what steps within the system you could simply delegate. Who will you delegate the simple, repeatable tasks to so that your time is free to focus on the important tasks?

_____

_____

_____

_____

There are many checklists already created for you in the book *Real Estate Investing in Canada*. Feel free to use those as a base from which to automate your investments.

SUCCESS STORY #39
FOCUS ON CHANGING OTHER PEOPLE'S LIVES, AND YOURS WILL CHANGE TOO!

Marco Santoro and Tanya Santoro

The reality is that opportunity is always knocking. But you only get to take advantage of it when you open the door.

Want to hear Marco Santoro's worst investment tip? Buy your principal residence just before the turn of the century, and then hope records of your mortgage responsibilities disappear when the world's computers crash during Y2K. "No really, that was my plan," he insists. "It wasn't a good plan, but I did dream of that happening."

Seven years after the millennium, he and his wife, Tanya, no longer need to dream of what could be. Instead, they're laying the foundation for an increasingly successful real estate portfolio solidly based on more than 30 revenue properties in eight Ontario cities. And this is just the beginning.

When Tanya got her real estate licence in the late 1990s, Marco supplemented her income working at a grocery store. Both were college graduates, but since the early days of selling real estate ran pretty lean, they counted on his work to pay the bills. Cashing in on what he'd been learning since he took his first real estate investment course at the tender age of 14, the Santoros bought their first three properties soon after graduating in 1995. "Opportunity had been knocking, and I was finally ready to open the door," says Marco, now 33.

By the time they married in 2000, Marco felt increasingly buried in debt. He knew their decision to buy revenue property was a great strategy for the future. But when Tanya learned she was expecting their first child in 2004, he was scared. He was also inspired. Not one to get too caught up wondering what might make sense to others, Marco took a paternity leave almost as soon as Tanya announced her pregnancy. "I knew I was never going back and I saw that period of time as a great opportunity to focus on Tanya's business and build our real estate connections."

Already a licensed mortgage consultant, Marco went to work full-time as Tanya's right-hand man. He accompanied Tanya when she took clients to view potential rental properties, and he arranged financing and helped people fix their credit.

By then, the couple owned several more properties, all professionally managed. That freed up Marco's time for other aspects of the business. It also proved a turning point as they both realized there was no need to try to do everything themselves. Before long, they were expanding the circle of people involved in their business. Today, Marco calls it his Power Team of home appraisers, lawyers, handymen and even other mortgage brokers.

The year 2004 was their best year ever, and not just because their son was born that September. In 2004, Tanya closed more than 100 transactions, 40% of them investment properties.

Marco had been building another side of their investment business, too. In 2002 he recognized another business opportunity when a tenant moved out of one of their properties to buy a home. Marco hit the phones. "I called every old and new tenant of ours and reminded them if they wanted to buy the house they were renting, we could help. We could also help them buy any other house."

That led to increasingly creative deals to help people set up rent-to-own (also called lease option) deals, with Marco and Tanya as their business partners. As that business picked up speed, Marco started hearing about other people who needed helping buying their own homes. One man, legally blind and still reeling from bankruptcies, now owns a house the Santoros helped him buy. Others started buying properties they had been renting. "Every time a tenant bought [the] property they had been renting, we would make a profit and move the mortgage to another home and do it all over again with a new family," explains Marco.

Marco smiles at the thought of it. "Every once in a while you get a chance to change a person's life. I don't take that for granted, but I sure like when it happens."

While he owns properties in eight cities, his current acquisition strategy focuses on Cambridge, Kitchener and Waterloo. Like other investors, he says he's learned the grass isn't always greener on the other side of the fence, especially if the distances he has to travel to buy the various properties compromises his focus on quality—and time with his family.

"In the end, there is no magic way to be successful at real estate investing," says Marco. "You've got to work hard, you've got to make money before you spend it, and you've got to be able to attract business partners who have money, but need your time and expertise."

Not one to compare himself to others, Marco likes knowing he and Tanya are building a future that's financially secure and will give them a chance to do the things they want to do. "Time is always more valuable than money. I've tasted 'freedom' by building wealth—and that equals opportunity."

Don Campbell's Observations

Marco and Tanya have combined their talents to create a top-notch professional investment team. It obviously didn't start that way, and there were many sacrifices along the way, but now they are true leaders in the real estate investing community. They have built their reputation with a lot of hard work, but more importantly, by focusing on how they can make others more successful in their life. I think Zig Ziglar said it best when he stated: "You can have anything you want in life just as long as you help enough other people get what they want in their life." The Santoros have really taken this to heart and changed not only their lives but also the lives of many others.

Here are the key lessons we can take away this story:

- They found a niche. They decided early on not to be generalists (good at a lot of things, but masters of none). In other words, they didn't get caught in the trap of trying to be all things to all people. That would have been the fastest way to mediocrity.

- They built a team upon which they can rely. Without a trusted team of professionals (lawyer, accountant, mentor, property manager, etc.) an investor is very limited in what he can create, as he/she gets bogged down in the day-to-day minutiae of being all things to all people.

- They became clear that they wanted to create financial freedom, but not at the expense of their relationship or how they treated other people.

This is a remarkable story of going from a grocery-store clerk to an investment real estate leader in a very short time. And most importantly of all, the Santoros' achievement did not compromise their values or their humanity.

ACTION STEPS

1. Knowing what you know today, what one niche within real estate investing do you want to become a master in?

_____

_____

_____

_____

2. What members of your real estate dream team are you currently missing?

_____

_____

_____

_____

3. By what date do you wish to have these open spots filled?

_____

_____

4. Where can you find these new team members and who can assist you in this?

_____

_____

_____

SUCCESS STORY #40
RESPECT IS A TWO-WAY STREET

Sharon Trenaman and Amy Jo Strutt

The big difference now is that I buy with my head, not my heart.

Sharon Trenaman is a stickler for detail. Just don't ask her for the specifics on the number of real estate properties she owns with her partner, Amy Jo Strutt. Tren, as she prefers to be called, knows it's around the 40 mark. But she enjoys buying properties to renovate and re-sell, so their portfolio bounces up and down a bit, depending on where those deals are at.

Most real estate investors dabble in the "flip" side of the business at least once, then move on out of frustration. Tren's different. She merges the creative side of improving a property's value with the all-business side of making money. Using contacts built over two decades of living in Calgary, she takes on renovations she knows she can do in a specific timeline. On a deal where she doesn't take possession for two months, she uses the time to order everything from paint to kitchen cabinetry. "On noon of the day we take possession," she says, "I'll have everything there and ready to go."

An Australian immigrant who came to Canada as a tourist in 1985 then stayed to coach squash for 17 years (a stint that included leadership of the national junior team), Tren admits she's always seen herself "as more of an owner than renter."

She and Amy started buying property together 12 years ago. Amy's full-time job often takes her out of the country, and when they were both working full-time, they shared their portfolio's management. Having left her position as a national-level squash coach, Tren now concentrates on the portfolio, which includes property from Lethbridge, in Alberta's deep south, to Fort McMurray, in the north. The latter is the only property she doesn't manage herself.

"We have fantastic tenants and that makes it easy," notes Tren, although she admits that wasn't always the case. She owned seven revenue properties before joining REIN in 2000. "I did have some bad tenants before that. But back then, I thought a bad tenant meant it was time to sell a property. Once I learned it was better to wait for a good tenant, we didn't have those problems anymore."

A more strategic approach to revenue property purchases also helped her and Amy fine-tune their search for property. "Before, if the mortgage was paid with rent, I figured it was a good deal." They now pay more attention to what's happening in a prospective property's neighbourhood and on a particular street rather than national or provincial headlines. While several of their properties are located in some of Calgary's toughest socio-economic neighbourhoods, they work hard to attract the kind of tenants who take pride in their homes—a sentiment that translates into taking care of their landlords' investment.

Amy, who moved back to Calgary from Vancouver, using money from her Vancouver home sale to fund property buys in her hometown, brings more of a bottom-line focus to their buys. "She is really good at analyzing a property and not getting caught up in the emotions," says Tren. "That's made a big difference for me because now I buy with my head, not my heart."

That serious approach to investment is evident in the "whole pile of addendums now attached to our rental contracts," she adds. Those addendums spell out what happens when rent deadlines are missed, including automatic late-payment penalties.

And those rules are applied across the board. One Edmonton tenant does a lot of their renovation and repair work on their properties in that city. Tren says she and Amy won't subtract rent from his cheques, nor would they skip late penalties if cheques bounce. "I explain to everyone that we have to pay interest to the bank regardless of whether their cheques clear or not. This is a mutual relationship."

Which doesn't mean it's without heart. When Tren and Amy learned one of their Calgary tenant's children had cancer, they changed their plans of selling that property. "We decided not to sell as that would have added even more chaos into this family's life. Now, out of the blue, he's painting the fence. We didn't even ask him to do that." Treating good tenants with respect will always come back positively to the property owner. They're also sticklers for treating tenants fairly, insisting on market rents and "gifting our tenants when we want to show them that we appreciate their business."

And make no mistake. When you're on the line for 40-some properties, real estate investment is a business, pure and simple. Twenty-two years after buying her first Canadian property, Tren doesn't foresee a future without real estate investment. "We don't need more rentals. But we're still looking, albeit more slowly."

With most of their second mortgages with vendors now being disposed of, cash flow looks better and better, especially alongside rapid equity appreciation. "I do want to be able to go to warmer places like Phoenix when I want to," she confesses, "and when I'm in Las Vegas, I think about buying a vacation property there. But Amy and I love what we do here. Friends joke about me going to some 12-step program for real estate investors, but I'm not sure it's really that funny. I like what I do and don't think I actually could just stop!"

Don Campbell's Observations

You might have first heard Amy and Tren's story in the back of the book *Real Estate Investing in Canada*. This update, almost three years later, proves that partnerships can work well if each partner brings their own unique strengths to the equation. The partnership continues to grow as each of them focus on what they do best, and what they enjoy most.

Like many successful investors, they've found their investment niche and take their business seriously. They have developed systems, forms and checklists that allow them to be at the top of their game every time they add a new property to their portfolio.

They have developed a reputation for doing what they say they're going to do. If they make a commitment, you can be sure that they will follow through. That is why they are surrounded by such a quality team, and this quality team supports their vision and wants to see them succeed. The team includes their tenants, which is very unique. They are proof that good people do finish first.

ACTION STEPS

1. What three people in your life would you like to partner up with to build your real estate portfolio?

_____

_____

_____

_____

2. Of the three above, who is the most like you?

    _____

    _____

3. Who has the most skills or assets that you are lacking?

    _____

    _____

It is important to remember that forming a partnership is a business decision, and partnerships work best when the two partners have complementary skills, not ones that are similar. So, the name you wrote in response to question #2 would be the least likely candidate for a successful business partnership, while the one listed for #3 has the most potential.

SUCCESS STORY #41
WORK HARD AND TREAT INVESTING LIKE A BUSINESS

Tasha Adams and Owen Shaw

You can have everything you want, as long as you help others get what they want, too.

"Hey! Do you mind if I ask what you do for a living?" The question caught 26-year-old Owen Shaw off guard, but he smiled when he saw the query came from a young guy whose pickup truck was parked beside him at a stop light in Calgary's trendy Eau Clair district. Looking up from the wheel of his mercury silver Aston Martin, Owen smiled again. "Real estate. I'm in real estate investment." This sounds like a story directly out of the movie *The Pursuit of Happyness* with Will Smith asking a successful person the exact same question.

The irony of that particular interaction is that, minus the vehicles, "we live a pretty modest lifestyle," says Owen, referring to the home he shares with Tasha Adams, 27, his life and business partner since they were 17 and 18, respectively.

While Tasha worked her way through a business management degree at the University of Lethbridge, Owen characterizes himself as a high school graduate "who learned that showing up to work in coveralls wasn't going to get me where I wanted to go." Moving on from installing car alarms and remote starters, he entered the warehouse distribution business, where his problem-solving skills and people management strengths set him on an upward track. It also brought him face to face with the realization that a lot of the executives he met didn't seem to like their jobs. Even though they were making good money, nobody ever thought it was enough.

"It was like I got high enough to look through the glass ceiling," says Owen, "and realized that as long as I was working for someone else, I would be letting them decide what my financial future would be. I didn't like what I saw."

By July 2003, a 22-year-old Owen had listened to his first Quickstart audio CD and handled his first real estate contract flip. For $25, he made

$19,000. The deal was structured so that he only had to put down $8,000. He lined up an investor to partner with him. By the time the condition period expired, however, Owen had found a buyer who gave him an $8,000 deposit on the property. Owen used that for the down payment and gave the first investor a sizeable cheque to thank him for backing the deal, even though his money wasn't needed. Not bad for three weeks' work. Owen was hooked, and that money went straight into another property.

By then Tasha had worked herself into a management position with a car rental agency. She was completing her degree on the side, and Owen, who was still employed by the distribution company, had negotiated a reduction in his working hours. By working through his lunch period and leaving work every day at 3 p.m., he could still help pay the bills and have more time for investing.

Having decided to pursue the buy-and-hold model, they started buying revenue property, quickly learning how climate changes impact rental market. "Properties are harder to rent or sell in the fall and winter, especially if it's cold, as people don't want to move," says Owen.

Before long they had a negative cash flow of $12,000 a month. Because they were reluctant to put other people's money at risk, they weathered their vacancy issues by offering people a short-term place to earn high interest rates. They paid back every loan. "That first year was a year of discovery," says Tasha. Owen is less philosophical: "Anything that could go wrong, did." Their first half-dozen properties were located in a diverse range of locations, from the new suburban neighbourhoods to older, blue-collar communities.

In what still stands as one of the worst experiences of their investing lives, they put $5,000 down to secure two townhouses in the fall of 2003. After visiting the vacant properties with prospective renters, Owen reported water damage from broken pipes that had frozen in the cold (another side effect of sudden weather changes). By the time the water was turned off, the complex was flooded. They expected the vendor to fix it up and proceed according to the deal. But that's not what happened. Instead, after several attempts to contact the vendor and Realtor failed, Owen was shocked to learn the seller had repaired the units then sold them to another buyer, keeping Owen's deposit.

Still perfecting their system, a lot of their first deals involved securing property $20,000 to $30,000 below market value, then finding joint venture partners to put up the cash. "Our goal was to provide a kind of plug-and-play program for investors," explains Tasha, using an expression familiar to those who grew up with personal computers and video gaming systems. "We found the deals and put in the time and arranged the financing. The investors just plugged in their money."

By November 2005, with Owen investing full-time, Tasha was working for Shaw Capital (she finished her degree in 2005) and their portfolio was growing—as was their reputation for success.

Today, Tasha manages their close to 100 tenants in a combination of single-family and multi-family homes. She also handles the administrative work for the entire portfolio and manages the people on a growing in-house team that includes a bookkeeper and operations manager. And to think it all started with one small deal.

Owen focuses on finding property and negotiating deals. Interestingly enough, he negotiates most of his deals over the telephone and has offers signed by fax. "When people first meet Owen, they are often surprised at how young he is," says Tasha. "But if they've dealt with him on the phone and have had a chance to see the paperwork behind his deals, they're much more confident." Dressed in flip-flops, jeans and a T-shirt, she also looks younger than her 27 years. But make no mistake: This young duo runs a professional operation. And they know what they're doing.

By mid-2007, their portfolio tallied more than $150 million in property and existing development and redevelopment projects. It stretches across their home province, with property in Calgary, Red Deer, Edmonton, Devon and Peace River, a northern-Alberta community of farmers, foresters and, increasingly, those attracted by the region's booming oil and gas industry.

The portfolio also includes a $32-million redevelopment of a mixed-use, 11-storey concrete building in downtown Calgary, and an $80-million land development project in the town of Devon, a thriving community southwest of Edmonton. That project will see the development of 187 acres of land zoned for a mixture of light industrial, multi-family and single-family homes.

"The reality for us is that the big deals are getting easier to come by," says Owen. In the coming months, he says the firm will adopt a more institutional administrative model. Ideally, he'd like that to include some way to get smaller investors into their deals.

He says it's important people realize that Shaw Capital's success isn't all about expensive cars and the freedom to travel abroad. "This is what I was meant to do and what I do doesn't feel like work. Is there stress? Of course. But 'failure' is not in my vocabulary. I like the challenge of making deals work so our partners make money."

His top advice to investment market newbies? "Join REIN." He credits the organization with helping him and Tasha stay on track with important decisions. He also cautions would-be investors to construct win-win deals. "The key to negotiating anything in business is ensuring that you meet the needs of the other party while trying to meet your own. You must always leave something on the table for the next person and you must give if you hope to receive."

"And don't quit your day job just yet," adds Tasha, who suggests new investors take some time to learn the market and figure out how they want to participate. "Seriously, you can be around people in the investment community and pick up a lot of bad vibes when all of the talk is about money. This is not a business that's about getting rich quick, but you certainly can become rich if you work hard, be patient and treat it like a business."

<hr />

Don Campbell's Observations

Theirs is a true story of lessons learned. First off, Owen and Tasha prove, once again, that no one can use age as an excuse. In this book we've heard from people who had to start over at 50, some who are now investing in their retirement years and now from a couple who are flying high in their 20s.

I have heard the "age excuse" too many times to count, and the entertaining thing about it is that it comes from all levels. From "I'm too young to start" to "I'm much too old to start now" to "I wish I had started earlier, I'm already 40." Life is about now and doing what you can with what you have in front of you. Regrets and excuses will not get you anywhere.

Owen and Tasha have a passion for what they do, and I'm sure there are many times where they are dealing with people much older than themselves who don't take them seriously. But they don't allow that to get in their way. They've built systems to work around it; for example, by initiating discussions on the telephone, where age plays no role in the conversation. When I started I was only 23 working part-time at a retail store. Nobody took me seriously at first either. But over time, by proving yourself and creating a reputation, anyone can get over the age hurdle.

The second lesson we learn from Owen and Tasha is that success takes time and effort—it doesn't occur overnight. In real estate, as with any true investing, you need patience as you let the market take care of you. It is in trying to reach the top in a single leap that most of the financial misery in the world is created. Strong, small steps towards your goal always work better than many large leaps trying to "grab the brass ring." To get to the top of the mountain, or to get to the end of any journey, you find your path, you plan your trip, and then you take the trip using the most efficient route.

Too many people believe the story of the get-rich-quick gurus and get frustrated when their dreams never come true. The odd person may get lucky and reach the top, but why put your future in the hands of pure luck? Why not, like Owen and Tasha, plan the journey take the steps and guarantee yourself you'll get there?

The third lesson, I believe, is their most important message: Don't quit your day job! Many dream of becoming a full-time real estate investor, so they lose sight of their critical path:

1. How are we going to eat, and where's the income going to come from while we build our portfolio?
2. Without an income, how are we going to qualify for the mortgages we need in order to buy the real estate we need to achieve our goal?

You will read of investors in this book who took the chance, jumped off the cliff and have done well in full-time real estate without financial backing or an income to fall back upon. However, that's definitely not the easiest path. Many who become full-time investors have done so successfully after creating a financial backing through part-time real estate or a buyout from their job. That way, they are not worried about how they're going to pay the bills. So they don't feel forced to take below-average deals just to make a small bit of money. Desperation is not a good place to be investing from.

ACTION STEPS

If you plan on making real estate investing your full-time source of income, make sure you have a plan in place that takes care of at least 12 months' worth of living expenses (don't count on taking any money out of your new real estate during that time) and a contingency plan for how you are going to qualify for mortgages on your new purchases. Talk to a professional, investment-focused mortgage broker to understand your qualification options. It may be that part of your plan will require you to work with joint venture partners. So you should learn all you can about how that process works. The REIN Joint Venture Secrets Program is a good place to start (details can be found at www.realestateinvestingin canada.com).

SUCCESS STORY #42
BEING BUSY IS A GREAT EXCUSE FOR CREATING SYSTEMS

Mark Healy

You have to know your own tolerance for risk, and then act accordingly. Personally, I subscribe to the "making your wings on the way down" philosophy.

At first glance, Mark Healy's business profile is hardly that of a guy who has time to own 72 doors on 30 properties. The CEO and owner and GM of Kensington Floors Carpet One, one of Calgary's oldest and most successful flooring companies, Mark works in an industry driven by a steaming hot market for new homes and renovations. With 33 employees and 42 subcontractors, he spends his days solving other people's problems. And he's good at it. Kensington Floors has racked up an outstanding collection of sales and customer service awards since Mark took over the business in 2003. He does it all with what he calls "systems." "The beauty of operational systems is that they free you up to do what you do best," notes Healy.

In 2003, he also became a director in Connaughty Investment Ltd., a family-owned company. Connaughty Investment was started by his father in 1981 and held a few revenue properties.

Several years earlier, Mark and his wife, Shelley, bought an R2 bungalow for $160,000. It was at least $40,000 more than they would have paid for a similar property elsewhere in the city, but an R2 designation meant they could legally rent out the basement, ensuring a tenant paid half their mortgage. It was a sign of things to come.

Not long after becoming a director with Connaughty, Mark joined REIN, an organization he'd heard about through a neighbour. From there, he set out to take Connaughty Investment to new heights. Together, Mark and his sister Betty Anne Tarini embarked on an aggressive campaign to implement the systems they were learning and closed on three properties by September 2005.

"I find the deals and handle negotiations and property management. Mark finds the money," says Betty Anne, who manages a diverse portfolio of single-family homes, duplexes, fourplexes, one fiveplex and three six-plexes, as well as three commercial properties. All are located in Calgary.

Mark laughs when asked about his favourite deal. "I guess it was the time I tried to entice a friend from Lethbridge into being a money partner. Within a month, I turned into *his* money partner, putting down $10,000 on a deal he had found in Lethbridge."

That $10,000 let the partners assume a $110,000 mortgage. They spent another $70,000 in renovations (carried out before they even took possession) and, just three months later, sold the property for $360,000.

"The lesson is about keeping an open mind," says Mark. "If you're always looking, you'll find great deals."

Betty Anne's favourite deal involves a careful negotiation to cut $100,000 from the asking price of a fourplex. Following a system shaped by REIN information, her offer included a cover letter and stipulated that the letter had to be read by the vendor, not just his agents. The information she provided detailed the current market and how she arrived at her price. She left the offer open and waited in her car for an hour while they looked it over. She got the property.

Betty Anne loves the nuts and bolts of the deal. She also likes knowing she can call Mark to take the next step. "I've called him and said, 'I put an offer in on five [properties], we got two. Now you find us the money.'"

What's easy now was harder in the early days. Betty Anne remembers having spent a lot of money on deposits on multi-family buildings when she found out the signed commitment from the bank contained an unworkable clause—a situation that required six more months, three different banks, and much anxious effort to remedy.

But there were no regrets. Despite the high-interest bridge financing they had to scrounge up, they resolved the issue with the lender. Mark and Betty Anne were perfectly positioned when the market took an explosive leap over the next few months. They target areas with strong economic fundamentals. So although the growth was nice, it wasn't a real surprise.

Like Mark, Betty Anne says the bulk of their success rests on a team approach. And her team is more than a bench full of lawyers, accountants and real estate contacts. "You become less intimidated when you surround yourself with powerful people," says Betty Anne, whose power team ranges from a personal assistant to the people who clean their houses and the guy who cuts their grass.

When her plumber told her he was too busy to help with an after-hours repair of a leaky water tank, she called another firm. When the first plumber heard she was being charged a $600 premium to get the work done, he juggled clients to handle her emergency first. "He was shocked that I was being taken advantage of, so he came and did the work—at regular rates! That's what a team member does."

Experience is a good teacher, adds Mark. He admits to times when a deal cost more than expected to get everything in place. "But it's all relative. If you're paying attention to what's happening in the market, you realize that a few thousand dollars is nothing compared to appreciation."

He also insists it's important to listen to people who know more than you do. The company has flipped several properties since 2005 and Mark remembers talking to a mortgage broker about financing these deals. "He was telling me how to make $40,000 to $50,000 on a deal. What he didn't know was that I was thinking, 'Wow. I'd have been happy with $10,000 or $15,000.'"

He's also learned to move on after each deal. In May 2006, he recalls, "we sold a house in Calgary for $255,000, walking away with $70,000 profit after just four months of work. A few days later, a house two doors down sold for $290,000. 'Oh well,' I said. 'I guess we left something on the table for the next guy.'"

That same attitude means they'll pay top dollar to get renovation work done if that's what needs to happen. "My dad used to say, using a stock market analogy, 'The bears make money. The bulls make money. The pigs get slaughtered.' We're here to make money, but we're not chasing every dollar."

Don Campbell's Observations

Mark is busy: He's running a successful business with 33 employees and still he finds time to build a very successful real estate portfolio. How does he do it while others in his position can't find the time? Simply, it is all in having systems that automate tasks.

Systems and checklists free up time for more important pursuits. Once Mark and his sister Betty Anne find something that works well, either in business or real estate investing, they create a system or checklist for it. That way they are not wasting time re-inventing their process every time. With these systems in place, they can find the time it takes to build the relationships that help them build their portfolio.

Their story could easily have been placed under the Friends and Family section of this book, but the key lesson their story teaches us is that no matter how busy we believe we are in our lives, if we are truly committed to building a strong financial foundation, we can and will find a way to release some time to make it happen.

Over the last 15 years, we have developed many investment systems and checklists to help our fellow investors automate their buying and holding of property. Many senior investors use these systems as a base from which to build their own checklists to fit their style of investing. So even though you may be starting at the beginning, there are always systems out there you can modify to fit your life.

Two warnings on systems:

1. Make sure the system you are going to use is proven to work in Canada as well as in both upward-moving markets and downward-trending markets. Don't get fooled by systems from elsewhere that don't have a decade of testing in the Canadian market.
2. Bill Gates states, "Bring automation to an inefficient business and it will increase the inefficiencies. Bring automation to an efficient business and efficiency will increase." This is very true with investment systems. If you build your system or checklist based on an inefficient model, it will not free up your time, it will take it away. Ensure your system does not have inefficiencies built into it. Follow a program that already has worked the efficiencies into it, then just duplicate it in your life.

Mark and Betty Anne also teach us that there is no need to grind the last penny out of every deal, or every transaction with their contractors or realtors. If the numbers make sense, they buy it at close to market; if the numbers are poor, they walk away. It's that simple.

If you are investing based on strong economic fundamentals, $2,000 here and there will not make any difference at the end. In the investment world it is important to remember the old adage, "The more you grind, the thinner your welcome becomes."

Work towards building your team, as Mark and Betty Anne have done, and be on the lookout for opportunities to increase your efficiencies so you can fee up additional time. Even if it is an extra hour per week, it will make a difference.

ACTION STEPS

1. How many hours per week could you devote to building your real estate portfolio?

   _____

   _____

   _____

   _____

2. Whether it is 1 hour or 40 hours, is there anything stopping you from starting today, then slowly adding hours as you go? If so, what is it and how are you going to solve this roadblock?

   _____

   _____

   _____

   _____

SUCCESS STORY #43
REMOVE EMOTIONS BY INVESTING HALFWAY AROUND THE WORLD

Todd Millar and Danielle Millar

An "overnight success story" in real estate will may take you 10 years to achieve. But it is possible. And it is worth it.

Husband-and-wife investor team Todd and Danielle Millar have a few stories to share about what can go wrong when you buy revenue property that needs major renovations before it's ready for tenants. There was the time fire code regulations changed as they undertook a reno, necessitating more expense than they planned for. They've also experienced the mind-bending levels of frustration linked to a contractor's decision to drop their multiplex renovation mid-stream to free his time for a larger multi-family project. They've worked through the aftermath of a fire that damaged several units of a building they were trying to buy. They've dealt with the financial and emotional roller coaster of learning the fire was set by a disgruntled tenant retaliating against the property's last owner. It gets worse: All of these things occurred on the same deal, which ended with the Millars losing a sizeable deposit, plus reno cash, all because they failed to meet legal deadlines and the municipal code, a problem that links right back to that contractor!

Complicating the situation was the fact Todd and Danielle launched their Canadian investment portfolio from the other side of the planet. Although trained as a classical French chef and a chemical lab assistant, respectively, Todd and Danielle live in Japan, where they teach English and satisfy a passion for travel, having journeyed to almost 20 nations.

They bought their first property, a duplex in Winnipeg, Manitoba, in 2002. They paid $32,000 and rented it for $1,000 a month. A second Winnipeg property followed and a multiplex in Hamilton, Ontario, was next. Its lessons were mostly scary and expensive, but that deal also spurred them to do more reading and to deliberately look for ways to make real estate investing less risky. "We took a few expensive real estate courses and bought a few more properties," recalls Todd, 35. They were also looking for ways to avoid the pitfalls of past deals. "At the same time," he adds "we were working hard to save more money to invest."

Still living and working in Japan, the Millars joined REIN in December 2005. That move paid off, big time. Operating as Glenn Simon Inc., the real estate company they launched in 2002 went from 5 properties in 2005 to 30 transactions by 2007. By the middle of that year, they were holding 25 properties, plus land. All of the properties are in Canada and most were purchased with joint venture partners. With investors in Canada, Japan, Singapore, Australia and the United States, the Millars have turned a $32,000 duplex into a multi-million-dollar investment portfolio, making their partners very decent returns along the way. "Most of them are repeat investors, I might add," says Todd.

Given the distance between their Asian home and their Canadian portfolio, the Millars rely on a team of trusted professionals, including property managers. They also protect their investors' interest with a healthy reserve fund and factor in potential negative cash flow, if needed. "That way, we eliminate cash calls. We never go back to our partners for additional funds." You can't afford surprises when your investments are halfway around the world and 15 time zones away. This distance has forced Todd and Danielle to automate their business as much as possible.

Keenly focused on growth areas within the Canadian market (they look for higher-than-average appreciation in areas of renewal combined with infrastructure and transit improvements), the Millars plan to double their portfolio by the end of 2007. That's aggressive, admits Danielle, 34, who figures they'll reach their target of owning more than 100 properties by the end of 2009.

"I think one of our skills is the ability to look at deals from a distance and really analyze what works and what doesn't. Part of our success is due to the research we run on our properties and the fact that we're often not there to look at the buildings and add emotion to the decision," says Danielle. "Analyzing deals from a distance makes us sharper. We do more due diligence, and that safeguards us and our partners."

With one eye on their exit strategy, their purchases are all located in the middle-class-plus neighbourhoods where new homeowners, families, executives and maybe even a few retirees will be looking to buy in the future.

"Todd and I have been in many unusual situations in all our travels," says Danielle. "But building this business from the ground up has been one of the strongest bonding experiences ever."

"I think our 'life dream' turned into our 'real estate dream,'" adds Todd. But with seven years of hard work behind them, including lots of late nights and early mornings (negotiations can be complicated when there's a full 15 hours' difference in time zones!), they remain committed to love, life and the business of real estate investment.

Down the road, they envision a family home in Edmonton (near Danielle's parents in Leduc), an island home on Vancouver Island (where they lived for seven years before moving to Japan) and the financial freedom to travel with their future children (whose grandparents hail from Barbados, South Africa and Scotland).

Topping that list, however, is a business goal that makes all the rest possible. "First and foremost, we want to make our JV partners successful," says Danielle.

—❦—

Don Campbell's Observations

There is an old and very wrong theory that floats around unsophisticated real estate investors, and that is to make sure you invest only within a one-hour driving radius from where you live. Well, if that were true, Todd and Danielle would be having a tough go of it rather than creating the amazing results they have so far.

What would happen if the region, encompassed in that one-hour radius, had poor investment fundamentals? Are you supposed to invest anyway, or on the other hand not invest in real estate at all? I don't think so. The key is to find a region that has strong economic fundamentals, no matter how far a drive, then find or develop a system that will allow your money to work harder in that region than you do.

Todd and Danielle teach us a lesson that we should all pay attention to even if we do happen to be investing right in our own backyard. That lesson is to develop systems and relationships to support your investment business. Just because you may live within driving distance doesn't mean you have to do all of the day-to-day work and nor should you. Your focus, like Todd and Danielle's, is best applied to building the key relationships in your business and finding properties to invest in.

Distance can also be your friend. Not having easy access to the property keeps you from continually driving by and obsessing about every little detail. Distance also forces us not to fall in love with a property just because of the way it looks. Both of these mistakes can lead us to make poor decisions. When distance enters the equation, investors are forced to look at the number and the numbers only, thus forcibly removing emotions from the equation.

Find ways in which to make your money work harder than you do by finding regions with strong economic fundamentals, no matter where they are located in Canada. Then once you identify the region, develop the relationships and follow a proven system to make it work.

ACTION STEPS

1. If you could invest your money in any property in any part of the country, where specifically would that be?

    _____

    _____

    _____

    _____

2. Are some of your current real estate investments located in this region?

    _____

    _____

    _____

    _____

3. If you're not sure of the answer to number 1 above, what unbiased resources will you tap into to find the answer?

    _____

    _____

    _____

    _____

SUCCESS STORY #44

Focus on the Numbers—They'll Take You Where You Want to Go

Daryl Zelinski

You have to keep running the numbers. You can sell a property and use the cash to buy more, or you can keep that property, leverage its value, and keep it working for you—while you buy more.

Forget all the talk about how pride comes before a fall. Real estate investor Daryl Zelinski figures pride has cost him cold hard cash that he could have earned through capital appreciation.

The corporate sales manager for the Edmonton Oilers Hockey Club, Daryl grew up watching his dad buy and sell real estate for a living in their home town of Whitecourt, Alberta. He and his brother Murray (now a realtor and an investor) also earned some of their first cash doing odd jobs associated with their dad's personal portfolio.

In 2000, the three teamed up to buy a rental property in Stony Plain, 15 minutes west of Edmonton. By investing together, they shared the risk of that first purchase. Since then, they've bought more properties together and other properties on their own. By July 2007, Daryl's own portfolio included 19 properties, most single-family homes in Edmonton and Stony Plain, plus a 17-unit apartment building in Whitecourt that he owns with his dad and brother. He and his dad are also completing a fourplex for the Whitecourt market. It should be open for business by the middle of 2008.

"I tell people real estate investment is the best thing I could have done for my family," says Daryl. That family now includes his wife, Julie, and their infant son. At this point, he tries to take care of the maintenance work himself while hiring out the major repairs, but still handles the nitty-gritty details of his own property management—which demands sacrifices in terms of time and labour. "It's tough to come home from a weekend camping trip and have 10 calls that need your attention," he admits. "But I look at it and say if it was easy, everybody would be doing it. At this point, I like meeting my tenants face-to-face, it helps me decide if I think they're the kind of people who will look after the place."

Like others already active in a prosperous market, Daryl's only regrets about real estate investment tend to revolve around the fact he didn't buy more before prices in the Edmonton market rose by 30% to 50% over the course of 2006–2007. "But who could have predicted the market would go up as fast as it did?" he asks.

Intertwined with those regrets is the knowledge he lost some deals because he got caught up in the excitement of the negotiation and traded, in the heat of the moment, a win-win strategy for one proudly based on "Me Not Losing." "I can't believe I let deals go over something as little as $2,000, or because the vendor would not include the washer and dryer," says Daryl with hindsight. One of those deals could have been his for $208,000, $2,000 more than his top offer. Less than two years later, that "property is probably worth $500,000."

In 2006, he took a bit of a break from buying real estate to focus on his wedding. He got into the fourplex (now under construction) in 2007 and he and his wife, Julie, took some time to settle into their acreage home on a golf course near St. Albert, just minutes from the Edmonton city limits. With all of the market fundamentals still making leveraged property a good deal, Daryl's in the market for more property—and looking forward to the passive income that's starting to come his way thanks to early purchases.

"We could have sold one property to put a down payment on our primary residence," says Daryl, "but if you run the numbers, it's better to borrow the money and let the property you could have sold keep covering its own payments and appreciate in equity. If you can make your properties pay for themselves, they're all yours, and you'll eventually own them free and clear."

Daryl figures passive income will one day give his family the financial freedom to make family time a priority and he looks forward to mirroring Julie's work schedule. A consultant with a local board of education, she gets extended Christmas and spring breaks, plus two months off in the summer. "I'd like to be able to work out a similar pattern," Daryl says.

With great deals tougher to find at the single-family level, he's looking at larger properties and more apartments. "It's kind of like playing Monopoly," Daryl admits, "but real."

Don Campbell's Observations

One of the messages from this story is that, even with a full time, high-pressure job you can create a solid real estate portfolio. Many believe that they must quit their job in order to get to their dream more quickly. Well, in most cases this not true, and quitting your job could hinder your ability to acquire properties, as banks love the security of jobs when they are approving mortgages for you.

Sure Daryl has regrets; most investors do. However, he has not allowed these "if only" thoughts to hold him back from looking to the future. I have noticed that those who live in the past focusing on what they could have done are destined to do nothing in their lives. Those, like Daryl, who are honest with themselves and openly acknowledge that there are regrets use these missed opportunities as motivators to move boldly forward. You can't change the past—you can only change the future.

ACTION STEPS

1. Be honest and ask yourself: "What past actions or beliefs are you allowing to hold yourself back?"

   _____

   _____

   _____

   _____

2. How are you going to turn this from an anchor into a motivator in your life?

   _____

   _____

   _____

   _____

3. Who are you going to ask to support you in this change?

   _____

   _____

   Start date for this change: _____

SUCCESS STORY #45
REAL ESTATE GRABBED HIM AT ONLY 16 YEARS OLD

Wally Janzen

I always try to stay ahead of the competition. So far, it's been working.

When 16-year-old Wally Janzen wanted to buy the neighbour's house as an investment property, people told him he was crazy. In the 30 years since, he's bought enough property to house 350 post-secondary school students in Ontario. He'd added another 100 doors in Edmonton, Alberta. by the middle of 2007. Crazy? Not by a long shot. Happy? Absolutely.

This spring, Wally, 47, celebrated his business success with a special purchase. A silver anniversary edition of the Acura MDX, marketed as the "driver's SUV," sits in the family driveway. Wally couldn't park it in the garage if he wanted to. That space has been converted to an office for him and Melanie, his wife and business partner. They've also got space for their real estate investment business's full-time computer specialist and part-time bookkeeper. The property manager comes in, too (usually on the days the bookkeeper's not using her desk).

"It's probably not big enough," concedes Wally, "but moving is not really an option." For one thing, the garage sits on three-quarters of spectacular land near the Niagara escarpment. It's also the home Melanie has lived in all of her life and the converted office, complete with a fireplace, is just 10 minutes away from the couple's 35 Ontario properties.

A former farm-labourer-turned-market-owner, Wally got into real estate soon after he decided to live what he calls "a mentored life" in 1998. He's still part of a mentor group that meets regularly and says greater awareness of why it's important to find people who share your interests also led him to join REIN, where he can be around people similarly enthused about real estate investment.

The first revenue property he bought was, in retrospect, a mistake. Still, he made money on the deal—and learned you can only call yourself a real estate investor once you're actually buying property.

Following a model whereby his portfolio holds the same number of properties, but increases its "per door" count, Wally built a stable of student housing in the St. Catharines area. Once he hit 75 students, he hired a property manager, a decision that let him concentrate on buying instead of managing properties.

Today, that part of his portfolio is managed by two full-time property managers, both committed to helping the company retain its share of a unique and highly-competitive market, where leases run May 1 to April 30. The trick is to "always try to stay ahead of the competition," says Wally. "I was one of the first to include utilities, then cable and Internet. Now everyone does that and so now we're upgrading our units with new windows, carpets and bathrooms. When there is a glut of these spaces on the market, the best units go first."

By 2008, he plans to have stepped up his web presence. Prospective tenants will even be able to take virtual tours of some rooms. Another step ahead of the competition.

Wally gets a kick out of people who think real estate investment is too complicated. While experience is a great teacher, he says, "You don't have to know everything. You just need to know where you can go for help, or to learn what you need to know."

Even with his success in his local Ontario market, that learn-and-then-go-for-it mentality led Wally to Edmonton in the fall of 2006. The market appealed to him because of the economics supporting the market. He duplicated the systems he developed in Ontario in this new market—no need to reinvent the wheel. An advocate of quality property management, he's bought poorly managed buildings and turned them around. He'd also tried his hand at development and learned that it wasn't for him. ("Everything just takes so long.") The Edmonton market gave him a chance to do what he does best: negotiate good deals for revenue property with a bright financial future.

His first full day in Edmonton locked up a deal for an apartment building that real estate agents valued at $75,000 a door. Wally negotiated a deal to pay $50,000 for each of 23 units, then sold them through an agent for considerably more, making $180,000; not bad for a guy who literally stepped off the plane in a city he'd never visited before, bought a map and a newspaper, and went to work. Following those kind of results, he's been in Edmonton a couple of times a month ever since, where he's completed condo conversions and re-sales.

"The toughest thing is finding the right financing," he says, "but even that gets easier. At first, it was all about my good credit. It got more complicated when I started doing bigger deals, so I had joint venture partners coming in with money."

Some of those JVs were years in the making. "I tell people you don't ask someone if they're interested in a joint venture partnership and take 'no' for an answer. People need a lot of information, especially if they're new to investing. I talk to people again and again."

Even keen JV partners can be complicated, adds Wally. One partner helped him finance seven buildings in about 18 months. "But he's the kind of guy who needs a paycheque to see where his money is going. He couldn't stick with it for the long term, so that partnership ended."

Wally admits his life is more successful than he ever expected. He remembers the days when he used to write "I want to buy big buildings" as part of a goal-setting exercise. Other times, "I thought it would be cool to get up in the morning and say, 'Which house should I work on today?' I feel like I got my wish."

The father of two teenagers, Wally often tells his kids, "I don't really care what you do. But if you don't love it, don't do it. I remember the days when I woke up and didn't want to go to work. Now, I'm happy."

Don Campbell's Observations

Wally and Melanie have the true entrepreneurial spirit, encompassed by the term "Let's go make it work and have fun doing it!" Their sense of perspective is quite unique. What he doesn't tell you in this story is that the Acura that they bought to celebrate their accomplishments cost the same as one of their first investment properties so many years ago.

Celebrating the steps along the path is a very important habit to build into your life. Whether it is an accomplishment at your job, in your business or in your real estate, make sure you acknowledge the accomplishment. Too many people wait until the end of a project to celebrate—why wait? Taking small celebrations helps make your life journey much more enjoyable. Small celebrations that others enjoy include dinner out with their favourite person, a quiet hour to themselves at a spa or coffee shop, going to their favorite beach in the middle of the week, or buying an expensive ticket to an event they really want to see but couldn't usually justify. The side benefit of holding these small celebrations is that you program your brain to create positive outcomes so that you receive the reward.

You can celebrate any accomplishment you want; the key is finding a way to make your life a series of small and large treats for yourself and your family. From finally cleaning out your garage, to sticking with your new exercise routine for seven days straight, to getting your next property's offer-to-purchase accepted by a vendor, the accomplishment is up to you. A side secret: You can often get a much better seat in a restaurant if you tell them that you're "celebrating." You don't have to tell them you're celebrating the cleanliness of your garage (they might think you're a little daft!). Don't wait for a huge accomplishment. It may never come in the form you're expecting it. Find something in your life right now to mark as an accomplishment; life is too short to wait.

The other myth that Wally has busted is the myth of the "student renter." He and Melanie have developed their systems so that they can handle 350 post-secondary students as their tenants. They identified their niche, bought their properties in areas where their niche market wanted to live and then kept duplicating their successes and fixing their mistakes. Despite what the average person believes, students can make wonderful renters. You can know this for sure by considering two obvious facts:

1. If you went to a post-secondary institution and you lived off-campus, did you destroy the property you lived in? I didn't think so. I bet if you asked most now graduated college students 99 out of 100 would tell you the same. Sure we were younger then and may not have treated it like the house we now own and live in; however, all rental properties take some form of wear and tear. Don't buy into the fear around investing in student housing; just build your system to handle it.

2. If it didn't make sense, do you think that Wally would have continued to add to their portfolio of student rentals? No, I don't think so either. There are many options out there for a person of his spirit.

Never believe generalities, especially if the generality is considered to be common knowledge. If it is considered common knowledge, especially if it is negative, you will often find that it holds massive opportunity for you, if you're willing to be contrarian.

ACTION STEPS

1. List three *small indulgences* you will reward yourself with to celebrate the small victories along the way.

   _____

   _____

   _____

   _____

2. List three *small accomplishments* you'd really like to achieve soon and use the list above to say what you're going to do when you complete the task (one must be something you already accomplished so you can celebrate right now).

   _____

   _____

   _____

   _____

3. List three large *indulgences* you will reward yourself with to celebrate major milestones in your life and your real estate investments.

   _____

   _____

   _____

   _____

4. List three *large accomplishments* you'd really like to achieve in the next two years and use the list above to say what you're going to do when you complete the task.

   _____

   _____

   _____

   _____

SUCCESS STORY #46
THE ULTIMATE SYSTEMIZER

Tony Peters

It's never too late to get involved with real estate investing. The key is to educate yourself—and then take action.

The first day of the summer of 2007 dawned hot and sunny. It was the kind of weather residents yearn for after a cold, snowy winter and wind-swept, wet spring. But Tony Peters was a little too busy to take much note. He was, after all, the guy behind the summer launch of a lease-to-own residential real estate company selling franchises to real estate investors across the nation. It was part of a personal promise to help 3,333 people realize the ultimate dream of owning their own homes. Tony was making it happen.

Tony, 46, got into the residential real estate business for entirely per-sonal reasons. In 2001, with more than 18 years of experience with the same company in the industrial construction industry, he left a manage-ment position and took some time off to spend with his family. "My life lacked balance," he says. "I knew I wanted to work, but I didn't want to work the way I had been working."

By that fall, he and his wife Jo-Ann were signed up for their first Quickstart program. Tony had already attended it. "I realized she needed to be there, too," he says. "I wasn't going to come back and do a sales pitch. If this was something we were going to do, it was important that we do it together."

Within weeks of that first Quickstart, they were buying property, with Tony headlining the property searches and acquisitions and Jo-Ann handling the books. They had transacted 150 revenue and lease-to-own properties by mid-2007 and were holding about 60 doors. They were also going full steam ahead on their plans to franchise Creative Housing Solutions Canada, the lease-to-own company they started in 2003.

Creating a Canadian version of a successful U.S.-based investment strategy, Tony and Jo-Ann had helped more than 50 renters buy their principal residences. By 2005, Tony was fielding a growing number of requests from others who wanted to use his approach. He liked the idea of sharing strategies, but was concerned about quality control. While the lease-to-own investment strategy isn't for everyone, Tony liked knowing he and Jo-Ann were making a real difference in people's lives. "With me," he explains, "it's not just about the investment dollar. It's not just about the house. It's about the people who want to buy that house."

Other people's interest in his own business success story made Tony realize he had a replicable product. He spent a year on legal issues and branding, then rolled the first franchises out in 2007. He figures there could be 10 to 12 across Canada by the end of 2007, 50 by the end of 2008 and 100 by the end of 2009. Tony's vision also includes taking his business model onto the international stage.

"There is a lot of interest," he acknowledges, "but it takes time to make sure we have the right people doing it for the right reason. Yes, they'll make money doing it our way, but they will also help others in the process." A creative way in which he can achieve his goal of helping 3,333 people across the country.

With his own kids now 11 and 14, that sense of altruism is more important than ever. Both kids own property and have portfolios that benefited from equity appreciation. "But," Tony underlines, "they also understand why it's important to help other people, too."

The commitment to help is why Tony asks those looking to buy a franchise if they are currently involved with, or are willing to be involved with, a charitable group or non-profit organization. He readily admits it's a due diligence question that might strike some potential franchisees as odd. He also knows it's a quick way to disqualify those who see the lease-to-own market as a way to take advantage of renters struggling to buy their own homes.

As franchisees come on board, Tony expects he'll focus increasingly more attention on helping this new group of entrepreneurs be successful. While he's busy doing that, he and Jo-Ann's portfolio will be busy doing its own thing, too. In other words, it'll be generating cash flow and equity appreciation. "That's what happens," Tony concludes, "when you take control of your own financial future."

Don Campbell's Observations

Tony left a solid job with no plans for the future. He decided that after 18 years it was time to review his life and spend some time with his family. Little did he know it would lead to building a family business based on providing housing for 3,333 people across Canada.

As we wander down the road of life, we often don't even see the forks in the road because we're too busy getting through the week. Have you ever noticed that when you do take time for yourself, for instance, a long holiday, your perspective of life begins to change? You start to see that there are options out there for you and your family.

This perspective also comes when a traumatic event occurs within our close circle of family or friends. We start to think about options we would never have considered. The lesson here is to *not* wait for a traumatic experience to occur. Start today to take specific time to sit back and look at what you have and the path you're on.

Imagine the reaction of his friends and ex-co-workers when he announced that he was going to change paths so he could help 3,333 people own their own home. You can just imagine how many people thought he had lost it. And now, here he is just a few years later and he is on the brink of launching a business that will achieve this outrageous goal. This is the second lesson we can garner from Tony's story. Set your goals high and then figure a way in which to make it happen . . . and don't let anyone steal your dream or dissuade you from it. Even if you don't hit the exact target, you will achieve more than if you set an easy target.

As Tony and Jo-Ann achieve their major goals, systems will play a major role in helping them hit their targets. Without the work they've put into their system, their chance of hitting the 3,333 target would be slim. But now that their systems are developed there are bound to be more than 3,333 smiling faces across the country.

ACTION STEPS

1. Do you believe your goals are big enough?

   _____

   _____

   _____

2. Which ones can you increase to make it just a little uncomfortable?

_____

_____

_____

3. How will you feel when you achieve these new goals?

_____

_____

_____

4. With this new level of goals, even if you don't quite achieve these new goals, you may still outperform your old goals. Will you be okay with this?

_____

_____

_____

SUCCESS STORY #47
ONE WORD: FREEDOM

Valerie Pawluk

What have I learned? Well, I learned never to let a vendor fill a suite just before I take over a property. There's no substitute for your own due diligence.

The door knobs used for interior doors in the 1970s residential construction industry are not the same size as those sold today. Valerie Pawluk knows. Indeed, she had four hours to think about it when she replaced the door knobs in a renovated home she and a joint venture partner were readying for market. She thought the job would take half an hour.

Valerie stuck with the task because she'd agreed to do it. Every hour spent in that house meant 60 more minutes thinking about all the great reasons she and her partner should hang onto it for long-term appreciation. But her partner's heart wasn't in it. "I thought it was more important to honour the agreement we'd made," says Valerie, "than to try and talk her into something else. A partnership is never about one person."

A farm girl turned teacher, Valerie married Grant Simpson in 1996. By then, she'd taught in two communities, finished a master's degree and was doing some substitute teaching. She started reading about real estate investment in early 2002, a couple of years after their son was born. That led her to a Quickstart program. In January she bought her first property: a four-suite house near the university. Before the year closed, she added a second property with four units, plus basement suites.

The second deal tallied $650,000 and involved some joint venture partners. "It was hard, because it took so much more money than I would have anticipated," explains Valerie. "But once I stumbled on the deal, I wanted to make it work."

Before long, she also owned a single-family home with two suites. Located near Edmonton's trendy Whyte Avenue, she bought it knowing it had all the markings of a quality revenue property.

The house she and a JV bought to renovate and re-sell, sold in August 2006 for a tidy profit. About the same time that deal wrapped up, Valerie bought another single-family home and a condo. Before long, economic indicators had her looking north to Grande Prairie and, by late August 2007, she owned revenue properties in that booming community. "Properties are a bit cheaper there [than in Edmonton] and rents are a bit higher," she says. Valerie anticipates bringing joint venture partners into the Grande Prairie deal.

In the meantime, she's also got a deposit on a condominium being built in Calgary's downtown core. "That may be a build-and-hold, but appreciation is also good there, so it's too early to say for sure. I'm just pleased the builder is sticking to his price because we got into that deal two years ago."

Valerie figures she'll be in acquisition mode for another five years and admits her earlier angst has diminished with practice and success. "I love buying property now. I didn't think I was going to enjoy it this much. Even though we haven't realized a lot of the profits, we can see on paper that we're doing quite well."

In 2006, however, Valerie realized that a decision to self-manage her properties was keeping her from acquiring more property, which is what she really loves to do. She set a business deadline, then followed through and hired two property management companies in 2007. One takes care of her Edmonton properties. The other handles Grande Prairie.

She also asked her husband to join REIN in 2006. Grant wasn't planning to give up his work as a business manager and chief financial officer for a group of companies, but Valerie appreciated his support of their growing portfolio and she wanted him to get, first-hand, the economic data she was bringing home from REIN meetings. "I would get so excited about what I was hearing," she remembers, "and I wanted him to hear it in that same environment."

Some of Valerie's toughest experiences were delivered by the hands of poorly chosen tenants. Those experiences have refined the way she screens tenants and, while no system is infallible, Valerie says she does a good job of finding good tenants if she sticks with her screening system. "You can negotiate almost anything if you're working with someone who is reasonable."

This past year brought home the risks associated with investments that take her into, what REIN terms, "grey areas." When she encountered problems with a tenant's smoking and he proved unwilling to change his habits, Valerie issued an eviction notice. The tenant countered by calling the City of Edmonton to report Valerie's nonconforming suite.

The end result is costly, since she lost $800 in monthly revenue. Capital appreciation is still at work, but there's less money to aid mortgage payments and cash flow. "I'll take less money," she reflects, "but gain some peace and control over who's living there." She'll also pay more attention next time around and she won't calculate grey-area income into her business plan.

In the meantime, she continues to love her new profession. "Investing, for me, is like a creative venture. I like working on the deal and then moving onto the next one."

She also likes knowing she has a direct hand in her family's future. "Freedom—if I had just one word to describe what real estate investing has done for me, that would be it. This is the tool that will lead to financial freedom and time freedom."

⋙

Don Campbell's Observations

Valerie now has the freedom to do what she enjoys doing, and that is being a full-time real estate investor. But Valerie also understands the need for balance. She says she enjoys the process and the creativity of the deals. You can see the passion she has for it. However, she also has a life.

Being a "full-time" investor is a bit of a misnomer because, once you have your investment and management systems in place, it is next to impossible to spend "full-time" 40-plus hours a week on your investment portfolio. You have a system that helps you save your time, your energy and your capital. Once you do progress to being a "full-time" real estate investor, the key is that you make a conscious effort not to fill up your week with tasks. This is especially important for those who come from working a 40-plus hour-per-week job and progress to being a real estate entrepreneur. Real estate investing is not meant to be a time-consuming process; let your systems and relationships take care of things for you. As a real estate entrepreneur, there will be weeks where you've never worked so hard in your life as you are analyzing and closing a big deal or solving a problem. However, most weeks you should be able to have the time and freedom to pursue what you want to pursue in life.

And this is a problem many come up against, "What do I do with my new-found time?" Because of our North American societal upbringing, we're trained to be busy all the time. Busy is good, it's productive—that's what has been drummed into our heads since we started working. And now, once your portfolio is large enough to support you and your family, you decide to focus all of your efforts on your real estate. Suddenly you start fighting the Time Bandits, those thoughts of having to stay busy and accessible all the time, in case you miss a deal. Or even worse, you get everything you need done early in the week; but rather than going out and living your life, you fill the rest of the week's time with real estate activities.

But what about life? It is the stated goal of most Canadians to have the freedom to choose what to do every day. Then when they get it, often guilt drives them to make tasks fill the time, rather than getting work done and then going on to follow other passions. For many, real estate is their passion, so that is a wonderful pursuit. For others, real estate is just a financial vehicle to get them to freedom so they can follow their passion. Bottom line: make sure you are honest with yourself about your passions in life and how you are going to manage your "full-time" real estate business if you get there. Remember: full time is not fill time.

A second valuable lesson we learn from Valerie is her sticking to her agreements even when it hurts a bit. Valerie has created a reputation for herself as someone who does what she says she'll do, which is really quite rare in society. Sometimes it hurts having to live up to an agreement that you didn't think all the way through at the beginning, but it sure teaches a lesson on not making agreements without careful thought.

Having systems to follow, an upstanding and trusted reputation and a passion for life are the catalysts for long-term success. Valerie has them all lined up and she's only just begun this journey.

ACTION STEPS

1. What three agreements or commitments have you made (large or small) that you are considering not fulfilling because it is too much work, too much effort or will cost you money?

    _____

    _____

    _____

_____

_____

2. Rather than not fulfill these obligations, what other options do you
    have that will help save your reputation?

    _____

    _____

    _____

    _____

    _____

    Once you start pushing yourself to do what you say you'll do, you'll
discover that you are much more careful about making commitments. The
fewer commitments you make, the more you will keep and the stronger
your overall reputation will become.

SUCCESS STORY #48
THE BALANCED PORTFOLIO STRATEGY—
A SHORTCUT TO SUCCESS

Shamim Rajan and Aman Rajan

*Real estate investment is one of those things that takes practice. But the
more you practise, the better you get.*

Shamim and Aman Rajan spent one month of their summer holiday in the
African country of Tanzania with their 10-year-old son at their side. Well,
that's not quite true, since anyone who meets Bilaal soon learns he's the
kind of kid who makes you run if you want to keep up!

Bilaal is quite an achiever. Even at his young age, he has conceived of
ideas that benefit UNICEF Canada's work in the world. The precocious
young Torontonian started raising money for international relief efforts
several years ago, partly through his own website: www.handsforhelp.org.
This summer's trip to Africa was a little different in that the whole family
spent a month working with non-governmental organizations dedicated
to improving life for Tanzania's poor. They also carried with them rapid
testing kits to test for HIV/AIDS. They were donated by a Canadian company and the Rajans gave them to an agency to hand out to those unable
or afraid to go to clinics. "I think we learn more from Bilaal than he learns
from us," concedes his mom, Shamim. "He inspires us to do things we
might not have done without his example."

In fairness, the example set by his parents has been strong, especially
since it includes teaching Bilaal about the benefits of the long-term wealth
generated by real estate investment. "He's done pretty good with his own
personal money and has a share in four condominiums," says Aman.

Those condos are part of a portfolio of 30 titles held by the family.
In Ontario Aman also runs a successful company that sells healthy food
products to educational institutions and related educational programs and
special events. Aman reckons that the venture records annual sales in the
seven-figure range. "Systems make all of the difference," he adds.

They also free his time to focus on a real estate portfolio that began
with what they now view was a kind of "haphazard" approach to investment with the purchase of a one-bedroom residential condo in Toronto's

Harbourfront area. With Toronto's condo market changing as more units came on line, they sold the property in 2005, not long after Shamim attended her first Real Estate Investment Network meeting and came home to tell Aman, "This is the system we've been looking for."

"Our investment business has grown by leaps and bounds," says Aman, describing their progress since Shamim's discovery of REIN. "I would say the turning point came when we ventured out of our geographic location; that was our springboard because it forced us to set up systems and to recognize that we were running a business which could generate significant long-term wealth, even though its assets were a long way away."

In 2007, Shamim and a fellow investor, Arden Dalik, formed Wealth Launch Investments. It sources JV partners to purchase multi-family properties, but enables each to build their own portfolios, too.

Running the business from a distance means Shamim makes regular trips out west, usually tying them to REIN meetings where she can build their investment network and check in on the western portion of their portfolio. "Edmonton has been very big for us, but we're always trying to investigate new areas of opportunity, too," she explains.

She and Aman are especially grateful for the way their knowledge of real estate investment has helped her brother invest. "Other family members are also coming to us and asking for help and advice," says Shamim. "In the beginning, it was kind of a tough slog to get people to come and invest with us. Now they're asking us, 'Where do we go next?'"

The first deal in Alberta was likely the toughest, she concedes, "but once we'd worked out the details, the confidence in what we were doing spread like wildfire."

But the Rajans do more than talk about their investments and seek joint venture partners; they also encourage others to start investing themselves. Last year, they paid for one person to attend his first Quickstart seminar in Ontario. In 2007, they will cover Quickstart fees for three people. They don't want to know the names of those who benefited from their generosity. "We think of it as a kind of scholarship," says Shamim.

"We know what real estate investment has meant to us. We just want to share that," adds Aman.

Don Campbell's Observations

Aman and Shamim have what would be called a balanced portfolio. They discovered that by spreading their investments in different geographic areas, they can develop a portfolio of properties that has the best of both worlds, strong cash flow and strong equity appreciation. They have placed some of their investment funds into Top 10 Ontario Towns in order to create strong current cash flow, while at the same time placing other funds into Top 10 Alberta Towns to take advantage of the strong equity appreciation.

They discovered this by paying attention to the economic fundamentals supporting each market. It usually takes three years for an investor's portfolio to begin performing well. With their balanced approach, the Rajans will shorten this timeline.

Because they're investing at a distance, having proven systems to follow, combined with strong relationships with professionals in each geographic area, is absolutely critical. In fact, I'd hazard to say that without these two components, their portfolio would not perform well at all.

Identifying the value of combining forces with someone who has different talents and expertise, their business truly began to take off. A great lesson, they found someone whose talents didn't match theirs; each party in the partnership brings their own unique assets, knowledge and expertise.

As they readily admit, their amazing 10-year-old son keeps them motivated. The difference he is making in other people's lives through his work with UNICEF is an eye-opener for anyone who wants to have an impact. Now that the Rajans' real estate business is doing so well, they're finding ways to help others, ranging from working with the disadvantaged to providing full Quickstart scholarships for up-and-coming real estate investors.

For the Rajans, as it should be for all real estate investors, real estate is just a vehicle to get them to where they want to be—to a position of making a difference in many people's lives.

ACTION STEPS

1. Who could you help get a head start on a financial education?

_____

_____

_____

2. How will you help them, starting today? (Books, courses, face to face?)

_____

_____

_____

_____

SUCCESS STORY #49
THE FIRST DEAL IS THE SCARIEST

Jas Kullar

Hot tips are great. But they are a poor excuse for due diligence.

Jas Kullar remembers his first deal like it was yesterday. But the memory is far from sweet. He figures the deal cost two-thirds of his $25,000 investment when the stock in a public company selling a real estate development hit the market—and collapsed. Compounding that stress was the fact that his parents gave him another $50,000 to invest in the same deal. "Consequently, they, too, lost two-thirds of their investment," says Jas.

The financial hit came as he struggled to find work not long after graduating from university. An accounting major, he entered the job market during an economic slump in 1994. Making things worse, the few jobs he landed that were related to his field didn't move him towards his dream job at all. Indeed, he was starting to realize he'd probably spent his university days walking down the wrong path!

Born in the U.K. and raised in Canada, Jas returned to Great Britain for his post-secondary education. He returned to Canada after he graduated from university, and it was four years before he got a job that felt like it had a future. In May 1998, he flew to Toronto for an interview and landed a position as a territory sales manager with a company that named him its Western Canadian rep. It was a world away from his accounting background, and it felt good. His first change of course . . . but not his last!

Able to work from virtually anywhere in Western Canada, he married and moved to Vancouver in April 2000. The job was interesting, but kept him on the road for days at a time. He was getting the experience he needed for career advancement, but felt robbed of time with his new wife, Kinder.

Filled with a growing sense of the need to do things that genuinely interest you, he moved to a pharmaceutical sales position in 2003. Change, of course, number two. With B.C.'s beautiful Fraser Valley as his territory, he left home in the morning and was home by nightfall. He was finally doing what he enjoyed, and able to see his family every day.

The job change came as Jas reinvestigated real estate investment as a long-term strategy to build wealth. By the spring of 2004, with their first baby on the way, he and Kinder opted to sell their condo in Burnaby and build a home in Surrey. They'd watched other young couples make similar investments, so they undertook the move with confidence.

Things didn't go as planned. The project took longer when several contractors proved less reliable than expected, and they eventually found themselves moving into a home that wasn't finished. The move was further complicated by the fact they made it with baby Aneil, a son born two months early, in their arms.

With hindsight, Jas figures the move up was a good way to build equity. But if he ever moves into a new home again, he will make sure a contractor handles all of the details. His big lesson? "'Never do something you can get someone else to do better.' That's what I learned building our house." As he sees it, at least some of the problems resulted from misguided efforts to save money. "Ultimately, you chase the money and that keeps you from doing what you should be doing."

As that realization was dawning over the course of 2005, Jas journeyed to a local bookstore to hear Don Campbell talk about his book *Real Estate Investing in Canada*. "Campbell challenged my thinking. I grew up believing you made money by saving money. He was talking about spending money to learn about making money, but it made sense, especially when he talked about economic fundamentals."

Jas joined REIN that November, attending his first meeting the night of Aneil's first birthday. Four months later, he bought his first revenue property, launching an investment business that held nine properties by mid-2007. The package includes five townhouses and two bungalows with four of the deals involving a joint venture partner.

"I have a property manager take care of the property and the tenants," notes Jas as he remembers his quote "Never do something you can get someone else to do better." While he doesn't always view a property before he buys, he does get his Edmonton-dwelling dad to take a look and to tag alongside the property inspector Jas hires as part of the deal.

"The first deal was probably the scariest," Jas concedes. Since then, he figures his family's net worth has already risen about $200,000. "I am highly leveraged right now, but you can't get something for nothing, and I can see long-term wealth building in those properties."

Short-term management of the portfolio means they'll be in their current home for at least five years, several years longer than intended in their original plan, which was made before they bought revenue property. Kinder is trying to work part-time, a schedule that still allows her the time to take Aneil to various medical appointments related to his premature birth.

Investing and Aneil's arrival, says Jas, "have changed the way I look at life. I used to focus on problems and now I look for solutions. I think that everything happens for a reason, and when I look back on my life, I can see how things have benefited me—even if it didn't seem like it at the beginning."

Applying that same approach to the future, Jas dreams of the day Kinder can be home full-time. But he's more focused on the present, a point of view that reminds him that sacrifices today pay off in the future. "I like the philosophy that you can get ahead by doing, for five years, what others will not do for one."

Don Campbell's Observations

Jas changed his life two times until he found the lifestyle he was looking for, while many are afraid to do it even once. The key is to develop that compelling vision, the ultimate goal you wish to create in your life. Once you have this firmly planted in your psyche, you can make all your decisions based on whether the choice takes you closer or further away from your dream.

Another important lesson Jas teaches us is to acknowledge your strengths and never do something that someone else can do better or more cheaply. His team, which includes his dad providing a second pair of eyes, is critical in his success. Without people he trusts to carry out key tasks, Jas would not have any time for his family or for future investments, which would dramatically hinder his ability to fulfill his vision.

One thing you do need to remember when delegating tasks to others is that ultimately you are 100% responsible for that property and your joint venture partner's money. So you must manage the managers and the team members through clear communications and direction. Acknowledge them when things go exceptionally well, and when, inevitably, things go sideways take swift immediate action to assist them in fixing the problem, even if you believe they are solely responsible. Ultimately, the buck stops with you. So grab control of a problem early so it does not escalate.

Developing systems is a cornerstone of any successful investor, whether they invest locally or afar. Jas knows this from his past training in accounting. So even when he changed paths away from accounting, he brought his education with him and now focuses on creating a cookie-cutter style of investing designed to protect his joint venture partners.

Jas and Kinder are on their success path, with their family focus continuing to be number one. They know the road is not straight and smooth, but the destination makes the journey worth the effort.

SUCCESS STORY #50
An Oasis in His Personal Belize

Dan Barton and Greg Gillespie

We trust the system we use to select properties that work. In fact, I've reached the point where I sometimes feel I'm doing a disservice if I don't sell a joint venture partner on a particular piece of property. That's how much I believe in what I'm doing.

Entire books have been written about the "hows" and "whys" of the corporate name game. Dan Barton sought his inspiration from a different kind of experience. Asked to think about where his real estate investment company would take him, the 22-year-old waiter and investor wannabe closed his eyes and visualized a tropical island paradise, a beachfront home on the Australian coast and a sophisticated, comfortable place to hang his hat in beautiful Victoria, B.C., the city he calls home even though his growing investment portfolio lies east of the Rocky Mountains.

The end result of his careful musings? A company called Oasis Properties and a downright clear vision of what he needs to do to achieve his "Personal Belize." Less than a year later, he used that vision to welcome a full-time business partner named Greg Gillespie—a young university-educated father who says real estate investment is giving him a chance to live the life he's always wanted but didn't know where to find.

Dan bought his first property right after taking a Quickstart program in 2005. (He actually tendered his first offer during the weekend workshop. It wasn't successful, but the experience boosted his confidence to take more action.) With his mother as his joint venture partner, he soon bought a property with two suites and a double car garage in a neighbourhood going through renewal, then rented out both suites, plus the garage separately. "I followed the specific strategy all the way and today now have a cash flow of $750 a month from this property alone," says Dan.

Two years later, the Oasis portfolio features more than 40 rental suites. All but two of the properties are professionally managed, and Dan figures the company's joint venture list tallies over 17 names, with several JVs in on more than one property. "I find most of our partners in B.C., because people have so much home equity here."

Which doesn't mean the JV is always an easy sell. "I talk to people about the fact they have $300,000 in dead equity just sitting in their homes. Some can't do it at first, but those same people tend to go away, do some research, then come back to me a year later."

The fact that people take some time to think about investing in real estate is okay with Dan, who bought his first property while working for a trendy bar and grill in downtown Victoria. He got that job after working for a year after high school, then travelling to Australia. He loved the trip, but learned a big lesson, too. "I came home $30,000 in debt—and I will never do that again."

Three years into his position at the restaurant, Dan was cutting his restaurant shifts to spend more time looking at properties and seeking out JV clients, some of whom he met while tending bar or waiting tables. "My excuse for working there was finding investors," says Dan. "I actually asked some patrons for their business cards, then called them up later." He obviously believed in what he was doing, and put a plan in place to make it happen. The job was part of the plan.

As a student of long-term wealth seminars and books, Dan welcomed Greg Gillespie on board in June 2006. "We want to grow the company and he's everything I'm not. Where I'm the visionary and a move-forward kind of guy, he's more analytical with a focus on the critical details and how they fit into the big picture." They make the perfect mix of business partners.

The father of two young girls, ages 10 and 4, Greg formally met Dan in March 2006. "At that first meeting, I actually gave Dan a pretty hard time," Greg recalls. "We were meeting to talk about me investing with him, and I pretty much made him go through the proposal, line by line. In hindsight, that approach showed me how mature and confident Dan was. The guy really knew what he was doing." Where others might take time to decide if they're in on a joint venture, Greg knew he was in—and wanted more. "I knew, hands down, that I wanted to invest with him," he says.

He also wanted Dan's mentorship and to partner with him in Oasis. Dan countered with a one-page proposal that covered what each partner wanted. And the rest is history.

With Greg's help, the company grew from 14 rental units to 40 units in about a year. More proof that a melding of differing talents can create an amazingly strong team. By mid-2007, they were looking for at least two more individuals to join the company as salaried or contract employees. One would be the operations manager. The other would help with financial analysis. "Without more administrative help," notes Greg, "we're stuck *in* the business rather than working *on* the business." With more time to focus on acquisition, the partners have moved their quest for JV investors into high gear. As of June 2007, they were also actively looking to consolidate their business in a full-time office in Victoria.

Based on his experience, Dan wrote a book titled *90 Days to Real Estate Prosperity* (available on Amazon.com). "I put this workbook together because so many people were asking me how I did what I did, and I knew I had a strategy that worked," says Dan. Published in March 2007, the book quickly sold out its first print run.

While still actively looking for more properties, Dan says Oasis could hit its portfolio peak in 2010. If that happens, and they start to sell a few properties, he may find his attention turning elsewhere. "I like creating stuff and want to be involved in different kinds of business ventures."

Greg Gillespie feels the same. But right now, he likes where he's at. Flexible working hours means that he and his wife, Pam, who works part-time as a preschool teacher, can both spend a lot of time with their kids. "Family is very important to me," says Greg, who chafed under the nine-to-five yolk of traditional employment. "I don't think of 'financial freedom' in terms of money. To me it's about time."

Time has value for Dan Barton, too. Indeed, he sometimes dreams of being a stay-at-home father. He may not be married yet, or even engaged, but those are mere details in the dream Dan is building, one decision at a time. "I like knowing where I want to go," he says.

Don Campbell's Observations

Systems, relationships and follow-through are the three components to success in real estate. Dan and Greg have built their success on this three-pillar foundation. They have a plan and are willing to do whatever it takes, morally and ethically, to make it happen. This partnership understands that real estate is just a stepping stone towards the financial freedom to pursue their other life passions.

This clarity of vision comes through whenever you speak with Dan and Greg; it is like they have a laser-beam focus. A great lesson they teach us is their ability to hold their vision clearly, tell others about it and make all of their decisions based on whether it takes them closer to or farther away from this vision.

There are many "serial distracters" in the world who have built whole businesses around selling us the latest get-rich-quick gimmick. They prosper because many of their customers don't have a clear vision of where they want to go; nor do most people have the ability to focus on one proven pathway to success. Greg and Dan use their laser-beam focus to cut through all of these distractions so they stay on their chosen path. Then, once they achieve their vision and financial freedom, they can afford, in both time and money, to chase as many of these distractions as they want. The lesson is to wait until the freedom is at hand before going off to chase the next craze.

The second lesson is that they formed the partnership based on both parties having different talents. This is critical to the long-term success of any partnership, each party admitting their own strengths and weaknesses, then building a business that focuses on enhancing the strengths.

Dan and Greg's clear vision, their willingness to do whatever it takes and their acute focus will quickly guide them to the freedom to pursue their true passions. Real estate is just the vehicle to get them there.

SUCCESS STORY #51
How to Turn One Cottage into Five Investment Properties by Opening Your Eyes

Felica Kelso

I try to take advantage of every learning opportunity that comes my way. The lessons aren't always easy, but they do pay off.

A self-employed couple desiring to get into the real estate investing game, Felica Kelso and her husband Chris Jackson thought they recognized the family's cottage for what it was: a run-down vacation property that needed the kind of repairs a buyer could afford to do only after negotiating a fire-sale price.

Felica and Chris loved the cottage, which had been a family retreat for generations, as did their three young children. But now that it was in the care of Felica and her sister Charis, holding onto a vacation property in need of so much work just didn't make fiscal sense for their two families. "For years, we rented it out sporadically to family friends for $400 a week to help cover off its annual expenses," says Felica. But, as they were unable to keep pace with necessary renovations, the ability to rent it out ground to a halt.

Felica says she always felt the cottage on Lower Rideau Lake, just outside of Smiths Falls, Ontario, could be used to do more for her family. But she confesses, "I had no idea *how* to do it." Looking back, her vision of what it could be also fell a little short!

Then it rained. Nope. Make that REINed. And their decision to join REIN gave them the in-the-nick-of-time education they needed to turn the cottage into a real money-maker—instead of a vacation property with a For Sale sign!

After taking her first REIN Quickstart program in 2003, Felica was determined to leverage her new knowledge to turn things at the cottage around. Being self-employed since graduating university and college, she and Chris had not always experienced success in dealing with banks. "When we first started negotiating for investment financing [for cottage renovations]," says Felica, "they wanted us to finance up our personal residence mortgage, and I wasn't willing to do that. From listening and learning from other veteran investors, I knew there were more powerful financial options for us."

What she was willing to do was give lenders a copy of her new sophisticated investment binder, a multi-page document she put together based on information she learned from REIN. While she did not want to refinance her and Chris's home, a move that would have added years of interest payments to the bank through amortization, she says, "I leveraged my new knowledge to negotiate better terms, shaving a full six years of our amortization and cutting our interest rate."

She figures the binder took her three weeks to complete. She also figures it's netted her family close to $17,000 in working capital for every hour she invested in its completion. One banker was so impressed she joked about showing it off to her colleagues. "It was a tipping point for our investment business. It helped me get the financing we wanted and I was beginning to see our investing options in a whole new light."

Before joining REIN, her family had been trying to scrape together $15,000 extra cash to renovate the cottage. Felica now saw the family retreat through investor's eyes. By leveraging some of the cottage's own value to finance the necessary renovations, they brought it up to rentable standards.

They also changed their approach to the cottage's value as revenue property. "We've learned to treat it like a business with proper rental agreements and security deposits," says Felica. "We market it on a great cottage owners' website and rent it out for market value rent of $1,300 a week. We're now beginning to build a roster of repeat clients."

Although turning the family cottage into a money-maker has been great, Felica says her favourite part of what they've accomplished so far has been applying her new-found real estate investing techniques to turn this one cottage property into five.

Using money pulled from the cottage refinance, "we bought four cash-flowing condos in Alberta in 2006 with the help of an excellent joint venture partner we met in REIN," says Felica. "Emotionally, it felt a risk at first. Yet intellectually, I knew they were solid buys from the education I was getting through REIN. And we have infinite trust in our JV partner."

While life is busy raising three young children and operating their successful advertising business in the Quinte, Kingston, Brockville and

Rideau Lakes regions of Eastern Ontario, Felica and Chris agree these first steps of real estate investing are important ones to expand on to reach their "Personal Belize" — matching their business income through passive cash flow. "I can see our next purchases might be in Alberta again, but we'll look at Ontario, too," says Felica. "There are tons of opportunities much closer to home here in Ontario. And thanks to our new focus on researching the fundamentals, we know now which real estate markets are appreciating best and which kind of investments make sense for us. For us it is all about focusing on fundamentals, playing within the rules and keeping our eye on our ultimate long-term goal."

Don Campbell's Observations

Felica Kelso and Chris Jackson have a reputation for never playing outside the real estate rules; you will never find them swimming in financial grey waters. However, that does not mean that they don't have the ability to think and invest creatively.

The Felica Kelso and Chris Jackson story is the perfect example of what can happen when our blinders are taken off and we discover a whole new perspective. Often, when we get too close to a problem, we can get caught up in seeing it from only one perspective. It is not until we take the time to step back from the situation and ask for others' unbiased opinions that we get to a real solution.

Instead of following the path that most would have followed, the family looked for and found a creative solution wherein both needs were met, without losing the family retreat.

They turned the cabin from a losing proposition into a strong and growing portfolio.

One of my favourite words is "and." Often, when approached by an investor with a problem, the investor believes he has to choose between one outcome or another. This is where I like to inject the magic "and" word into the conversation. I'll say something like "Have you considered the option of having both solutions?" At first I'll receive a dumbfounded look because all through life we've been taught that we must make a choice, when in fact sophisticated investors know that a third option exists:

that we can have both. In Felica's case they chose to have both—a family retreat and a growing real estate portfolio—when they first thought they had to choose between the two.

Many investors commonly state that they want to quit their job to undertake real estate full-time. Now, as exciting as that may sound, it's often the wrong course of action. Why? Simply put, you have to eat (and it is difficult to eat equity) and without a job you'll have a very difficult time getting financing at the banks, which will then put your investing on hold because you can't buy anything. Sort of defeats the purpose, doesn't it.

So why not look at the "and" solution? For instance, find a way in which you can work part-time, maybe as an outside contractor to your employer, or work four longer days instead of five regular days. In both cases you still keep income coming in and you'll have much more time to pursue your real estate investing dream. In other words, you get to have both choices. Often, all it takes is a little creativity and a different perspective on a problem.

It really is all about re-examining your perspective on a situation and looking for ways in which you can have your cake and eat it, too. You deserve it, despite what you may have believed in the past.

ACTION STEPS

1. What important choices or decisions are you trying to make in your life right now?

   _____

   _____

   _____

   _____

2. How can you combine your choices to come up with an ultimate solution for each decision?

   _____

   _____

   _____

   _____

REAL ESTATE
INVESTMENT
NETWORK™

#1018, 105 – 150 Crowfoot Cres. NW, Calgary, Alberta T3G 3T2
phone (403) 208-2722 fax (403) 241-6685 www.reincanada.com

Property Goldmine Score Card

Property Address: _____

Town: _____ Prov: _____

Source: _____ Tel:_____

Property Specific Questions

- ❑ Can you **change the use** of the property?
- ❑ Can you buy it <u>substantially</u> **below retail market value**?
- ❑ Can you <u>substantially</u> **increase the current rents**?
- ❑ Can you do small **renovations** to <u>substantially</u> increase the value?

Area's Economic Influences

- ❑ Is there an **overall increase in demand** in the area?
- ❑ Are there currently **sales over list price** in the area?
- ❑ Is there a noted **increase in labour and materials cost** in the area?
- ❑ Is there a lot of **speculative investment** in the area?
- ❑ Is it **an area in transition** – moving upwards in quality?
- ❑ Is there a major **transportation improvement** occurring nearby?
- ❑ Is it in an area that is going to benefit from the **Ripple Effect**?
- ❑ Is the property's area in **"Real Estate Spring or Summer?"**
- ❑ Has the **political leadership** created a "growth atmosphere?"
- ❑ Is area's **average income increasing** faster than provincial average?
- ❑ Is it an area that is attractive to **"Baby Boomers?"**
- ❑ Is the area **growing faster** than the provincial average?
- ❑ Are **interest rates** at historic lows and/or moving downward?

_____ = Total ✔'s

Does This Property Fit Your System? ❑ yes ❑ no
Does It Take You Closer to Your Goal? ❑ yes ❑ no